A Lover's
Quarrel An Autobiography

My Pilgrimage of Freedom in Churches of Christ

Leroy Garrett

Leroy Garrett

A Lover's Quarrel, an Autobiography: My Pilgrimage of Freedom
in Churches of Christ

ACU Station, Box 29138
Abilene, TX 79699

Cover design and typesetting by Mark Houston.
© 2003 Leroy Garrett

Printed in the United States of America

ISBN 0-89112-074-2

Library of Congress Card Number 2003110647

1,2,3,4,5

Table of Contents

v   Preface v

xi   Introduction: What The Quarrel Was About xi

1   My Family 1

2   Growing Up In Dallas 11

3   My First Love 17

4   A Banner Year At Freed-Hardeman College.......27

5   Two Years At Abilene Christian College 35

6   Those Who Can't, Teach 41

7   With Presbyterians At Princeton 47

8   With Unitarians At Harvard 55

9   On Becoming An Editor & Landing In Jail 67

10   Pioneering In High School Philosophy 81

11   Teaching All Women & All Blacks 97

12   Editor of *Restoration Review* 111

13   My Unity-In-Diversity Heresy 125

14 High Adventures Abroad...................................141

15 More Adventures Abroad, Now With Ouida ...163

16 Discovering My Stone-Campbell Heritage.......183

17 My Magnum Opus—& Doors It Opened........203

18 When Brethren & Enemies Are The Same.......225

19 The Sunset Years 243

Addenda:

1 My Testament Of Faith 259

2 What I Want For Churches Of Christ..............267

Index 285

Preface

– by Allen Dennis, Ph.D., professor of history and chair of the history faculty, Troy State University, Troy, Alabama

I was born into the "everybody's-going-to-hell-but-us" Church of Christ, and I bought into it completely. I began preaching by the time I was eighteen. At twenty, I was preaching full-time in East Tennessee, and there wasn't much I didn't know. I might have been wrong, but I was never in doubt. Looking back on that experience, I am convinced that there is only one thing worse than a boy preacher—an old one who hasn't learned anything!

After finishing college, I moved to Mississippi for graduate school with all of my legalism still intact. That's when I learned that the only way to remain a legalist is to refuse to think. Graduate school forces thinking, and the critical method used in my studies spilled over into my religious life. By the end of my first semester, my religious house of cards had collapsed. Legalism is like fog—it cannot survive heat and light.

For a few months, I dropped out of church entirely. After all, I thought, "If the Church of Christ isn't it, there is no 'it'." Then my major professor—also a disillusioned member of the Church of Christ—said to me one day, "Well, I think you're ready for this." He handed me several issues of *Mission Messenger*, edited by Carl Ketcherside, and a copy of *Voices of Concern: Studies in Church of Christism*. That was more than thirty-five years ago. I remember it well. I read them all, staying up all night to do so. I was amazed to discover that I was not alone in my thinking. It was a turning point in my life.

From *Mission Messenger* I learned of a similar publication, *Restoration Review*, edited by one Leroy Garrett. Once I received back copies of this journal, I had another sleepless night! I found Leroy's paper feisty. It named names and was quick to cut to the chase. Armed with my new thinking, I declared holy war against my legalistic Church of Christ friends and relatives. After all, if I could shuck my sectarian past, so could they. That's when I learned that legalists are sometimes fearful and suspicious—even dangerous.

While I have never been jailed for my convictions like Leroy, the ostracism I suffered for three decades was no less a prison. It may have been partly my fault, for dogmatism is a disease—whether disguised as legalism or progressivism. I exchanged one kind of dogmatism for another—dogmatic legalism for dogmatic progressivism. In one case, I couldn't see why Baptists and Methodists couldn't see that "we" in Churches of Christ were right; in the other I couldn't understand why my own brethren in Churches of Christ couldn't accept the "new truths" I had discovered.

In 1973, Leroy visited me in the small Mississippi town where I was a college professor. The incredible events of that occasion are told in this book. We were verbally assaulted that day in a manner that only those who have endured such treatment can understand. I actually feared I might suffer bodily harm.

This was followed by one of the most shameful things I ever did—I "walked the aisle" at that congregation to ask forgiveness for inviting Leroy. I did it because I was scared. But I eventually reclaimed at least a portion of my honor.

For the next several years, I was that congregation's resident liberal—its resident heretic. I was "sound" enough to lead the singing or to lead in prayer, but not to teach a class. My frustrations grew. I would "drop out" for months at a time, and then go back and try again—always "going forward" to make a "confession" for having "forsaken the assembly."

For a time I preached for a small Baptist church while it was without a preacher. It was a refreshing experience in that I was loved and accepted. But I was soon back at the Church of Christ where it seemed I was less loved and less accepted. By now I had more courage. In yet another meeting with the elders, all my frustration and anger of fourteen years spilled out. In no uncertain terms I repudiated the times I had "gone forward" to ask for forgiveness at their congregation. I emphasized one thing: "I specifically repudiate the time I went forward after Leroy Garrett visited me. We were not wrong that day, you were!" I'm not sure how much of a Christian I was on that occasion, but I had at least been a man.

It was at that meeting that I asked the elders to define my place in the congregation. I was sick of being a second-class member. I wanted full and equal treatment or none at all. While they did not give me an answer at that time, I felt that I had at last drawn a line in the sand. That confrontation was a milestone in my life.

More than three months passed. Finally, in still another meeting they told me that their decision was that I should go before the congregation and confess sin for having fellowshipped the Baptists!

My response to that may have been my finest hour: "Gentlemen, before I do that hell will freeze over and Satan will skate on the ice." With that I walked out a free man. I did not set foot in that church again for the next eighteen years that I remained in that town.

That is what this book is about. Leroy Garrett's quarrel with the Churches of Christ was a comfort to me during those trying years. I saw that I was not alone.

The rest of the story is that two of those elders eventually apologized for the way I was treated, and

vii

thereafter treated me warmly. Nonetheless, for some years to come, I was not only estranged from Churches of Christ, but from organized religion in general. For more than a decade, I didn't attend church anywhere at all. I eventually tried the Presbyterians, only to discover that Churches of Christ have no monopoly on sectarianism. They nominated me to be a deacon, but I would have had to sign the Westminster Confession of Faith! So I left them too.

My peripatetic church life in those days reminds me of the story of the lonely castaway on a desert island who was being rescued. The rescuers noticed three small huts built along the tree line, and asked him about them. "The one on the left is my house," the castaway explained. "The one in the middle is my church—and the one on the right is where I used to go to church!"

My only contact with Churches of Christ during those years was Leroy's *Restoration Review*. I was impressed that while he suffered more abuse than I, he responded with love and kindness.

I have at last found what I was looking for all those years—and it is a Church of Christ! When I moved to a new university position in Alabama in 1998, my wife and I began attending the Landmark Church of Christ in Montgomery. In an orientation for new members, an elder told us that they did not allow their pulpit to be used for personal attacks. I was accepted as I was. I was even asked to teach. It was clear that Landmark was not the kind of Church of Christ I had left thirty years before. I felt like Rip Van Winkle waking up after a long sleep.

At Landmark I am not only free to teach about Churches of Christ history, but to examine our traditions as well. I have even challenged our sectarianism! I am at last in a Church of Christ where I can talk about having sisters and brothers in other churches. I have even said that I had much rather face God in judgment having accepted someone whom He rejects than to have rejected someone He accepts.

I am at last free in Christ—in a Church of Christ! I am so overjoyed that I sometimes weep, even while teaching. While memories of the past still haunt me, I rejoice that there are no longer any "church cops" out to get me.

Again, this is what this book is about. Were it not for Carl Ketcherside's persistence and Leroy Garrett's quarrel there might never have been a Landmark Church of Christ in Montgomery—or a Woodmont Hills in Nashville or an Oak Hills in San Antonio. Carl and Leroy blazed the trail for the likes of Rubel Shelly, Max Lucado, Rick Atchley, and Jeff Walling. There is a long list of our free churches and free preachers who are indebted to them. And were it not for Leroy, I would never have come back to the Churches of Christ—a testimony that countless others could give. He is one reformer who has lived long enough to see much of the fruit of his labor.

And I was able once more to invite him to my congregation. It was a great day for me when in 2001 Leroy visited Landmark, and was welcomed to the pulpit with these words from our minister: "We're very glad to have Brother Garrett here tonight. He hasn't been treated very well by some of our brethren, but he's a kind and gentle man who needs to be heard." What a difference twenty-eight years can make! That time I didn't have to "walk the aisle" and make a confession! Thank you, dear Leroy, for lighting the path. May you yet have many years to see the fruits of your labor. When the time comes for you to cross that River, please leave your torch behind. We need it to find our way.

Introduction:

What The Quarrel Was About

You may recognize that the title for this book is borrowed in part from the poet Robert Frost, who instructed that his epitaph read: *He had a lover's quarrel with the world.* It occurred to me that the poet's quarrel with his world and my quarrel with my church have similarities.

The poem that best depicts my own pilgrimage is *The Road Not Taken.* Frost describes himself standing at the fork of a road. One road is well-traveled, well-worn, and is the way of ease and certainty. It is the road the crowd takes, the way of conformity. The other road is less-traveled, perhaps because it may be lonely, uncertain, and venturesome. He takes "the less-traveled way"—"because it was grassy and wanted wear." Frost places all of us at the fork of the road, noting that it makes a big difference which road we take:

> *Two roads diverged in a wood, and I—*
> *I took the one less traveled by,*
> *And that has made all the difference.*

Frost saw his quarrel as a *lover's* quarrel, as do I. If a quarrel is vindictive and divisive, it only compounds the problem one is seeking to solve, whether in the world or in the church. That must be the kind of disputation Paul had in mind when he urged, "The Lord's servant must not quarrel" (2 Timothy 2:24). But there is lots of quarreling in the Bible, even God with His people. We may presume that it was usually done in love, certainly on God's part.

But love isn't always evident. The urgent cry of a prophet or a reformer may appear to be madness more than an expression of love. Jesus was thought to have a demon, and Paul was accused of being beside himself. Did Luther's quarrel with the Roman church appear to be a lover's quarrel? Alexander Campbell admitted to being "tart and severe" in his exposure of clerical abuses, but could it not have been in love? Mother Teresa embarrassed politicians and dignitaries—including a sitting President—at a Washington, D.C. prayer breakfast when she scorned our nation for its millions of abortions. Was her quarrel a lover's quarrel?

Perhaps the best case I can make for my quarrel being a lover's quarrel is that made by Raccoon John Smith back in the 1820s. When some Baptists were fed up with his efforts to reform them, they urged him to "go on and leave us alone and join the Campbellites." His response was "I love you too much to leave you." The argument is persuasive: *One doesn't leave because he loves too much to leave.*

Once you realize the extent of my quarrel, you may wonder why I didn't just leave the Churches of Christ. As I have said for fifty years, and I say once more: *I will never leave the Churches of Christ, never, no matter what, for I love my people too much to leave them.* Even if they kick me out, I'll stay around!

There is more involved here than love. When a reformer stays with his people and works for change, he is saying that he believes in them and expects better things of them. His quarrel is a compliment.

And what was the quarrel about? Freedom! I was urging my church to join me in a pilgrimage of freedom:

Freedom from sectarianism, legalism, and obscurantism;

Freedom to embrace the grace of God fully, and to be joyfully confident of our salvation;

Freedom to exult in the indwelling presence of the

Holy Spirit—whose mission is to conform us to the likeness of Christ;

Freedom to accept the Spirit's gift of unity with forbearing love—in spite of all our differences and hangups;

Freedom to accept as sisters and brothers all those who are devoted to Jesus Christ as Lord, wherever they may be;

Freedom to think for ourselves and to question the dogmas handed down by our forebears, including the dogma of anti-instrumental music;

Freedom from the tyranny of opinionism—making opinions and methods tests of fellowship—and from a herd mentality and blind conformity, which hinder growth in Christ;

Freedom to examine new ideas, to venture beyond party lines, and to march by a different drum beat;

Freedom even to be wrong in the quest for truth;

Freedom to pick up the broken pieces and start over—whether a tragic divorce, drug addiction, a gay lifestyle, or a wavering faith—and to be loved and accepted during the struggle;

Freedom to take a critical look at our history and admit where we've been wrong—and to get back on course;

Freedom to bring women into the church as equals in ministry, and to bring an end to male domination;

Freedom to make use of modern biblical scholarship, and to be honest about the difficulties one faces in the interpretation of Scripture—without being called names or having one's motives impugned;

Freedom to participate in Body life in the assembly—with believers sharing their joys and sorrows, and encouraging each other in the faith—with professionals serving more as facilitators than as performers.

Our Lord assures us that it is truth that makes us free, and truth may call for change. And change is often painful. I agree with Thomas Jefferson that no person, church, or nation can expect to move from despotism to liberty in a feather bed.

And in stating what my pilgrimage of freedom has been about, Jefferson said it better than I can: *I have sworn upon the altar of God, eternal hostility against every form of tyranny over the mind of man.*

I am indebted to several people for this modest contribution to the reading public. Had it not been for my dear wife Ouida—who for years stayed after me to tell my story "before someone else does"– it would not have happened. And it was she, along with a few other persistent friends, who convinced me that perhaps mine is a story that should be told, for it is the story of a church as well as a person.

I am especially indebted to the insightful guidance of Dr. Wayne Newland of Falmouth, Maine—a teacher, preacher, and school administrator now in retirement. Well acquainted with Churches of Christ, he was most helpful, not only in what should be told, but how it should be told.

I also thank Dorothy Koone, a fellow member of the Singing Oaks Church of Christ in Denton, Texas and a writer of study materials for the ACU Press. An English teacher now in retirement, she offered both helpful suggestions and encouragement.

I am grateful to Dr. Allen Dennis, professor of history and chair of the history faculty at Troy State University in Alabama, who not only critiqued the manuscript but also wrote the Preface. His own story— partly told in his prefatory remarks—is a testimonial to what this book is about. I take heart that his story—itself a pilgrimage of freedom in Churches of Christ—could be told a thousand times over.

Chapter 1

My Family

There were always a lot of us around. Ten of us in all, counting our parents. Seven boys, one girl. I recall being teased as a lad about there being fourteen of us kids: "There are seven of you boys, and you each have a sister. That makes fourteen." It was awhile before I could answer that one!

My father, Benjamin Joseph Garrett, was born in Marshall county, Alabama in 1874 and migrated to Palo Pinto County, Texas with his family in about 1895. He had no formal education. His mother taught him his ABCs from a blue back speller and taught him to read from the Bible. He claimed never to have read any book but the Bible, and he made that one book his lifetime study. He was also an avid reader of the daily newspaper—usually the *Dallas Morning News* or the *Fort Worth Star-Telegram*.

To this day, I can see him squinting and shading his eyes with one hand as he read the Bible or the newspaper—as if he needed glasses. But I never saw him wearing any, though in his old age he sometimes used a magnifying glass. While he enjoyed talking about the Bible, he was not dogmatic about his views.

He was in his eighties when he pecked out on a typewriter—in almost indecipherable copy—his view of the church through the ages. I was able to make out that he concluded that Jesus was talking about the church in John 14 when he said he was going away "to prepare a place for you." He also saw the New Jerusalem that comes down out of heaven (Revelation 21) as the church. He never seemed to have a sectarian view of the church, which I find surprising as I look back on my own sectarian past. I learned my sectarianism in our churches and colleges, not at home.

My father was a dirt farmer in his earlier years, barely eking out a living for his growing family. In about 1905 he took my mother and my two or three oldest siblings, then but babes, by wagon to west Texas in hopes of claiming title to government land near Lubbock, then frontier country. Unable to remain on the acreage for the required number of years for entitlement, they returned to Palo Pinto County, poorer than ever. My parents not only described that experience as one of the most arduous of their years together, but observed that they eventually would have been rich if they had claimed title to the land that became part of west Texas ranch and oil country.

Pop—as we always called him—eventually got into the real estate business in Mineral Wells, in Palo Pinto County. This town—25 miles west of Fort Worth—became our family home. All eight of us children were born there. Pop made a decent living as a realtor so long as he remained in Mineral Wells. It was when the family moved to Dallas in 1927 that things changed for him. He never succeeded as a realtor in Dallas. For awhile, he commuted back to Mineral Wells. Then came the Depression, which laid a heavy hand on our family. Pop seemed to give up. During the Depression and in the decades to follow, until his death in 1957, he was content to let "the boys" — as we called my older brothers—take care of the family. The Depression seemed to kill his spirit.

My mother was born Annie Olive Heath near Hillsboro, Texas in 1883. Her father died when she was of a tender age, and her mother then married a man named Zinn, an odd name that one of my brothers inherited—which he deemed a dubious honor. This made for a passel of maternal aunts, uncles, and cousins—some Heaths, some Zinns. But my mother never made any distinction between her full siblings and half siblings. Nor did we. We had only aunts, uncles, and cousins—not half aunts and uncles or half cousins.

My mother's family moved to Palo Pinto county in the 1890s. There she married my father in 1899 when she was 16. She was a mother at 17, but lost her first child in infancy. Growing up a farm girl in what was still a virtual wilderness, she too had almost no formal education. As it was with farm girls in those days, her duties were in the field as well as in the home. Her stories were tales of hard work and gnawing poverty. She cradled her babies on her back or in the shade of a tree while she hoed cotton—or while she picked cotton, dragging a long tow sack. She was in the baby business—ten in all, counting two lost in infancy.

Unlike Pop, once Mom learned to read she read rather widely. I was impressed that, even in her mature years, she studied grammar and the dictionary in an effort to improve her verbal skills. She was taken with what the schools then called "Expression" and wanted my sister to enroll in such a course. She would have taken it herself! Had her station in life been different, she would have borne wealth and status well. She had a class and dignity that even ignorance and poverty could not hide. And she was a fighter and a survivor in the face of hard times.

My oldest brother, Olin—who died in 1987 at 84—did not marry until he was well into his sixties, but then he had a surprisingly happy marriage. He served in the Army during World War II, but did not go abroad. He had a "Garrett's Coffee" business for a time, which consisted of preparing his own blend and marketing it to restaurants. With sufficient capital, it might have survived. Afterwards, he was in lawn care and landscaping. He helped the family endure the Depression, since he was the only one at home that had a job. He lived at home with our parents during most of his years. He helped me buy my first bicycle. We had a good relationship, and I always thought of him as having high ideals. I especially enjoyed visiting him and his new wife in their "old age," as I then saw it.

Ray—who died in 1990 at 86—was a golfer from his teenage years, and became a professional of some reputation. He served as pro at the elegant Wichita Falls (Texas) Country Club for some 35 years. He was a friend of—and played with—some of the great golfers of his day, starting with the famed Walter Hagen, whom he considered among the greatest golfers. As a kid I thought it was something to see on his desk a picture of him and Hagen in a golfing pose. There were stories about Ralph Gudahl, Dick Metz, Byron Nelson, Ben Hogan, Sam Sneed. Ray knew them all. And he helped nurture one near-great golfer—Don January—on his own Wichita Falls course. Three of us younger brothers each had our turn working for him in what was called "the golf shop" at his various courses, all in Texas. He too married later in life and had no children.

Clyde lived to be 91, passing on in 1997. During the Depression, he did well in an unusual business, coin machines—"marble tables" we called them—placed in businesses. He made his money a nickel at a time. He was a Navy officer during World War II, serving on the home front. For years after the war he vigorously sought to work out a system "to beat the horses" (race track betting), which of course was to no avail in spite of an incredible effort by a sharp mind. He was confident his system would one day make him rich. He eventually made a decent living as a mechanic of bowling machines. In his sixties, he worked for Ouida and me as manager of our fried chicken-to-go business in Denton, and in his latter years he *did* become relatively rich by starting his own fried-chicken outlet. He had two failed marriages in his younger years, but later in life he married and had two sons. He was one of only two of my five older brothers to have children.

4

Zinn died in 1984 at 76. He married at 19 and after ten years was divorced, with no children. In those years he was a druggist. He was an Army officer during World War II, and he remained in Germany for some years after the war, serving with distinction on General Mark Clark's staff in rehabilitating that war-torn country. I performed his wedding ceremony for his second marriage while he was in the service. From this marriage came two children. After the war he served as an Assistant to the President of the Institute of Paper Chemistry in Appleton, Wisconsin. He was a particularly handsome man and uniquely gifted in social skills. It bothered him that he had so little formal education— not even a high school diploma—especially when he had college graduates under his command in post-war Germany. He told me of a conversation he had with James B. Conant, former Harvard president, who was ambassador to Germany. Zinn expressed appreciation for the Harvard men who were his associates. The ambassador responded with "There are a lot of them around!," as if their presence was no big deal. He might have supposed Zinn was a Yale man! I assured my brother that it is better for people to assume you are an educated man by the excellence of your performance than for you to have to convince them by producing a degree.

Beeler, whom we all called Doc (he was named for the doctor who delivered him), died of lung cancer in 1976 when only 67. That smoking cost one of my brothers his life made me all the more diligent to try to turn people from that habit, especially my students. Doc served as a medic in World War II in the decimated 36th Division, made up mostly of Texans. He never talked about it much, but he did tell of the fearful landing at Salerno, Italy, and of occasions when he dragged wounded soldiers to safety under barbed wire. He was a war hero who said little about it. After the war, he joined Clyde in his ill-fated venture to beat the horses.

He later worked as a pressman for the *Los Angeles Times*. A fair golfer and proud member of the PGA, his best years were probably as an assistant pro to Ray at the Wichita Falls Country Club. He was an excellent golf teacher and, in later life, married one of his students. They had no children. He had a winsome personality and made friends easily.

Joann—my only sister—was born Gwendolyn Olive, a name she understandably didn't like. That she dared to change her name while still a teenager speaks for her independent spirit. From the outset the family called her "Sister," which somehow in time became "Toer" – pronounced *two-er*. Her parents continued with "Sister," but her seven brothers never called her anything but Toer—an endearing nickname to us and numerous others. She and I were close—probably closer than any other two in the family—due largely to our Christian walk together. She was with us at Wynnewood Chapel, a story told in this book. She was a dear friend as well as a precious sister, a delight to be around.

Toer was at home as wife, mother, and grandmother most of her life, but worked as a secretary for the Dallas Community College System long enough to draw retirement. It was a terribly sad day for me when she died at 79 in 1992. She willed her body to medical research, perhaps because I had done so. Ouida and I were with her children at the hospital where she died when the man came from the Southwestern Medical School in Dallas to take her away. It was done with reverence and dignity.

William J.—whom we all call Bill—is still going strong at 77. While only in his early 20s during World War II, he worked as an electrician in the building of AT-6A trainer planes for the Navy and Air Force. He has since done well as a real estate manager and developer in Dallas. But his claim to fame is being a Texas A&M "Aggie" *par excellence*. I was present back in 1954 when Bill—as president of the Dallas Aggie Club—introduced

6

a new coach who had come to A&M "to make a difference." His name was "Bear" Bryant. Among Bill's favorite photos is one of him standing between Coach Bryant and the president of A&M. He has long been a friend to Coach Gene Stallings, and to anything that is A&M. He was on the grounds to do what he could the night of the bonfire tragedy in 1999 that killed twelve students. He has, in fact, retired to College Station just in case the university might need him! He has one daughter and four grandsons.

Bill also has zeal for the Lord's work. He served 30 years as a deacon at two Churches of Christ in Dallas, and is often a teacher and promoter of various programs. He even succeeded in bringing the Men's Bible Study Fellowship into a Church of Christ in Dallas. Sometimes his passion for A&M and the church accommodate each other. He recently came to our congregation in Denton raising money for building an "Aggie Center" at the A&M Church of Christ in College Station!

Born on December 11, 1918, I was six years old when Bill joined the family on April 23, 1925. I was sent to an aunt's house that night. What still amazes me is that I had no idea that my mother was pregnant. In our family there was no preparation for newcomers! I recall looking in on little Bill when he showed up in bed alongside Mother. I had no choice but to accept him. I was not consulted about his entrance into the family. We were "stuck" with each other!

To Bill's delight, I have often used my being "stuck" with him as an illustration of accepting our spiritual brothers and sisters. "If they are begotten of our heavenly Father, and born of our spiritual Mother, who is the Jerusalem above," I have often said, "we have no choice but to accept them. God determines who is in His family, not us. Wherever God has a child, we have a brother or sister. We are gloriously "'stuck' with each other!"

While our older siblings grew up on farms near Mineral Wells, by the time Bill and I came along, the family lived at the edge of that town on an acre or two. We had a cow and chickens, a garden, and a sugar cane patch. We'd catch the fryers by way of a long wire with a crook on the end. My most vivid memory is being witness to the cow reaching across the fence and catching baby Bill's dress on her horns and tossing him into the barn yard. Dad rushed to the scene with a club to drive the cow back. It was a clean toss for the cow, for not a scratch did Bill have!

My parents' conversations always seemed to be about how to pay the bills or where the money would come from to buy groceries. On one such occasion, I went to my "bank" I had hidden away and brought a handful of change to place in my mother's hand. I learned that money solved problems. I just didn't have enough of it! Even as a boy I always had some kind of job and a little money stashed away.

Entertainment was simple and inexpensive. There were free movies, in the open, at a nearby park. A small radio provided my parents with Will Rogers, Fibber McGee and Molly, George Burns and Gracie Allen—and Amos n' Andy, whom they never missed. The Amos n' Andy program was so popular in the 1930s that the movie theaters would interrupt whatever they were showing to allow their patrons to listen by radio to the famous comedians.

During World War II, my parents listened religiously to Gabriel Heeter, who brought nightly news from the war zones. Having a son on each of two different fronts, my parents had special interest in what Heeter had to report. Even after the war, Pop would recall the doleful cry of Gabriel Heeter, "There's bad news tonight." But sometimes the news was good, and Heeter would cry out in his inimitable way, "Ah, there's good news tonight!," which became his trademark. Through it all my parents had a faith, quietly taken for granted more than verbalized, to sustain them.

———— —— ————

The family called me "Buster" until I was more than grown, presumably because I was a chubby baby. My brother Zinn at last put a stop to it, insisting that "You can't call a Harvard Ph.D. 'Buster'!" But some in the family called me "Buster" until their dying day, including my parents. Toer shortened it to one syllable, "Bu." That is what she called me, right down to my last visit with her in the hospital. Bill obeyed Zinn and started calling me Leroy. So I don't hear my nickname anymore.

I was apparently a good little boy. I wasn't a problem at home or when I started to school. One naughty thing I do recall was when at about age seven, I got into the family Model T Ford, started it, backed it, and had started down the road when my brother Doc put a halt to it. A more serious transgression was when several of us boys swiped the left-over wafers from the Communion table at church one Sunday.

With the family Model T Ford, Mineral Wells, Texas, age 7

Religion at home was more implicit than explicit. There was grace at meals—especially on Sundays—but no family devotionals or teaching that I recall. But we went to church and Sunday school at the Church of Christ in Mineral Wells. I was along when my parents dropped off an offering at the preacher's house—a mother hen and her biddies! We were giving from about all we had. The "collection" at church—which they said was for the Lord—was a curiosity to me. I remember asking my mother during one collection how they managed to get the money to the Lord!

I must have had something of a religious impulse. I was once some distance from home with several other kids—older than I—when a fierce storm came up. They all started running for home, leaving me behind since I was pulling my little red wagon. I gave it all I had with my wagon bouncing along behind me, but they got farther and farther ahead. I distinctly recall stopping my wagon, getting on my knees, and asking the Lord to help me. Answered prayer! I was home before the storm set in. I sometimes saw my Dad kneel beside his chair, and men at church sometimes knelt to pray.

It was about this time that our family made a drastic change—a move to Dallas—the wisdom of which was long debated once we were caught in the throes of the Depression. Two of my older brothers had moved to Dallas to work, and my mother was afterwards blamed for insisting that the family follow them, leaving the modest security of our native town.

It was 1927 and I was eight. The dark clouds of the Depression were looming . . . .

Chapter 2

Growing Up In Dallas

The Depression took a heavy toll on our family—as it did on families across the country. Pop no longer went to Mineral Wells in search of real estate deals, and there was little for him in Dallas. While still comparatively young, he appeared to give up. For the rest of his life—even after the Depression—he left it to my older brothers, for the most part, to care for the family. Since he wasn't indolent, it was always a mystery as to what happened to him.

This meant incredible hardship for my mother in particular. She accepted such help as she could from my older brothers, who were barely making it themselves. She took in roomers and boarders, which brought its own problems. One time we had two handsome young men renting a room who turned out to be a problem. We didn't know they were using our home for their robbery operation until the police came calling.

Then there was a retired Methodist preacher and his wife who took a room with us. He had but a meager pension and could find only occasional work. Sometimes he couldn't pay the paltry sum we charged. Though an honorable man, he was caught stealing bread from a nearby food place. Shades of oppressive times!

When a room was vacant, Mom would long for a traveler to heed our "Room For Rent" sign, if but for a night. One day a man from New York rented a room for the night. I was greatly impressed to see someone from New York. I was impressed even more when he gave

Mom a dollar for the night's stay when the charge was only fifty cents.

We were on welfare part of those years. Pop would go to the county agency and bring home a box of groceries. We could pay our utility bills only occasionally, so the electricity and gas were sometimes turned off. Toer was too proud to tell a date why we had no lights when he called. So she feigned a romantic reception for him with several candles burning in the living room! That is a story we had fun sharing through the years.

Though unemployment was frightfully high, as a lad I always had some kind of job. At age eight I helped a big boy with his paper route. Then I had a route of my own. I sold magazines. I set pins in a bowling alley before they had automatic setters, the hardest work I ever did.

One after-school job was selling donuts house to house. Bill, at about five, would go with me. The donuts were still warm and smelled heavenly. Bill would only need to lift a bag under the nose of a prospective buyer. We always sold all we took, and we made a nickel a bag. The baker kept urging more upon us. We always managed to save a bag or two for the family.

Another after-school job was at King's Cafe near our home for a dollar a week and my meals, but it had a shady side. The owner was a bootlegger, and he used me to fetch bottles of beer—a few at a time when customers called—from the hiding place on a nearby vacant lot. One night the police were watching. The owner was arrested, and I was summoned to appear before the juvenile court. I went alone and was lectured by a policewoman. That is what impressed me most about it all: a police*woman*, the likes of which I had never seen.

I also worked on weekend nights as a bartender at a tavern near another place where we lived, an area now part of Love Field airport. I probably set a record in that I drew countless mugs of beer without ever drinking a drop. I hated the stuff. My first bottle of beer would be

65 years later in China when Ouida and I felt that we had no other choice but to accept what our hosts placed before us, "asking no questions for conscience sake."

My brother Olin, who had a coffee route, arranged for me to buy a bicycle from one of his customers—a dollar down and a dollar a week. With the bike I got a job delivering orders for a pharmacy. I had a little dog named Pudgy that would ride with me, balancing himself on the crossbar and placing his paws on the handlebars.

I came to be pretty well known in our neighborhood. One time when the family had no food, Mom asked me to go to the A&P manager to see if we could "borrow" some items she requested. When I brought back the groceries, I broke down crying, telling her that I didn't want to do that anymore. She too cried, assuring me I wouldn't have to do it again. In the ensuing years, when times were better, we talked little of those days. It was too painful.

Some friends who shared those hard times say they were poor but didn't know it. I was poor, and I knew it. I cannot forget how Mom would do the washing out in the backyard over a boiling black pot, followed by hours of ironing. The drudgery was such that a joke was passed along in the family. When one of my brothers was helping with the washing, he would ask, "Mom, are they all wet yet?"

That joke lives on in our own family. In mailing our newsletter, the first big task is to apply over 2,000 labels, then comes the sorting by zip codes. Ouida will sometimes ask, since I'm the one who does the labels, "Are they all wet yet?"

The few small bills we had to pay seemed gargantuan in size. We rented a sizable home for some years, but were hardly ever able to pay the $25 monthly rent. The landlord allowed us to stay nonetheless, for he had no one else to rent it to who could pay the rent. In later years, amidst affluence I would shake my head in disbelief, wondering how we made it.

The Depression years—however painful—bequeathed to me some helpful lessons for life: I learned to work; I learned the value of a dollar; I learned to save. When just a kid I always had a few coins stashed away from my various jobs. On those occasions when the family was in dire straits, I could sometimes come up with a few coins from my coffee-can bank.

While getting an education was not particularly encouraged in my family, I had some encouragement from teachers early on—such as being selected to give the class oration when I graduated from elementary school. My performance so impressed my family that they talked about my becoming a lawyer. But it never was my ambition. In fact, I don't recall having any particular goal back then—except one day to be free of poverty. Money solves problems, I learned early in life; therefore, have money.

Secondary school was a virtual zero for me, perhaps because I was more interested in some job than in studying, which I didn't know how to do. I had no motivation. After two years or so, I dropped out and began helping three of my older brothers who were now working outside the law as bookies—the fine art of taking bets on horse races.

I worked the phones and took bets. We had phone contact with race tracks across the country, and races would be called over our speakers as the horses left the gate. It was fun passing along the results to the customers, especially when they won. My brothers did very well indeed, for the Depression years, but sometimes they lost—and lost big! The police would call occasionally and arrest somebody, but never me as a minor. We'd pay a fine and go on with our business. No one ever went to jail.

It was messy—no place for a teenager, if for anyone. My brothers went on to better things: first the war, where two became officers, and then respectable civilian pursuits. There was something about the Depression that seemed to forgive less exemplary behavior, so long as it wasn't violent.

But at 17 I was hardly on the right track. I had been baptized the year before at the Oak Cliff Church of Christ by W. L. Oliphant, and church had some meaning to me. But I lost interest and wandered, even when my mother would urge me to go back to church. More than that, I was ignorant, immature, and insecure. I was being chastened by life. I was a high school dropout, void of any skill, terribly poor, had an inferiority complex, and was scared. I had no mentor, no one to guide me. I did not then have the faith to look to the Lord. I had lost my way.

Two things soon happened that turned my life in a different direction. Was it providence? I met two women: first, a girl who soon became the most important person in my life at that time; then there was a woman in Brownwood, Texas, who insisted that I go to college, a high school dropout or not.

Chapter 3

My First Love

I met her at a party in Oak Cliff, a suburb of Dallas. She was 16 and I was 17. She became my first real girlfriend. The chemistry was right—she was as poor as I was and almost as ignorant. A virtual orphan, she lived with an older sister, and, like me, she always had a job of some sort. After all these years I can still see her behind a counter at a dime store or "jerking soda"—as we called it—at some pharmacy.

She was pretty, smart, and engaging, as if she might be royalty. So, I was soon calling her The Duchess. The nickname stuck. A duchess behind a soda fountain! As duchesses have a way of doing, she stole my heart. It was a relationship that would last into our young adulthood—and I supposed then that we were in it for life.

Early on in our relationship, while we were yet just kids, I "borrowed" my brother Zinn's new Oldsmobile sport sedan from the parking lot near his work and took The Duchess for a ride over much of Dallas. I even put her at the wheel. With the top down and the wind blowing, we had quite a ride! As our sins so often find us out, Zinn, while making business calls in a taxi, espied his sports car in the distance and gave chase. When he overtook us and saw that his car was in the hands of such sublime innocence as a young duchess, he was virtually speechless. He said only that I should return the car to the parking lot.

It was difficult to leave The Duchess and move to Brownwood to work for my brother Ray in his golf shop. He was the pro at the local country club. It was here that still another woman would influence my life— even though she was never more than a casual acquaintance. She was a customer—a golfer—which meant she was a woman of some affluence. I would clean and store her clubs, and have them ready for her when she came to play, as I did with all the golfers. That was part of my job.

She took an interest in me, and one day suggested that I should go back to school to Daniel Baker College, which was in Brownwood, though it is now defunct. I told her that there was no way, that I hadn't even graduated from high school. Not to be deterred, she kept after me and finally arranged for me to be interviewed by college officials.

The college allowed me to enroll on the condition that I take certain high school aptitude tests and pass my college courses. I was never given the tests, and while I was no whizz in my courses, I did pass. I was now in college. It did worlds of good for my sagging ego. Not all that far from Dallas, I would go home periodically to see the family, and, of course, The Duchess.

It was while in Brownwood that I came back to church and to the Lord, though I didn't yet really know Him. I even began to think about being a preacher, receiving encouragement from W. L. Wharton, the local Church of Christ minister. It was at that church that I did my first public act of ministry, which was to serve the Lord's Supper at night for "those who did not have opportunity to take it at the morning service." I don't think I did it well, but that became part of who I was. I always dared to do, even if I failed.

My year at Daniel Baker may have also fanned the sparks of one gift I may have, writing. The girl who edited the student paper drafted me to write a sports column. I didn't know all that much about sports, but I dared to do and became the school's sports writer—not all that bad a one, if I may say so! Part of my column was to predict upcoming college football games across the nation. I got so many of them right—by pure luck—that my brothers in Dallas accused me of writing my column *after* the games were played!

Back home in Dallas, The Duchess and I moved to higher ground in our relationship. We became more spiritual, and she encouraged me to be a preacher. At a service at the Oak Cliff Church of Christ, we were singing the invitation song together. She closed the hymnal and started down the aisle. It was a beautiful moment—one forever etched in my mind. I watched through tear-dimned eyes as W. L. Oliphant baptized her into Christ, just as he had me a few years before.

She was present at the Sunset Church of Christ in Dallas when I made one of my first talks at church, maybe my very first. I was 18. J. L. Hines, the minister, had two or three of us would-be preacher boys make the effort at the service on a Wednesday night. G. A. Dunn, Sr.—a veteran evangelist and a member of the congregation—was present. After we had done our thing, he spoke up from his seat, "Brother Hines, is this the first time these boys have made talks?" The Duchess assured me afterwards that no less a person than G.A. Dunn was impressed by my effort. Having her approval was enough, but Brother Dunn's didn't hurt any.

As my interest in "preparing for the ministry" grew, it was a given that I must continue with college—a Church of Christ college this time. Abilene Christian College, relatively near, was the logical choice, but Brother Oliphant advised that if it was a preacher I wanted to be, I should go to Tennessee and study under N. B. Hardeman.

Money was a factor, and I was as poor as ever. At Freed-Hardeman College there was an "Akin Fund" for preacher boys. I could study under the great N. B. Hardeman for nothing, and that's what I could afford, nothing. For train fare and incidental expenses, my mother cashed in an insurance policy for $40, and my brothers added a few dollars more. I was ready to enroll at Freed-Hardeman at the beginning of the next semester.

It was January, 1939. I had turned 20 the month before. The Duchess and I were now well into our third year together. She and Pop were at the train to see me off on my first train ride and my first trip out of Texas. It is one of those scenes one remembers: there stood The Duchess waving goodbye, alongside Pop; I waved back with my New Testament in hand, indicating that it was only such a cause that would separate us for so long.

By the time I would see her again five months hence, things would be radically different. It would become one of the most trying experiences of my life. But for now, my lot in life was changing for the better.

Freed-Hardeman College was a new world for me. I studied under men long respected among Churches of Christ. Beside Hardeman, who was at that time the most prominent preacher among us and president of the college, there was W. Claude Hall, C. P. Roland, and L. L. Brigance in Biblical Studies. Mary Nell Powers, Hardeman's daughter, was the tough-as-nails teacher of "Preacher's Grammar." A local Baptist, R. W. Stewart, coached basketball and taught history. E. R. Endsley was in science. I came to love and admire all these people.

That year's class of preacher boys was star-studded in terms of the influence they were to have in subsequent Churches of Christ history. These included Earl West, who became one of our prominent historians, and James Baird, destined to be president of Oklahoma Christian College. Edward White would become a professor at Harding University, and Eugene Clevenger a professor at Abilene Christian. Several others became successful preachers.

By now I knew more about how to study, and made decent grades. I lived in Paul Gray Hall, across the street from the First Christian Church, which was "hard to" the campus. I walked past it hundreds of times, unaware of the role it had played in our history. But even then Brother Hardeman told us boys that the time was when he had led singing in that church while "Miss Jo," his wife, played the piano.

I would later in my writings point to the irony that the congregation used a musical instrument in worship for 17 years before it divided over it—which meant it wasn't the instrument that divided it. In this case, as in many others, it was an "editor-bishop" from Nashville, but that's another story. I little realized then that I was in one of the most significant places in Churches of Christ history, and among people who were making that history.

This was evident in the notable editors and preachers who came to speak in chapel. I heard the aged Daniel Sommer and the youthful Homer Hailey. Then there were B. C. Goodpasture, H. Leo Boles, C. L. Wilkerson, G. K. Wallace, G. A. Dunn, Gus Nichols, and L. O. Sanderson. Dorsey Hardeman, the president's son who served in the Texas senate, was a Commencement speaker.

Claude Hall took us preacher boys to a nearby lake and taught us how to baptize. We practiced on each other! In his classes he also gave us an appreciation of the Old Testament. We had a preacher's club where we preached to each other and were preached to by faculty members and visiting preachers. One old preacher gave an annual talk on how we were to behave ourselves around women.

In Brother Hardeman's classes, we not only studied the Bible—and his published debates! —but we got the lowdown on what was going on in Churches of Christ—some of which was ill-conceived for youthful minds. We learned that things were not going well between Hardeman and Foy E. Wallace, Jr. —another eminent preacher at the time. Hardeman also told a story that made R. H. Boll out to be a hypocrite, but we already knew that Brother Boll was an enemy to the cause, being a premillennialist. We learned both how to spell and pronounce that word, as well as how to expose the doctrine!

We all loved and admired Brother Hardeman. Some of us were even in awe of him. He was always elegant, well-groomed, and a gentleman—but he didn't fraternize with us. One preacher boy made a point of memorizing Hardeman's sermons and practicing them in his room. Several of us gathered outside his door, and when "Brother Hardeman" gave his flowery and persuasive invitation, we sang an invitation song!

Things were rather regimented. "Miss Jo" played the piano, always the same march, "Country Gardens," while we filed into chapel to assigned seats, with Brother Hardeman standing regally at the podium to welcome us. We stood at our places until all had filed in, and when he nodded we all sat down at the same time.

A "date" —if it could be called that—was hardly more than walking a girl to church, and perhaps sitting with her in the parlor of the girls' dorm for a while afterwards. Romances nonetheless bloomed, and several found their lifetime mates. We boys had the distinct impression that some girls had been sent there by their parents to find a husband. Even a preacher would do!

It was the table fellowship in the dining hall where lasting friendships were made. We shared our joys and sorrows, and came up with lots of stories. One preacher boy regaled us with endless jokes about J. D. Tant, colorful Texas evangelist, many of which were probably apocryphal.

During these months at Freed-Hardeman, The Duchess and I were in constant touch by mail. She shared the new world that I had found. I hadn't the slightest interest in any other. Everyone knew that I had a girl back home.

The crisis came near the end of the school year. Suddenly, the flow of letters from The Duchess ceased.

22

I kept writing, but there was no response. Some of my friends observed my consternation, and one of them— Norman Vaughn—who became one of our excellent preachers, had the bright idea of writing to The Duchess to see if he could find out what was up. I had no better sense than to let him do so, solicitous as he was.

But that did it! I soon had a letter from her. She didn't appreciate Norman's letter, saying that we should be able to take care of our problems without outside help. Problems? My next letter was an inquiry as to what she could possibly be talking about. I didn't know we had any problems. But I didn't know what she knew!

By now school was out and it was time to go home. I was so eager to see The Duchess that I had forgotten that there was supposed to be a problem.

I hitch-hiked home. I hitch-hiked most everywhere in those days, including my preaching appointments. It inspired a sermon outline that I submitted in one of Brother Hardeman's classes— "The Gospel Hitchhiker." When I placed the title on the blackboard, it brought a roar of laughter from the class and a chuckle from Brother Hardeman.

At last I saw The Duchess, and it could not have gone more beautifully, nor could she have been lovelier. We went to the Sunset Church of Christ together that night. The church knew that I had been away "studying to be a preacher," so I was something of a hero. J. L. Hines called on me to lead the prayer, with The Duchess at my side. Brother Hines was a friend and a mentor. He had quietly sent me money to help me along while I was at Freed-Hardeman.

Walking back to her nearby rented room (she no longer lived with her sister), she began to cry, which, I think, I had never or seldom seen before. I feared she was going to tell me of a serious health problem. I was actually relieved, for the moment, when she told me that she was in love with someone else.

I didn't believe her. I couldn't believe her. Once we

were in her room and she recounted the details of how it all happened, and talked of how I was now free, it dawned on me that it was for real. It was a severe blow to the solar plexis. I was devastated. Free? I didn't want to be free of her.

Heartbroken, I went across Dallas by streetcar that night to my parents' home. Mom was ready to hear me out for as long as I needed to talk; but Pop, once he sized up the situation, told me that if I really loved that girl, I should go back to her at once and lay out my claim for her in a no-nonsense kind of way.

I liked the idea. She was, after all, *my* girl. And so—if you can believe it—I took a late night streetcar back to her house. Once I had aroused her from sleep, I proceeded to make my speech, which may have been kin to one of Brother Hardeman's exhortations. It had the desired effect. She relented—even repented—telling me that I was always lifting her out of a pit, which wasn't the case. If during those three years there was any lifting going on, it was she lifting me, as she did that night. I was the one she loved, after all.

So, the same night we were separated we were reunited. She passed the word along to her would-be suitor, and we continued our relationship. But things were not the same. A solid, longtime romance was now beset by uncertainty.

It called for wisdom that I did not have. I suggested that we go on and get married, even if that ruled out further education. But she insisted that I go on to college. She would wait.

I am confident she meant that, but it was not to be. She soon broke off the relationship, telling me that it was the other fellow that she loved after all. That may appear fickle on her part, but she, too, was in crisis—caught in a dilemma that was a bit too much. At the time, I was too concerned for my own feelings to realize what she was going through.

She married one night that same summer. At the

time, I was in my first protracted meeting with the Amy Church of Christ near Cooper, Texas. I couldn't bear the thought of The Duchess being married to someone else. My world came to an end that night—or so it seemed.

But amidst all the gloom God was working for good—for hers and mine alike. Even then God was growing a wife for me only 70 miles away in Athens, Texas—one cut to order like a diamond—even if she was then but 15 years old. She was to be my sweetheart wife for 59 years and still counting. But I had no way of anticipating such a joyous eventuality on that lonely summer night back in 1939. I faced a long, black tunnel, and it would be years before any light appeared.

That traumatic experience taught me that, while life can be beautiful and exciting, it can also be deceptive and cruel. What one sees as the betrayal of a loved one is the bitterest of all pain—as our Lord himself experienced. I thought that I would never get over it.

I learned lessons that I've passed along to my students. If you have frogs to swallow, swallow the big ones first; and if you are run over by a Mack truck, you have to get up and keep going. I doubt if we ever completely recover from such devastating experiences. Indeed, they become part of who we are, and God uses them—if we allow Him—to hone us for a ministry of tender loving care. I've always been there for those crushed by a failed romance—not that I know what to say, except to tell them to give God time—but I can always cry with them.

The Duchess did well for herself. She has been married to the same man for 64 years—also a Church of Christ preacher! She has a passel of children and grandchildren, and she has stored up treasures in heaven all these years as a mother in the church and as a preacher's wife. Besides, she belongs to the "loyal" Church of Christ. Not bad for a girl who might have married Leroy Garrett!

25

When I see The Duchess in heaven—where there is neither marriage nor given in marriage—will I see her as the 16-year old who was my first love and who is forever etched in my memory, or as the gracious 84-year-old woman she now is?

Yes.

Chapter 4

A Banner Year At Freed-Hardeman College

After a summer of heartbreak, I badly needed to get into the win column. My first full year at Freed-Hardeman provided a series of successes that buoyed up my sagging ego. It was born largely of my own initiative. As the rental car ad has it, I was number two, so I tried harder.

For reasons now made clear, I had little romantic interest in the girls, but it was not beyond me to use them for "devious" ends. Several of them were daughters of elders in country churches in Tennessee and surrounding states, small churches that did not have resident ministers. At mealtime I would sit with such girls and con them into writing their dads and asking them if I could come and preach. I received several appointments this way—at a time when they were hard to come by.

Hitchhiking to these country churches on Saturday afternoons was an education all its own. However helpful the college classes may have been, I was learning to preach by preaching. I was wise enough to use sermons by some of our great preachers of the past— such as J. W. McGarvey and F. G. Allen, which was good stuff. "Little Mac" McGarvey, as they called him at the College of the Bible, would have been pleased with the way I did his "The Conversion of the Ethiopian Eunuch" and "Believing a Lie."

Another favorite, lifted from some such source, was

"Not a Hoof Shall Be Left Behind," reminiscent of Moses' standoff with Pharaoh. I could really ring out that line—possibly rivaling Moses himself! I made my points with the zeal and confidence of a Fuller Brush Man, which I once was. My enthusiasm may have provided more heat than light, but I gained a reputation for being able to "rev it up."

Besides the preaching experience, I was in the homes of hardy farm folk who were Christian to the core. And did they ever feed me! It was somewhat beyond the fare back at the college. I recall a table of hot food served in a dining room that was so cold I shivered. They kept house for the Lord each Sunday—the men making the fire and the sisters preparing the Lord's supper.

Etched in my mind is a dear sister stepping down from a pickup truck bearing the Supper, and making her way into the old country church well ahead of the congregation. There she would lay out the unleavened bread she had baked herself, fill the Communion cups, and then cover the table with spotless white linen that she had washed and ironed that week—even when it didn't need it.

They didn't always have preaching. But they always gathered around the Lord's table. That's who we are!

Word got back to N. B. Hardeman that I was out amongst the brethren and making tracks. He said to me one day, "Leroy, I hear you've been out preaching here and there." Then he added, "How about preaching for me next Sunday night?" He often filled the pulpit at the Henderson Church of Christ, which then met in the college auditorium. He was scheduled for the next Sunday, but he had to be away. He asked *me* to take his place!

If Franklin D. Roosevelt—who was then in the White House—had called inviting me to Washington, the impact on me could have been no greater. I was to preach in Brother Hardeman's place! What preacher boy had ever had such an honor?

I preached in Union City, Tennessee that Sunday

morning, but was back in time to fill the appointment at the Henderson church that evening. I did not lack confidence for the occasion, but it did help that Brother Hardeman was not to be in the assembly! But the auditorium was filled with faculty, students, and townspeople. It was the crowning moment in my young career up to that time.

I again made use of one of McGarvey's sermons, "God Is Not Mocked" (Galatians 6:7), but by now the sermons were becoming my own. The response was sufficiently positive—from faculty and students alike—that I was beginning to see myself as a bona fide preacher and not just a preacher boy.

There were other ego-building successes. I was elected president of my social club, Sigma Rho. I spoke in chapel and in the Preacher's Club. Moreover I was learning a lot, especially in Brother Hardeman's classes—which included Bible geography—and in Claude Hall's Old Testament class. There was also excitement in the coach's class in American history, and in zoology with E. R. Endsley. I had an advantage over the others in that I had no way to go but up.

L. L. Brigance was the professor the students may have loved the most. We saw in him the tender compassion of Christ. One day in his class we were studying 1 Corinthians 4 where Paul describes the suffering of the apostles— "We are fools for Christ's sake... We both hunger and thirst, and we are poorly clothed, and beaten, and homeless... We are the filth of the world, the offscouring of all things."

As Brother Brigance went over these lines, tears rolled down his cheeks. Applying a handkerchief, he at last said that it troubled him that preachers today have it so easy when the primitive preachers had to suffer so terribly. I was awed by what I saw. A teacher of preachers weeping over a text! I saw it as strength, not weakness, and it remains among the tenderest and most poignant scenes in my memory bank. It was a case of tears

29

conveying more than words ever could. That text has special meaning to me to this day.

During the spring term of 1940, a call came to the college from the Church of Christ in Blytheville, Arkansas. Their preacher was to be away, and they wanted someone for two weeks to fill the pulpit on Sundays and to do a daily radio program. I don't know why I got the call, but I accepted, even if it took me away from college for two weeks.

My teachers permitted me to take books and assignments with me to Blytheville, and to keep up my college work while filling the church assignment. I had a busy two weeks. In typing out my radio sermons, I discovered that one can say a great deal in 15 minutes. It was my first experience in writing sermons, and I came to see what Francis Bacon meant by "Reading maketh a man full, writing maketh a man exact."

Blytheville was an important success—not unlike a military victory for a soldier. I now had radio experience, and I was delving a little deeper into what I had to say. My sermons were becoming more my own. While I preached the gospel, such as Peter did on the day of Pentecost, the emphasis was upon the church, baptism, and the plan of salvation. It would be a long time before I really discovered the gospel of the grace of God. I wasn't exposed to it in the offerings at Freed-Hardeman.

Back at the college, I continued with my studies as if not having been gone. I even had time to respond to an emergency call from the faculty director of the senior play, W. O. Davis. The one who was to play the villain—a major role—had to check out for some reason. I agreed to do it, even if the time was short. When you're Number Two, you try anything.

Professor Davis later wrote in my college yearbook, "You *did* Moulton!" At one point in the play, titled "Attorney for the Defense," Moulton grabs the hero of the play—who happened to be James Baird—by the throat and really roughed him up, while telling him off at the same time. I was so mean a villain that it excited the audience. Brother Hardeman told me the next day that I had stolen the show, and that his little grandson stood up in his seat and clapped with excitement each time I came on stage.

As the year drew to a close, a number of us preacher boys did a special chapel program. It was a stage play that laid out our lives as sacrificial servants of the Lord for many years to come. In the final scene—with our hair grayed by flour and leaning upon canes—we sang "In A Land Where We'll Never Grow Old." That the girls sat there blotting their eyes with their hankies was reward enough for our rather considerable effort.

There was one negative in that banner year at Freed-Hardeman. I made a talk in the Preacher's Club on Paul's desire to preach where Christ had not been named, rather than to build on another man's foundation (Romans 15:20). I questioned the system that employs men to do what elders and others should be doing, when they ought to be in the field doing the work of evangelists, like Paul did.

Claude Hall—the sponsor of the club—responded to what I had to say with, "Leroy is wrong. Never mind why he is wrong, but he is wrong!" While I never took it up with him, I let the other preacher boys know that I wasn't satisfied with such a response. If I were wrong, I wanted to know why.

When noted evangelist C. L. Wilkerson visited the college, I shared my concern with him about our modern pastor system. I laid before him what I saw to be the New Testament pattern—that elders cared for the churches and the preachers served as evangelists in the field. While he agreed with me, he said, "But we don't do it that way." That a respected evangelist would say quite candidly that we in Churches of Christ were not doing it the New Testament way was not lost on me. Hall's rebuke and Wilkerson's admission were the

Graduate, Freed-Hardeman College, 1940 (courtesy of Freed-Hardeman University)

beginning of my lover's quarrel with my own people in Churches of Christ. It was to last for much of the rest of my life.

Because of the work I had done at Daniel Baker College, I was able to graduate from Freed-Hardeman College in June of 1940. That spring, Don H. Morris, vice-president and soon to be president of Abilene Christian College, came to the campus to offer generous scholarships to those who would like to do their last two years of college at Abilene. I was one of several who signed on.

Freed-Hardeman was a big plus for me—coming into my life at just the right time. An important part of it was the friendship of N. B. Hardeman. We continued to correspond for years to come. He encouraged me to do graduate work— "Take your proper title," as he put it, referring to a graduate degree.

A few years afterwards, when I was back on campus for a lectureship, Brother Hardeman invited me to his home for dinner. I was at the Hardeman table with G.

K. Wallace, Homer Hailey, and Gus Nichols, big-time preachers among us. I never understood why Hardeman was so gracious to me, a nobody, but I sensed that he was expecting great things of me.

At that time I could not have imagined any scenario that would cause that same college—under a different administration—to have me arrested right on campus when I was there for another lectureship. During one visit the president of the college honored me at his table. Some years later the president of the college had me jailed!

Chapter 5

Two Years
At Abilene Christian
College

By the time I enrolled at ACC in the fall of 1940, I was suspicious that I might not make it as a professional preacher. Not that I would lack the ability, but I might not fit into the system. I should be prepared to do something else. I would be a schoolteacher. Besides, I had already loaded up on Bible courses at Freed-Hardeman. At ACC I would major in Education, with a teaching minor in Social Studies.

Not that I would not preach. I would support myself as a classroom teacher and be free to preach on weekends and during the summers, especially in needed areas. In his letters, N. B. Hardeman encouraged this course of action for me.

It was a fortuitous decision. In 60 years of ministry, I have been able to support myself financially and yet give considerable time to the church as preacher and editor. For a while I refused any pay for church work, but I soon saw that would not do, for church leaders are embarrassed when a laborer doesn't accept what they offer. I decided to take whatever was given me and pass it along to my publication efforts—which are now 50 years and counting. My publications might not have survived if not for the money the churches paid me during those years.

More than that, financial independence gave me the freedom to say and write what was on my heart and mind, without fear of being fired by anyone. There probably has never been an editor freer than I, thanks to a decision made early on that I would not depend on the church for my livelihood. Nevertheless, in my ministry I have felt constrained by the love of Christ—and by what is appropriate—in a ministry of reconciliation. We are all captives of the Word—or should be.

ACC differed greatly from Freed-Hardeman. It was much larger and more like what I thought a college should be. Freed-Hardeman was more like a big family, and I missed the intimacy. At ACC, I didn't have a mentor like N. B. Hardeman. I did, however, take courses from Charles H. Roberson and Homer Hailey, respected leaders among Churches of Christ. I especially related to Brother Hailey, who also served as minister to the Highland Church of Christ in Abilene.

My studies in Education led to a permanent high school teaching certificate, which I was to use for several years before going on to graduate studies. Gilmer Belcher, a veteran Education professor, taught me many tricks of the trade that proved helpful, not only for high school teaching but for college as well. One tip was that it is sometimes best not to see some things that go on in the classroom—at least until you know what to do about them. Not a bad rule for life in general!

One year I lived in an apartment behind the home of W. R. Smith, the beloved vice-president of ACC. My roommates were Townsend Walker, Richard Walker, Charles Mossman, and Rex Kyker—who would later be a professor at ACC. But my closest friend was Ralph Graham, older and married, who came in from nearby Tuscola for classes. We would later serve churches in New Jersey together, and be together at Princeton Seminary.

And there was J. W. Roberts, who became a longtime, distinguished professor at ACC. He and I were competitors of sorts. I won the James F. Cox Speech Contest—sermons by ministerial students—and he won second place. I also won a preaching job at the North Park Church of Christ in Abilene. But when it

36

came to academics, J. W. won hands down. While I was at ACC, I was too busy reforming the place, as well as the Baptists, to bother with grades.

An unfortunate confrontation with the Baptists grew out of my efforts to convert some of them while preaching at the North Park Church of Christ. When a nearby Baptist church barred me from talking to some of their people, I set up a loudspeaker one Sunday night in the front yard of the house next door and preached to them as they filed out of their building. Ralph Graham was at my side, but he didn't speak. The police came about the time I had finished, and took me to the station. Contrary to rumors, I was not jailed, for I had violated no law. The police chief did call Don Morris, the president of ACC, and told him "I have part of your institution down here." The police dismissed me for lack of a charge.

Since the incident made the Abilene paper, I was branded as something of a radical. I may have been sectarian, but not radical. My sermon to the Baptists was reasonable and biblical—even pleading. It was the same gospel Peter preached on the day of Pentecost. I didn't call them names or condemn them to hell. But I did exhort them to be baptized for the remission of their sins, and to be Christians instead of Baptists!

When the campus was in an uproar over this, I recall J. W. Roberts saying that there was a time in our history when what I had done would have been taken as quite appropriate by our people. But he could have also said that I was long on zeal and short on wisdom. I may have been naïve, but I was also sincere. I believed the Baptists were seriously in error—as my mentors had taught me—and it was my duty to preach the truth to them.

I would, of course, live to regret such indiscretion. But that is who I was back in Abilene at the age of 22 years, a victim of our embedded sectarianism. If my methods were more daring than my fellows, it was because, like Saul of Tarsus, I was more zealous for the law than they.

As if the encounter with the Baptists in Abilene were not enough, the following summer I had another confrontation with them while preaching in a brush arbor in Taylor, Arkansas, where a Church of Christ had recently been organized. As we made inroads among the Baptists, I was challenged to debate Dr. D. N. Jackson, a prominent Arkansas Baptist preacher and debater. He had a reputation for debating "Campbellites" —and with marked success to hear the Baptists tell it.

Since Jackson was twice my age and a veteran debater, it was daring for me to accept the challenge, probably foolish. But I had the advantage of being a possible David before a Goliath.

Elmer Goble, the evangelist who had started the Church of Christ in Taylor, and Jack Hawkins, one of my fellow students at Freed-Hardeman who worked with Goble, insisted that I should not engage such an experienced debater as Jackson. The truth might suffer. It was my first debate, and I should not start at the top, they urged. While I was eager to take on the old war horse, I yielded to their better judgment. O. C. Lambert, one of our noted debaters in those days, agreed to take my place.

But Jackson would not have it. I was the one who had stirred up the Baptists in Taylor, and I should be the one to debate. My friends agreed that, under those circumstances, I should go on with it.

In the debate, which was held at the Baptist church, Jackson talked about "spanking" me, but I nonetheless pressed the arguments that I had learned from our experienced debaters, including Guy N. Woods, who tutored me by mail. It was likely an uneven playing field from the outset, but I nonetheless felt that I had the advantage in that the truth was on my side.

That episode further reveals my youthful audacity. There was no star I would not reach for, no ocean I would not cross, no mountain I would not climb. Or at least try to. I was still Number Two—trying harder!

There were hundreds of beautiful girls at ACC—any number of whom were probably looking for a serious relationship. But I had not yet recovered from the disappointment of my First Love, so I did not have a single date at ACC. The Lord was still growing Ouida for me, who was by now a tennis star at Athens High School.

I was at the North Park Church of Christ in Abilene on December 7, 1941—preparing to preach at the evening service—when news came that the Japanese had bombed Pearl Harbor. The next day we listened to President Roosevelt as he spoke of "the day that will live in infamy." We all knew that our world would radically change. Some students were already caught up in the war effort; many others soon would be. I was a conscientious objector to service in combat, but I would consider serving as a medic or as a chaplain.

I graduated from ACC the next spring. The nation was at war, the future uncertain.

Graduation, Abilene Christian College, 1942; Golden Anniversary Reunion of Class of 1942, Abilene Christian University, 1992 (Courtesy of Abilene Christian University)

Chapter 6

Those Who Can't, Teach

I eventually responded to the war effort by applying to the Navy recruitment office to be a chaplain. I passed the tests, and they indicated that I would probably soon be called. I never was. I figured it might be because all five of my older brothers were already in the service. But I doubt if I would have made a good chaplain. I was not then ecumenical enough, and I still had too many hangups. I wondered what I would do about instrumental music in military chapels!

It was just as well. It was better that I spend the war years preaching, teaching school, and going to school. I preached during the summer months, usually in out-of-the way places, and on Sundays.

My first teaching job was at Richardson High School, which in 1942 was part of a small, poor school district fifteen miles from Dallas, but is now one of the largest and richest in the metroplex. The grade school and high school met in the same dilapidated building with a leaky roof.

With the war on, we were poorly staffed. I served as principal, teacher, and the girls' basketball coach—a job I learned by doing. There was bad blood between some of the teachers and the superintendent, who was the de facto principal as well. My salary was meager, far below what my students were making working in war factories.

Such a grim start as a teacher reminded me of a dictum from Professor Belcher's classes at ACC: "Those who can, do; those who can't, teach." My humble beginning suggested that I was indeed one of those who couldn't. But my first job had its rewards. I was getting needed experience in the classroom and learning something about school politics. And I managed to purchase my first car, a 1936 model Chevrolet, which gave me wider range for preaching.

Equally important, I began work on a master's degree at nearby Southern Methodist University. Part of my work was in the School of Education and part in religion at Perkins School of Theology. Perkins was my first encounter with liberal theology, which I absorbed fairly well since I was interested in what it was all about. It was also my first taste of serious scholarly work. I studied with professors who had taken doctoral degrees from leading eastern universities.

There were a few set-tos in Professor John Davis' class in New Testament. I defended the use of a biblical text by observing that it was inspired. "Inspired?" the professor responded, ever so graciously, "Wasn't Shakespeare inspired? Wasn't Emerson?" I said something to the effect that they too might have been inspired, but in a different way; but it didn't seem to fly.

My answer would be different today. In the first place I would defend the New Testament's uniqueness on the grounds of its apostolicity, not its inspiration. Shakespeare was not apostolic and could not therefore be equal to Scripture, even if inspired.

I was something of a curiosity to the liberal Methodist students, who had probably never studied with a Church of Christ minister before, even though Carl Spain had been at Perkins before me and Homer Hailey after me. The Methodists seemed intrigued—perhaps even a bit envious—of my conservative approach to Scripture.

My lifetime interest in Alexander Campbell began at SMU, one reason being that they had in the library—to my surprise—a complete set of the *Millennial Harbinger*, which Campbell edited for 34 years. I conned the faculty into allowing me to do my master's thesis on *The Educational Philosophy of Alexander Campbell.* When I took my oral exam, the faculty conceded that Campbell was in some respects ahead of his time, particularly in his emphasis on health education. They were also impressed that he called for the education of the heart as well as the head.

It was while I was teaching at Richardson and attending SMU that I met my wife-to-be—the one the Lord was growing for me in Athens, Texas. It had been more than four years since I had had my first and only serious relationship, and I was now 24—old enough to at least be on the lookout.

Teacher, Richardson (Texas) High School, 1943

I was in Athens for a preaching appointment, and I stayed in the home of Mr. and Mrs. D. B. Pitts, who had a daughter at Texas State College for Women (now Texas Woman's University) in Denton, only 25 miles from Richardson. Impressed as I was with the dignity and beauty of Mrs. Pitts, I was interested in meeting her daughter. Brother Hardeman had advised us preacher boys: "Find the mother first, then the daughter."

After several visits to Athens, Mrs. Pitts asked if I would take her daughter's typewriter to her aunt's in Dallas, from where it could be conveyed on to her in Denton. I volunteered to deliver it to Denton myself. I was afterward to tease Mrs. Pitts, whom I came to call Mother Pitts, for setting me up for the kill!

It was on a cold January night in 1943 that I first laid eyes on Ouida Pitts. It may not have been love at first sight, but I was interested. I soon after invited her to go

43

on a preaching appointment with me. Regular dating followed, including bicycle riding around Denton. We married thirteen months later on February 18, 1944 in the Little Chapel in the Woods on the college campus.

After 59 years, I can say that marrying Ouida was my greatest hour. It would not have done for me to have missed Ouida. I had come a long way since that sad summer in 1939 when my First Love turned me out in the cold. I was coming to realize that the Lord had been working for my good all along. Ouida had it all: goodness, beauty, intelligence, and she was to graduate from college in only three years.

There is a "story" from our dating days. We were late one night for the 11 o'clock curfew at her dorm and were locked out. The dorm windows were being painted, so the screens were off the windows, and there was a ladder lying nearby. Under Ouida's supervision, I lifted the ladder to the window of her second floor room. She scooted up the ladder, tapped on the window, and her roommate raised the window and let her in. She was no more than inside when the dorm matron entered for room check, unmindful of Ouida's blushing face. It was something of a moral dilemma for the roommate, who served on the discipline committee. Apart from any pressure from Ouida, she decided not to report her. Situation ethics!

That was a fun story that I would tell the girls each year, once I returned to that same university as a professor. They loved it! They delighted especially in the fact that it was Ouida who led the assault against the rules!

By the time we married, I was teaching for the Dallas Independent School District—a one-year assignment at W. E. Greiner Jr. High in Oak Cliff. I was then living with my parents only a few blocks from the school. I walked to work each day even though I had a car. I was also preaching at the Hampton Place Church of Christ.

I took my bride to our very own home, one that I

had just purchased from G. A. Dunn, who was both friend and mentor, an aged minister who became a significant part of our lives. I paid $300 down on the house and $35 a month. We made a substantial profit when we sold it, which became a pattern for us. We've done well all through the years buying and selling the homes we've lived in.

For a time, with school teaching behind me, I worked for the *Dallas Times Herald* and took classes at Dallas Theological Seminary. This was my first experience with dispensational premillennialism, which is different from classical premillennialism. It was quite a contrast to SMU. From the outset, I was not favorably impressed by Dallas Seminary. They required a prospective student to sign what I saw as a creed, which included not only dispensational premillennialism but the whole nine yards of fundamentalism. Since I was at such variance with their creed, they debated among themselves about accepting me.

Their main concern was that I was not premillennial and did not believe in what they called "eternal security,"—one of the five points of Calvinism usually named "perseverance of the saints." When later at Princeton, also historically Calvinistic, I told a professor of the creedal requirement at Dallas, he thought it odd that a seminary would make such a demand of a student. He thought it more appropriate for both seminary and student to be open and to follow truth wherever it led.

When Dallas at last decided that I was open and teachable, they accepted me. But I came to see them as neither open nor teachable. Nothing exciting ever happened, not even a course I had with Lewis Chafer, who was Dallas' only claim to fame in those days. I eventually came to see the work I took at Dallas a virtual waste of time. The more I was exposed to the likes of Princeton and Harvard, the more obscurant and sectarian Dallas Seminary appeared to me.

In December of the same year we married, I was at

work at the *Herald* when a call came from Athens that Ouida's father had died suddenly of a heart attack at only 54. It was triggered by his frantic but futile effort to save a fellow hunter who had accidentally shot himself. His untimely death was to affect our own lives, for Mother Pitts lived on as a widow for another 47 years.

She still had two children to finish raising and get through college. This she did with uncommon courage and resolve, but as she grew older we felt a responsibility for her—first to watch out for her in a retirement home, and for the last decade of her life in our own home. She and I always had a special relationship, for I loved her as if she were my own mother.

In the summer of 1945, an invitation came from old ACC friend Ralph Graham to join him in New Jersey. We would minister together at the Liberty Street Church of Christ in Trenton and with small, struggling churches in the area. Ouida was all for it.

And we might study theology at nearby Princeton Seminary!

The year before we married, 1943, ages 24 and 18

Chapter 7
With Presbyterians At Princeton

I had heard Lewis Chafer, president of Dallas Theological Seminary, describe Princeton as the greatest seminary in the world, but I never imagined I would ever be a student there. At Princeton I was to study with world-renowned theologians, the ones who were quoted by other scholars, and who wrote the books that were studied in other seminaries.

It was founded by Presbyterians in 1812, and while the majority of faculty and students were of that denomination, it was unashamedly ecumenical, with many denominations represented both on the faculty and in the student body. While Ralph Graham and James Baird were students there before me from Churches of Christ, I was the first to take a degree (1948). There have been many from Churches of Christ since then, and a few have served on the faculty.

While the professors held doctorates from leading universities of the world, I was impressed by their humility and openness. It was evident that we were all engaged in the search for truth—faculty and students alike. If any of us had a chip on our shoulder, no one cared to knock it off. It was a common search for truth, with the faculty serving as senior colleagues, the students as junior colleagues.

Princeton was special because Ouida was able to take classes with me, though not officially a student. With her business training, she took down the lectures in shorthand. I was to be known for years to come as the student who had his personal secretary in class with him!

Princeton instilled in me a respect for theological scholarship. The professors were and continued to be leaders in their field. I had a class in ecumenics with John A. Mackay, president of the Seminary, that enlarged my vision of "the church catholic." He had a way of saying, "The road to tomorrow leads through yesterday." He was the epitome of grace and dignity—the ultimate Presbyterian.

Lefferts A. Loetscher, who taught American church history, alerted me to the early connection between Stone-Campbell history and the Mormons. "No Campbellites, no Mormons," he claimed. Andrew W. Blackwood taught homiletics (sermon preparation). He emphasized the importance of soul-stirring, meaningful public prayers: "If the pastor doesn't know how to pray, the people will go elsewhere," he insisted.

I had my introduction to Hebrew under Charles T. Fritsch, who took us through the prophets in the original language. He told us that we didn't need to rely on commentators. We could interpret for ourselves, right from the text. On our final he had us translate and comment on Malachi 2:1-9 from the original Hebrew text. Its application to ministers was clear enough. From that day, those verses have had special meaning to me.

Edward J. Jurji, a Syrian, introduced me to the great non-Christian religions. Joseph A. Hromadka, whom I had trouble understanding, came from Czechoslovakia to escape Nazism. He lectured on theology. Otto A. Piper, a German who also fled Nazism, took us through Romans. Norman V. Hope, a Scot and a student favorite, taught us church history. He was encyclopedic. The favorite of Ouida and me was Bruce M. Metzger, who taught Greek and New Testament. He was then in his early 30s and was destined to become a world-renowned New Testament scholar, especially in the field of textual criticism. His classes were always interesting, replete with stories on the history of the Bible.

We still tell stories of our own about Professor

Metzger. In a course on the book of Hebrews that Ralph Graham and I took with him, he conceded that the author was not a Calvinist! Ralph once questioned him on his interpretation of a Greek text, noting that Professor Roberson back at ACC had explained it in a different way. After studying the text further, Professor Metzger acknowledged that our Abilene professor was correct and that he was wrong.

When the Presbyterians gathered for chapel each day, Ralph, Ouida, and I would spend that time in the library. On our way to the library, we'd often meet Professor Metzger who was dutifully headed for chapel. He told us one day, after learning that we were from the a cappella Churches of Christ, that he had misjudged us and wanted to apologize. He first thought our truancy from chapel was a lack of conscience, and now he realized it was a matter of conscience. He would afterwards refer us to sources in the library, scholarly and ancient, that supported the non-instrument position.

I was impressed by what might be called Presbyterian dignity. I recall that when I went to a professor's home for some assignment I saw him slip on his jacket before meeting me at the door. It was more like England or Scotland than Texas!

While at first we were disinclined to accept our Presbyterian friends as equals in Christ, we came to see them as Christian as ourselves, if not more so. We were not used to teachers in Churches of Christ schools who could so easily yield ground to others. And whoever heard any of our teachers say they were wrong about anything at all! I learned from my graduate studies, especially at Princeton, that true learning and scholarship makes one humble and childlike rather than proud and arrogant.

One of the most rewarding Princeton experiences was a Bible reading course from Donald Wheeler, who had a reputation for coaching Broadway stars in New York. He entertained the Princeton community each year at Christmastime with his inimitable rendering of Dickens' *Christmas Carol*.

He stressed the importance of effective public reading of the Bible—that it should be prepared for and taken seriously. He insisted that one cannot read aright without understanding aright. We spent the entire course learning to read interpretatively the Sermon on the Mount, using the King James Version.

He pointed out, to our amusement, that "Whoever looketh upon a woman to lust after her hath committed adultery with her already in his heart" is not to be read as if there is something wrong with *looking* at a woman. Jesus is talking about lust, and in lusting one *has already* committed adultery *in his heart*.

But he would not have us dramatize. Reading is to be in a normal voice—clear, distinct, and with understanding. Bible reading, he insisted, should be a major part of public worship, for when it is done effectively it both informs and inspires.

The course gave me an enthusiasm for the fine art of the public reading of Scripture, an enthusiasm I have sought to pass along. I am hopeful that we will make greater effort in Churches of Christ to encourage men and women alike to cultivate their God-given gift of excellence in Bible reading. It remains an untapped means of grace in most of our assemblies.

Henry S. Gehman, who taught Old Testament, introduced me to a new term, the fertile crescent, that fruitful strip of land that wraps around the Arabian desert in the form of a great crescent. In that place were the ancient empires that became the context for the Biblical story—Babylonia, Assyria, Mesopotamia, Syria, Phoenicia, and Palestine.

This is where it all took place—in a crescent that wrapped around a desert. God did not deal with his people Israel in a vacuum. Their history was intertwined with the pagan nations around them: Nebuchadnezzar, the Babylonian king, was called the Lord's battle-ax;

Cyrus, the Persian, was named the Lord's anointed or messiah; the Assyrians were the servants of the Lord. God used nations that did not know Him to fulfill His purposes for Israel. For me, it was breaking new ground in biblical study.

When it came to biblical chronology, Gehman would warn, "Don't try to date Adam." While he taught us to respect modern biblical research, there was no question but what God spoke to us through those ancient documents that we call the Bible. I was to realize, once I was at Harvard, just how conservative Princeton was, a fact I have always appreciated.

While I completed the requirements in the winter of 1947, I did not graduate until June of 1948. I received the Bachelor of Divinity degree—now called Master of Theology. It represented three years of graduate theological education beyond college. I've always considered it my most rewarding educational experience, even more than Harvard. I'm deeply grateful to the Presbyterians for providing it. It cost me nothing financially, not the first dollar.

Ralph Graham and I were busy at other things besides our studies at Princeton. While Ralph's ministry was largely confined to the Liberty Street Church of Christ in Trenton, which was our main supporting congregation, I gave my time to several small Churches of Christ in New Jersey, including a congregation that met in an army chapel at Fort Monmouth.

Here we met with young service men from all over the nation, and we formed lasting friendships. Eventually this work became part of the Church of Christ in Eatontown where I frequently preached. One summer I held a meeting under a tent in that town. I baptized Warren and Norma Van Tuyl. Warren eventually studied at Abilene Christian College and became a leader in our northeast churches for many years. The Eatontown church later moved to Tom's River where there is today a substantial congregation.

I also made frequent visits to an older but still small Church of Christ in Tabernacle, New Jersey. Here we met the influential Cutts family—Jack, Ross, Walter, Ernest—who were blueberry and cranberry growers. They and their children and grandchildren became pillars in Churches of Christ, especially in the northeast. Ernest's daughter Alice married Wayne Newland, who served the Trenton church in various ways for 25 years, and now worships with the Greater Portland Church of Christ in Maine. In recent years, Ouida and I have visited with the Newlands in Maine, and I have had assignments at their congregation.

During the Princeton days, I also helped start a new congregation in Seaford, Delaware, which eventually settled in Laurel and is today a substantial church. Here I met the family of Charles Hudson. When I baptized the four Hudson sons in a pond near their home, all on the same occasion, Mr. Hudson cried out praises to the Lord. That family too has provided leadership among our churches in those parts all these years.

Ouida and I left New Jersey in the winter of 1947 in time to serve on the faculty of Montgomery Bible College during its spring semester of 1948. Ouida taught secretarial courses, and I taught Bible. Rex A. Turner and Leonard Johnson, founders of the college, served as co-presidents. This college eventually evolved into what is now Faulkner University. Southern Christian University, also in Montgomery, is largely the result of the efforts of Rex Turner, who served as its first president. Leonard Johnson completed his distinguished teaching career at Freed-Hardeman College.

In Montgomery I also preached at the Church of Christ in nearby Chisholm and conducted a 15-minute morning radio program on station WJJJ. During those months, I did a number of protracted meetings in that part of Alabama, some of them where we had no church.

During this time, Ouida also worked as a secretary for the state highway department when "Big Jim"

Folsom was the popular governor. I was with her one time at a reception at the governor's mansion. When it was time for Ouida to shake the governor's hand, he blurted out, "Ain't she pretty!" "Big Jim" gained a measure of national notoriety when he kissed girls on the streets of New York City. It is just as well that he wasn't in a kissing mood at the reception that day!

While it was tempting to remain in Montgomery where we had interesting things to do, I felt the need to do still more graduate work: a doctorate at either Yale or Harvard. But I would first study for a year with Lutheran scholars at Concordia Seminary in St. Louis. Concordia would provide a strong German touch to my studies. But it was only part-time, since I also had to make a living by serving as a busy substitute teacher in several St. Louis high schools. Ouida again worked as a secretary.

Not unlike the Princeton professors, the Lutherans at Concordia were quiet, unassuming, and studious. They were accused of thinking in German. They were more Armenian in their theology, while Princeton was more Calvinist, and, as Missouri Synod Lutherans, they were more conservative.

Martin Luther, of course, was writ large around the place, but, oddly enough, one professor admitted to me that it bothered him that his church bore a human name, even if it was Luther's! Another professor assured the class that no one understood Paul's doctrine of grace in Romans like Martin Luther, which may be true. At least none has acted upon that doctrine the way Luther did.

The most eminent professor at Concordia was the genial William F. Arndt, who became known in the theological world as co-editor, along with G. W. Gingrich, of Bauer's *A Greek-English Lexicon of the New Testament*. But I introduced Professor Arndt to a subject somewhat removed from Greek lexicography: Alexander Campbell, who believed he was called of God to finish

53

what Martin Luther had begun. Arndt was interested.

I gave some thought to pursuing the Th.D. (Doctor of Theology) offered at Concordia, but I knew it wouldn't sell in the academic marketplace like a Ph.D., especially one from Yale or Harvard, even if it were as demanding. I applied to both Yale and Harvard.

While Yale was still considering my application, Harvard wrote and said "You're accepted."

Harvard! A Ph.D. student at Harvard! This high school dropout had come a long way! If I could make it, I'd likely be the first Harvard Ph.D. who could not produce a high school diploma. I was still Number Two. I would try harder.

After a summer of gospel meetings, Ouida and I returned to the northeast in the fall of 1949—all the way to Boston this time, and by train. We crossed the Charles River by subway and arrived at Harvard Square in Cambridge. It was a new world to us.

By now Ouida had begun to quote her mother to me: "If you marry Leroy, you might die of excitement but never of boredom!"

Chapter 8
With Unitarians
At Harvard

"Founded in 1636 so that New England might have an educated ministry." So reads an engraving on an entrance gate into "The Yard"; yet Harvard University does not impress one today as an institution founded for religious purposes. It is the oldest university in America and, with an endowment now exceeding a trillion dollars, it is the richest. Its libraries are the greatest repository of knowledge in the world. Its faculty is world-class, with more than its share of Pulitzer/Nobel prize winners. Its reputation arguably makes it the most renowned university in the world.

It might also be the freest and most liberal, open as it is to every conceivable area of study and research—fiercely competitive and cosmopolitan. It is a marketplace of ideas. Its schools of medicine, law, education, business, and engineering are always out on the growing edge.

And yet it welcomes criticism, and is even self-critical. A most scathing criticism imaginable against the university, having to do with its presumed coziness with Communism, I read on a bulletin board in "The Yard" for all to see, posted there by officials. Equally impressive is its parsimony, as if committed to getting the last penny's worth out of every dollar, and in little ways, such as using both sides of note pads in the library! Their money-managers, among the best in the business, believe that people will give to an institution that is frugal with the donors' money. In fund drives they go after hundreds of millions at a time, and usually get it!

With all this said, Harvard could hardly be more secularistic, or post-modern if that is the term, but perhaps no more than most American universities. Courses are taught and knowledge is pursued as if there were no God. Deity is irrelevant, and anything supernatural is suspect. It is a secularism that ignores God more than it denies him.

When I was at Harvard a half-century ago, James Bryant Conant, a noted scientist and skeptic, was president. He referred to the part of Harvard that interested me the most as "my superstitious colleagues at the Divinity School."

While the Divinity School has undergone substantial change in recent decades, it was ultra-liberal, or so it seemed to me, when I enrolled in the fall of 1949. During my first two years there, I may not have had a single professor who believed in the deity of Christ. The professor who taught theology was a professed atheist! At least he had no sectarian bias!

The students were mostly Unitarian. One year, when it was time for the students to do the Easter service, they thought it appropriate to have someone speak who believed the Easter story. The lot fell on me, the one believer they knew. There I was to speak in the renowned Divinity Hall chapel where Ralph Waldo Emerson gave his famous "Divinity Hall Address" back in 1836. I was to speak to both faculty and students— with hardly a believer among them—on the Easter story! It rivaled Brother Hardeman's invitation for me to preach in his place back at Freed-Hardeman College.

In the presentation, I put the witnesses to the resurrection of Christ on the witness stand. One by one—the women, Peter, James, Paul, all the apostles— they gave their testimony, as if in a court of law. I reviewed some thirteen appearances of Jesus following his resurrection—evidence that demands a verdict! I then referred to Goethe's *Faust*, in which Faust, the infidel, hears Easter bells, and says, "Oh, Easter bells, I hear your message, but I cannot believe," as if maybe he wanted to.

My point was that Faust could have believed if he wanted to, for the evidence is there. I concluded with my ace card. I pointed to the tower of the Harvard Law School out our windows and referenced Professor Greenleaf, the famous jurist on that faculty in a bygone day. He made a study of the testimony of the evangelists from a legal point of view, and concluded as a jurist that their testimony would stand in any court of the land.

Following my presentation, my major professor, Henry J. Cadbury, eminent New Testament scholar and a quiet Quaker (a theist but not an orthodox Christian), came by, took my hand in his, smiled, and—as a good Quaker would—said not a word. As the students filed by, one of them smiled and quoted Goethe back to me, "I hear your message, but I cannot believe." But that was my quarrel with them. They could believe if they wanted to. They didn't want to!

While I did not refer to it at the time, another Harvard great, William James, in his essay on "The Will To Believe" argued for belief in God on the ground of willing to believe. The evidence for believing is at least as strong as for not believing, so why not will to believe? "It is a matter of what one wants to believe," he insisted, "and there might be advantages to believing. Suppose it turns out that there is a God," he warned.

At Harvard, the issues were different from those back in Tennessee and Texas. Instead of baptism or instrumental music, it was the gospel itself, the Easter message.

Professor Cadbury's classes often provided for substantial give and take. Once when we were into texts on the resurrection of Christ, one student said a good reason for not believing was that it was too good to be true. The professor agreed that, yes, some stories told are too good to be true. The entire class seemed to accept such a conclusion. At last I had my say, that, yes,

57

some things may seem "too good to be true," but that was why I am a Christian. I believe to be true what is "too good to be true."

On one occasion Cadbury, a man I came to love and respect, allowed that "the empty tomb" is a compelling story. "Something must have happened," he conceded. On other occasions he would question the role of the clergy, as one might expect a Quaker to do: "When Peter fished and Paul *span*, where was the clergy*man?*"

Gentle Quaker or not, he could be devastating in his criticisms. He walked into class one day telling us he had a letter from Texas. "They're having a big debate on instrumental music, and they want to know what the professor of New Testament at Harvard has to say about the Greek word *psallo*—as to whether it includes or excludes the instrument." When he left it at that and went on with his lecture, I at last asked him how he responded to the question from Texas.

After all, it must have come from one of my Church of Christ brethren, but I didn't mention that. He slyly told us that he would not likely please either side, for his answer was that *psallo* simply means to sing, and it neither includes nor excludes an instrument!

Cadbury was a social activist and believed that passion for the marginalized of society leads to inner religion rather than the other way around, as is commonly held. As chairman of the American Friends Service Committee, he had gone to Stockholm the year before I met him to receive the Nobel Peace Prize on behalf of the AFSC. At least among the Society of Friends he was as renowned for his expertise in Quaker history as in biblical scholarship. When Margaret Hope Bacon, a Quaker writer, authored *Let This Life Speak: The Legacy of Henry Joel Cadbury* (1987, several years after his death), she asked me—as one of his graduate students—to share some of my Harvard memories of him, some of which she used in her book about him.

One touching memory is of a speech he gave to a

58

Harvard peace organization. A consummate pacifist, he held all human life as sacred— "There's something of God in all of us" as the Quakers like to say. In his speech that night, he said something I found riveting: "It isn't so bad for a man to die, for he is going to die anyway, but it is terribly bad for me to kill him." It wasn't only what he said, but the passion with which he said it that caused it to stay with me all these years. One of his comments about the nature of religion I also find challenging: "Religion is not only the beatific vision, it is getting on without it." He was observing that even the mystics, who profoundly feel the presence of God, sometimes have their dry, blank periods.

I once asked Cadbury what he supposed would happen if Jesus were among us today. "He would be killed or imprisoned," he said assuredly. When I asked him who would do it, he answered with the same assurance, "The clergy." I thought it strange. There I was in a renowned divinity school where clergy were being trained, and one of its leading professors was telling us that if Christ were among us today he would again be murdered—and by the clergy!

Cadbury seemed quite taken, if not shaken, by "the Jesus story," one of his books being *The Peril of Modernizing Jesus*. He emphasized that to understand Jesus we must see him in the context in which he lived. In class he would sometimes speak of Jesus, as if talking to himself, "I wonder what went on in that mind of his."

He would point out that we really do not know all that much about Jesus—nothing like a biography. We know much more about Paul, he would say. I sensed the professor was awed by Jesus—one that he could not quite accept as Lord and one he could not quite ignore! He admitted that the evidence for the resurrection of Christ as set forth in the New Testament documents was impressive, and he never appeared willing to reject it completely.

Into his 90s, long after retirement from Harvard,

Professor Cadbury died when he fell down a flight of stairs in his home. I have often thought to myself, "What would Professor Cadbury say about Jesus now?"

I studied Roman and Hellenistic Backgrounds with A. D. Nock, who had a reputation for being something of a tyrant. He certainly didn't start each class with a prayer as the professors did at Princeton! There was a saying around the Divinity School that "One takes his Ph.D. by the grace of Cadbury and the wrath of Nock." I found that the best way to survive in his class was to stand up to him and argue one's case. I did so and survived, but he once asked me, "Are you a Baptist?" I told him no, but didn't tell him what I was. With Nock, I answered only what I was asked!

The theology professor referred to earlier as an atheist was J. A. C. Auer, a gentle, gracious soul even if an atheist. An atheist teaching theology! It struck me as an amusing contradiction. But after studying with him awhile I decided that that might be as good a way to do theology—from a distance. He asked me one day in class if I believed in immortality, and if so, why.

Realizing it was not a time to be biblical, I gave what I thought was a reasonable argument based on the universal tendency of man to believe in another life—something innate in all of us, and which may well be true. He stroked his bald head, as he usually did when pondering an issue, and at last said ever so gently, "Mr. Garrett, you will forgive me for not believing for such a reason as that."

While I was not particularly impressed with my argument either, I came to see that there was nothing that I nor anyone else could have said that would have made any difference in his thinking. He was an atheist with a closed mind. I realized that at Harvard, too, as liberal-minded as they presumed themselves to be— there were those who believed only what they had made up their minds to believe. And never mind evidence!

Professor Auer was fascinated with Texas and liked to

ask me about my home state. He told me one day that if he were a young man and could start over, he would go to Texas!

I had a course on the Inter-Testamental Period, or the Maccabean Age, with Robert H. Pfeiffer. Though a Harvard professor, the class was at Boston University. The course was one of my less exciting ones, but it meant something to study with a noted scholar. What I remember most is that while I took a subway to Boston U. for the course, I rode back to Harvard with Pfeiffer himself. Even on cold nights, he had a sports car with the top down. He would hold his beat-up hat with one hand while speeding along with the other, while I shivered. Some way to cross the Charles!

I would occasionally go to "The Yard" (the main campus, one-half mile from the Divinity School) for something special. One such occasion was to hear Perry Miller lecture on Alexander Campbell, which he did each year. After the lecture, he told me that he saw Campbell as "part of the great West," and one unfortunately neglected by historians. In his own lectures on 19th century America, he sought to correct this. Arthur Schlesinger, another noted Harvard professor at the time, went to Bethany College to lecture on Campbell.

Reading courses were new to me, but vintage Harvard. These consisted of required readings and periodic consultation with the professor. They had the advantage of one-on-one contact with the professor. I took two of these, the most significant being with Harry A. Wolfson, a Judaic scholar whose specialty was Philo. I read with him on Judaism. He assigned me the scholarly two-volume set on *Judaism* by George Foote Moore, a Harvard scholar of an earlier day.

When I reported to him on my reading and readied myself for the next assignment, he said, "Read George Foote Moore again." He made the point that it is better to master a substantive work like Moore than to dabble

61

in multiple lesser works. It confirmed a point Cadbury had made about European scholars, who may study fewer books than we, but they study them more thoroughly. Wolfson's point stuck with me. If it is really a meaty book, linger with it before moving on to something else.

While Ouida worked in Boston during most of our time at Harvard, she was free at the outset to attend some classes with me, particularly Cadbury's, whom she came to admire as I did. She could join me in drawing comparisons between Harvard and Princeton. Perhaps it was that the former spoke more to the head, the latter more to the heart.

I finished my resident requirements at Harvard by the summer of 1951, lacking only the thesis. We returned to a home we owned in Dallas where I again taught school, preached, became an editor, and gathered data for my thesis. It was five years before I got back to Harvard to write the thesis. Some unexpected things happened during that time, which I chronicle in the next chapter.

One thing that happened is that we started our family by adopting our first child, an infant we named Phoebe Anna Garrett. She is now Phoebe Trammell and a grandmother. She and her husband live only a few miles from us. Ouida's having to stay in Dallas to care for Phoebe meant that I had to return to Harvard alone to write my thesis, which took most of 1956. It made a big difference not having Ouida.

By the time I returned, the Divinity School had undergone quite a change. Nathan Pusey, a lifelong Episcopalian, had succeeded Conant as Harvard's president. Unlike Conant, he had a heart for the Divinity School and made it his first priority to initiate a campaign "to save it from obscurity." Pusey had been active in the World Council of Churches, an experience that persuaded him that Harvard should have a Divinity School that would be both academically challenging and yet congenial to the churches. Such a priority on the part of a Harvard president was to the dismay of many in the university community. But Pusey made it work. The Divinity School was now more ecumenical and less Unitarian, and more in touch with the church at large.

Pusey not only raised millions to strengthen the School's endowment but brought in such promising young faculty as Krister Stendahl, John Dillenberger, and Conrad Wright, along with the more seasoned Amos Wilder. Most of the older faculty I knew had retired, including Cadbury. I was to be doubly blessed in that I was exposed to the new faculty as well as the old.

It meant I would have a different professor to guide me through my thesis. This would be Stendahl, recently imported from the University of Uppsala in Sweden. He was young, forceful, demanding. He brought with him the high standards for graduate study of Scandinavian universities. Only 35 years of age at the time, he was destined to be a highly acclaimed New Testament scholar. A high church Lutheran, he would, after Harvard, become archbishop of Stockholm.

And he was a believer. One story they told on him was his response to a rather colorful question from a student: "Suppose on Easter morning someone was there at the tomb with a Brownie camera, what kind of picture would they get?" Pondering the question as good scholars do, he at last answered in his Swedish accent, "I suppose he would have a picture of the resurrection!"

One thing Stendahl insisted upon was that no one should do a thesis on his or her own; research should be shared with others in seminar discussion. He therefore met with the Ph.D. candidates, and we gave reports to each other on our progress. That enabled us to help each other in our search for data. My thesis was entitled *The New Jerusalem: A Study In Jewish and Christian Apocalypticism*. When I gave my first report, Stendahl seemed pleased that I was off to such a good start. We

63

graduate students helped each other. One of my colleagues was researching the Jewish temple in the time of Christ. If I came upon data that he could use, I passed it along, and he in turn would help me. That is what Stendahl wanted, which apparently was not the way Harvard had been doing it.

But I was in for a rough ride. When I submitted my first chapter for his inspection, he wrote across the cover page, "This is not a thesis! I want to know what *you* think!" I had given enough data, but I was not drawing my own conclusions sufficiently. Once I saw what he wanted—and, of course, he was right—I had no further difficulty.

I gained something of a reputation at the Andover Library for my industry. The custodian opened for me in the mornings even before staff arrived, and I was the last to leave at night. I was accused of spending my nights there! Stendahl told it around that I was the most industrious student he ever had. He didn't say the smartest, just the most industrious. Translated that meant that I was Number Two, but I tried harder!

I had hardly started before I came down with acute pain in my back and right arm, so bad that I had to go to the Harvard Infirmary during the night. They had no problem controlling the pain, but they didn't know what was wrong with me. Doctors from the Medical School came by and poked around on me trying to come up with a diagnosis. At last I told one of them that I was probably suffering from anticipatory anxiety. He thought that maybe I had correctly made my own diagnosis. They dismissed me the same day that old friends Richard E. Smith and Max Watson came up from Bridgeport, Connecticut to check on me. But I had lost a week, except for such reading as I could do in the Infirmary. Now I had to work even harder, anxiety or not.

Stendahl was apparently pleased with my effort, once the job was done. When LeMoine Lewis returned to

Harvard from teaching at Abilene Christian to write his thesis in 1957, he asked Stendahl, who would also direct him, to name four or five Harvard Ph.D. theses that he might read to see what was expected of him. Stendahl said he would name but one, and recommended mine. LeMoine told me that story several years after the fact. Coming from Stendahl, that was the ultimate compliment.

Dean Willard Sperry told us at the outset of our Ph.D. studies that we should not let it be drudgery, as it so often was. Theological research should be joyous. "Have fun!" he preached. For the most part that proved true for me. It was fun turning up ideas and weaving them into a thesis. That writing is easy for me didn't hurt any.

I had passed my "generals" exam upon completing the resident requirements five years earlier. Stendahl invited professors from "The Yard" to join him for my thesis exam. It may have been just as well that they had little notion of what apocalypticism was about. But they still knew the right questions to ask.

Usually the thesis exam is not critical. It is the "generals" where they might tell you to forget it, and give you a master's degree as a consolation prize. That *did* sometimes happen, and it put fear in us.

I was in a preaching series at a Church of Christ in Vincennes, Indiana when Harvard wired me that my thesis had been accepted. I would receive the Ph.D. hood in elaborate ceremonies in "The Yard" in June of 1957.

But I couldn't afford another trip to Harvard for the ceremonies, so I graduated *in absentia*. Sometime later the postman handed me my Harvard Ph.D. at the front door, special delivery. Ouida and I got a bang out of that. *At last I received my Ph.D. from Harvard—from the postman at the front door!*

Just another mail order degree!

65

Chapter 9
On Becoming
An Editor & Landing
In Jail

One of the earlier historians of the Restoration Movement, W. T. Moore, observed that while the Disciples of Christ do not have bishops, they do have editors. He at least meant that editors, for whatever reason, have had an inordinate influence among our people—a power not unlike that of a bishop in other traditions. And so, from the outset, we have had what can arguably be called editor-bishops.

Moore was not speaking pejoratively, but matter-of-factly, as he saw it. Whether for good or evil, our editors have had the aura of bishops. After all, three of our "four founding pioneers" —Barton W. Stone, Alexander Campbell, Walter Scott—were editors, and their leadership was comparable to that of good bishops in other churches. They were "bishops" who blessed us by getting us off to a good start. In darker periods when divisions came it was again the work of editor-bishops.

When I started *Bible Talk* in October of 1952, I was not aware of the influence an editor could have in Churches of Christ. When I sent out the first issue, I was an unknown commodity, but in less than a year I was a controversial figure of some dimension. Beginning with a handful of subscribers and a few hundred sample-copies, I soon had thousands of readers.

It was shortly after becoming an editor that I became acquainted with Carl Ketcherside, also an editor. In 1953, I attended his debate with G. K. Wallace near Paragould, Arkansas. He impressed me as sincere, persuasive, and eloquent. We discovered that we had much in common, and that our papers were pursuing similar ends. For the next 37 years, until he died in 1989, we would do considerable work together.

While I wrote in *BibleTalk* on numerous subjects, some of them drawn from my research at Harvard, my main purpose was to challenge two related practices in Churches of Christ, professionalism and institutionalism. The first had to do with "the pastor system," as it came to be dubbed, and the other with institutions, colleges in particular, doing the work of the church. They were related in that they depended on each other. The colleges produced "the clergy," which in turn influenced the churches to support the colleges.

My objection to the minister system was related to the larger issue of the proper function of the body of Christ. Drawing upon Ephesians 4:11-16, I pointed out that God has set the church in order "for the equipping of the saints, for the work of ministry, for the edifying of the body of Christ." And that this is realized when "the whole body, joined and knit together by what every joint supplies, according to the effective working by which every part does its share, causes growth of the body for the edifying of itself in love."

Based on this apostolic mandate, I saw the ministry of the church in terms of what I called "body life," where every member shares in building up the church, each according to his ability. When a professional is imported—brought in from outside the body—to do what the members themselves are to do, it is a harmful departure from the Biblical order.

The same passage calls for pastors (elders) and evangelists. The elders, I observed—drawing on Acts 20:28 in particular—were to "feed the flock" while the evangelists (preachers) are to take the gospel to the unsaved. The apostle Paul did not instruct the elders to hire it done, but they themselves were to be pastors to the flock, aided in the work by all the members—each according to his or her talents. The Scriptures thus called for a mutual ministry, led by duly appointed elders—not a "one man" hired minister.

The scriptural order is distorted, I claimed, when evangelists (preachers), who are mandated by Scripture to "do the work of an evangelist," are employed to be "the minister" of the church. Pointing to our claim to be "the New Testament church" and a people who have "restored the Biblical pattern," I challenged our leadership to find "the minister" in any New Testament church. Elders and deacons, yes, but where is "the minister"? We were as unscriptural as the denominations, I charged, in that, while they have their pastor, we have our minister. In pressing this issue, I rattled not a few cages.

The battle was joined when in March, 1953, I mailed out 25,000 copies of a special issue of *Bible Talk*—composed mainly of excerpts from Restoration pioneers on the minister system. I also had cartoons depicting "the System" from the time the candidate goes through Bible college to being hired by the elders. One cartoon illustrated how much of the church's money goes to the minister and edifices, and how little to missions and benevolence.

I quoted from Alexander Campbell: "To employ men to preach the gospel to a Christian congregation is a satire upon that congregation that employs them." And from Tolbert Fanning, the founding editor of the *Gospel Advocate:* "The system of converting evangelists into pastors of the respective flocks is from without and is plainly popish in all its bearing." And the more recent G. C. Brewer: "What we call the 'located preacher' usually does the work required of elders, and really if we follow the New Testament pattern, there is no official position in the church for a preacher."

There were similar excerpts from David Lipscomb, James A. Harding, Benjamin Franklin, and Moses E. Lard. One of my favorite quotes was from a contemporary, Guy N. Woods, perhaps because he so

69

well summarized what I was saying: "The elders are the pastors of the flock, and not the evangelist; and it is their duty to care for it and tend it. Evangelists are to carry the glad tidings of salvation to the lost, and preach the gospel in regions where it is not known." I think Brother Woods forgot that he ever said this until I reminded him of it in a debate we had!

If I was by now an editor-bishop, after only two years, I was a controversial one. While there were many who rallied behind my efforts, the powers that be were out to minimize my influence. There were instances of preachers taking *Bible Talk* into the pulpit and advising the people against it—which proved to be my most effective advertising! I became "the issue" in most of the Churches of Christ journals, including the *Gospel Advocate*, edited by B. C. Goodpasture—the leading paper among us at the time.

Editor Goodpasture editorialized me with abandon, characterizing me as a hobbyist and a radical. He published an attack on me by Rex A. Turner under the title "An Open Letter to Leroy Garrett." He also ran a series by Guy N. Woods, with front-page prominence—exposing my teachings, which was mostly misrepresentation.

I could never persuade the *Advocate* editor to allow me equal space to respond to the attacks. So, in one of my editorials I nicknamed him "Brother Hit and Run"! Since he was so interested in exposing my views, I made him an unusual offer. I would debate our differences in our papers with him without saying anything on my own. I would answer him by references to former, renowned editors of the *Advocate*, his predecessors. He wasn't impressed.

By this time I had debated Guy N. Woods in Stockton, California and George DeHoff in Nashville on these issues. While the Woods debate was congenial enough, the DeHoff debate, which was held under a tent, became so explosive that I thought there might be a riot.

The attacks against me during these days led G. A. Dunn, Sr. to express concern that I might suffer bodily harm, and he reminded me of what Erasmus said about Martin Luther: "Luther's problem was that he hit the pope's belly and the priests' pocketbook."

This is enough to give you a feel for the climate when I arrived at Freed-Hardeman College for its lectureship in January 1955. As probably the most controversial figure among Churches of Christ at the time, I created considerable curiosity wherever I went.

Due to other appointments, I was there only for the last day of the lectures, but that was all the time it took for my presence, which was unexpected, to catapult the lectureship into a virtual firestorm. As one of the college officials said later when I asked what my offense was, "Just being here is offense enough!"

When I walked into the Administration Building that morning—at the college where I had been a student 15 years before—I immediately greeted old friends and classmates, such as Doyle Banta, Charles Holt, William Hull, and C. W. Brannum. Our conversation was as friendly as in years past. No problem. But when the student ministers of the college began to gather about me—probably out of curiosity to see what kind of an animal I might be—and began to question me about what I believed, the administration became concerned.

On my way upstairs to hear a lecture by Denton Neal, the preacher whose place I took on the radio in Paragould, Arkansas, back when I was a student at the college, I was met by H. A. Dixon, the president of the college. He told me, in a less than friendly way, that I was welcome to attend the lectures but I was not to cause a disturbance by talking to the students. Surprised by his attitude, I told him that I was doing only what all others were doing, visiting in the halls. *What was he afraid of?* I asked.

After Neal's lecture, when I once again was visiting

among students and lectureship guests, I received word that President Dixon wanted to see me in his office. With the president were C. P. Roland, dean of the college, a man whom I loved and respected from my days as a student, and Robert L. Witt, a faculty member that I did not know. The purpose of the meeting was to issue me an ultimatum. They had heard that I had been invited by some of the preacher boys to come to their dormitory and discuss issues further. *I was not to go!*

It got ugly. Dean Roland was especially agitated. He threatened to call civil authorities. When I asked him what I had done that was all that bad, he said, "Just by being here!" He assured me in no uncertain terms that he had the power to take care of the likes of me. Professor Witt, who taught psychology at the college, proceeded to analyze my mental state, concluding that I must be schizophrenic. He advised that I see a psychiatrist at once—even before I returned home.

I told the professor that if his diagnosis was correct, I was hardly being treated as a brother in need of mental therapy. Threats, shouts of abuse, and ultimatums were hardly appropriate for one mentally ill. They heaped upon me threats of reprisal if I proceeded to visit with the students. I reminded them I was a free man in Christ—that I was within my rights and was violating no law—and if the students did not withdraw their invitation, I would go to their dormitory.

I let them know that I was puzzled by their behavior. They had the students all year, and I was to visit with them only an hour or two. What were they afraid of? I even suggested that they go along with me to the dorm, and we could talk it out in brotherly fashion—that the students would love that. Their answer was if I tried to go to the dorm, I would be met by the police.

I could not believe they would do such a foolish and reckless thing, however much they might be displeased with me. I was wrong.

As the volatile day drew on, there was an open forum

conducted by Guy N. Woods, a lawyer as well as preacher, who had a talent for such assignments. Since I was present, the agenda was changed. A student wrote out a question "*Is Freed-Hardeman College doing the work of the church?*" for discussion and asked me to sign it, which I did.

A lively discussion followed, and sometimes the attitude was no better than that shown in the president's office. I was both surprised and disappointed when Earl West—an old classmate at both Freed-Hardeman and Abilene and now a professor at the college—told the forum that the problem with Leroy Garrett was that he has a martyr's complex. But Brother Woods allowed me to speak and to answer questions that were raised. There was lots of excitement, and it was visceral.

I had at least injected life into a lectureship that might otherwise have been boring!

The students did not withdraw their invitation, but I didn't get as far as their dormitory. I was arrested in the afternoon by the town police for disturbing the peace on the campus of Freed-Hardeman College. I was driven away in a police car while hundreds watched as they were lined up at the cafeteria for the evening meal. Since I could not post the required bail, I was incarcerated in the town jail, which, I was to learn, had the reputation of being the dirtiest in the county—but with the best food!

Unfortunately for me—and the town drunk who was now my cell mate—the cook of reputation was at home ill. By law the incarcerated have to be fed, so we were taken to a restaurant in town by two armed officers for the evening meal, as well as the next morning for breakfast. For a small Tennessee town full of lectureship visitors, this created something of a spectacle. The officers told me I was the first preacher they had taken into custody, and they were kind enough to allow me to call Ouida from the restaurant phone.

It took some explaining for Ouida to understand

that I was both in jail and at a public restaurant. It made more sense when she realized that I was flanked by two armed officers of the law. She could hardly believe what I was telling her.

Later that evening Dean Roland and Professor Witt came to the jail. They said the college would withdraw the charge filed against me and allow me to attend the lecture that night at the local Church of Christ, if I would comport myself according to their wishes.

I declined the offer. They had arrested me in the presence of hundreds; they would not now release me privately. They had made their charge. I would meet them in court. I told them it would be interesting to see how they would sustain the charge that I was disturbing the peace when all I did was to talk to people who wanted to talk to me. And when I spoke in the forum it was only when I had permission. They were out of sorts with me when they left.

At the church that night they prayed for me. It was now generally presumed that I was a mental case. I suppose that was the proper thing to do for a mentally disturbed brother—pray for him—once you have secured his safety in the local jail. I was praying for them, so we had something worthwhile going after all!

In the meantime, some rather interesting things were happening. It was reported that James D. Bales, professor at Harding College, was in his car ready to return home when he heard what had happened. He changed his plan and stayed for the rest of the evening. A visitor to the lectureship wouldn't believe what he had heard until he saw for himself. He persuaded the jailer to allow him to look in on me. He came to the basement jail and looked in with gaping disbelief, and without a word to me turned away murmuring something to the effect that he'd never send another daughter to Freed-Hardeman.

My cellmate—there was but one cell—told me that the police were looking for the town's bad guy, who was suspected of another crime. If they find him, he warned me, they'll throw him in here with us, and he'll likely whip both of us. So, we were pulling for the bad guy! He also warned me about the bedding—too filthy to sleep under. So, following his lead, I used my overcoat for a pillow and slept in my clothes. We had a fairly good night.

It was the first and only night I ever spent in jail—and at Freed-Hardeman College! My mind would, of course, go back to my student days there when I had it so good, and to some years later when the president of the college entertained me in his own home during another lectureship. And now the president of the college had put me in jail! It all seemed so incredible, so ironic—even bizarre.

The next morning, the college officials unconditionally withdrew the charge they had filed against me, and paid the court costs, which included my meals. I was free to go home. Before I left, I consulted with a local lawyer who told me I had cause for legal action—false arrest. The college's withdrawal of the charge was an admission.

"But I can't take the case; I have to live with these people," he told me. I had no intention of suing. I only wanted to know what my rights were since I would soon be applying for a university teaching job—and such an episode as this on my record might well raise questions about me. And I was still a Ph.D. candidate at Harvard. I don't know how Harvard would have responded to Freed-Hardeman's charge that I was mentally deranged. They might have agreed!

The *Gospel Advocate* had a full-page spread entitled "Leroy Garrett's Visit to Freed-Hardeman," written by President Dixon, in which he claimed he had no other choice but to jail me, adding, "We cannot believe he is a normal man." An attending affadavit, signed by 26 preachers who were at the lectureship, stated that they believed I had been treated fairly.

Virtually every editor among Churches of Christ had something to say. Jack Holt had fun with it in the *Gospel Guardian* under the title, "The Ins and Outs of Leroy Garrett." But Jimmy Lovell, in his paper from California, called it one of the most disgraceful things ever to happen in Churches of Christ.

Once I told the story in *Bible Talk* to my thousands of readers, the reaction was shock and disbelief. President Dixon got some negative mail, and a few wrote to tell me that I got what was coming to me. It was a story that I would tell for the rest of my life—even to a generation not yet born.

A common reaction at the time was dismay that a Christian college would respond to a problem so injudiciously. The president of Johnson Bible College wrote to me sympathetically, conceding that what had happened to me at Freed-Hardeman was reason enough to reevaluate the role of our Christian colleges.

The college officials did not have to do what they did. They had an easy way out. Allow the students to talk to me all they pleased—even encourage it. It would all end that day. I would be gone, and the college would be no worse off for it. Since they were decent people and exemplary Christians, why did they behave so irresponsibly?

Carl Ketcherside—who at first responded humorously with, "You lucky dog! All these years I've been trying to get those fellows to put me in jail!" —at last gave a more serious analysis. "It could not have happened anywhere else except at Freed-Hardeman College," he said, "a school with anxiety in its genes." It was panic-prone. Only a few years before, hundreds of students staged a sit-in strike in response to what they perceived as tyranny on the part of the president. They shut the school down and forced the president's resignation. It was a drawn-out spectacle that attracted national media attention.

There was also a long history of infighting within the

administration that goes back to its founders, leaving some people badly hurt in its wake. The college seemed to run on nervous energy, harboring unrealistic fears. This would explain why it overreacted—even irrationally—and to its own harm.

I had some understanding of this, and I have never in all these 48 years since then had much of a problem with what happened—not even at the time. While those involved never apologized, I had no problem forgiving them. If anything, I've had compassion, for I realize that irrational fear can be a cruel master. Those involved have now gone on to a better world, and when we all meet in heaven we will have the maturity to laugh about it—if it comes up at all!

Freed-Hardeman College, now a university, is not that way today. I have returned to the campus once since that dramatic event back in 1955, and it was as if nothing had ever happened. It is still my alma mater, and I still treasure my banner year back in 1939-40. I find some satisfaction that the college librarian recently wrote asking for some copies of my newsletter missing from their files. She plans to bind the first 50 issues for permanent reference. And Ouida and I were pleased to have a present-day faculty member as a houseguest when he was in Denton recently on business. All this happened before he was even born! Time does make a difference, doesn't it?

I had fun with this when Abilene Christian University honored me with an award during its 2000 Lectureship. I told them, "This shows what can happen if one lives long enough," and I added, "I intend to live long enough to receive such an award from Freed-Hardeman! How long did Methuselah live?"

As for the issues that triggered such a dramatic series of events—the minister system and the role of Christian colleges—I still hold the views I did then, albeit more moderately. Or, to put it another way, I have shifted my priorities, deeming other issues more important.

77

Carl Ketcherside and I, who soldiered together on these matters for many years, saw that if we pressed these issues to the point of division, we would only create another Church of Christ sect. The alternative was to work peacefully within the system, bearing with things we did not approve, in hopes of helping to effect meaningful change in the long pull.

While we were accused—once we launched our renewal efforts—of swinging from one extreme to the other, it wasn't that way at all. We changed our priorities, not our convictions. The best way to minimize the negative influence of the pastor system and to curb the power imposed by the colleges, we concluded, was to make the Churches of Christ themselves what they ought to be. Seeing the futility of fighting a system that was genetically a part of Churches of Christ, we deemed it best to work within the system for such renewal as might be possible.

I have lived to see promising signs of change in these respects. The house church movement, prevalent in most denominations, is present in Churches of Christ in the form of cell/study groups, which meet in addition to the main assembly. These small groups capture much of the body life that is obstructed by the one-man minister system.

They are laity-centered rather than clergy-centered. Since they are free of the trappings of a "sanctuary" environment, real body life is possible with mutual sharing and encouragement, including the women. They have the feel of "the church in thy house" of New Testament times.

Our task is to transplant the spirit of these cell groups to the main assembly. Once this is done, we will have less need of a professional to minister to us. This would free our preachers to do the work of evangelists, starting in our own communities.

There is also change in what I have seen as a harmful, unscriptural dependence upon the colleges. In recent decades, many of our churches have experienced exciting changes, such as becoming less sectarian and having more to do with other churches. We are also more attuned to things spiritual, more responsible in Biblical interpretation, more aware of our own distinct history. This has come about through renewal in the churches themselves, with colleges having only a limited impact.

As we face the future as a church, we owe it to ourselves to be critical as to what role the colleges play. They are admittedly human institutions, and yet their mission in part is to do what is clearly the mission of the church: teach the Bible, train ministers and missionaries, send out evangelistic teams, hold church conventions (lectureships), conduct seminars for elders, etc.

It is understandable that we have always had among us those who have opposed this alliance between church and college. In my work in *Bible Talk,* I joined them in appealing for the biblical principle of "one Body," the church, as the entity ordained of God to carry out his mission on earth.

In their 1967 Plan of Restructure, the Disciples of Christ sought to solve this old issue by defining the church more broadly—which made colleges and like institutions "manifestations of the church." While this may raise other theological issues, it is a solution to be considered. That the Christian colleges *are* the church at work may be a supportable thesis, allowing for certain changes on the part of the colleges.

The great universities of Germany have chairs and departments of religion that are under the control of churches. The universities offer the environment and the venue, but the churches run the program.

Churches of Christ should insist on some such solution. We can at least be more honest than we have been, and quit claiming that the colleges do not do the work of the church. The problem will be with the colleges. They will not want to give up any of their

79

power.

I continued *Bible Talk* until 1957, the same year I took my Ph.D. from Harvard. Also that same year, except for the semester I taught at Montgomery Bible College, I took my first college teaching position, at MacMurray College in Jacksonville, Illinois, a Methodist-related women's college.

I had embarked upon a new and eventful dimension of my life—a career as a college and university professor.

Chapter 10
Pioneering
In High School
Philosophy

My first college teaching position after finishing my doctorate at Harvard resulted from a grant by the Lilly Endowment of Indianapolis to MacMurray College in Jacksonville, Illinois. Lilly funded an experimental course in philosophy for gifted seniors at Jacksonville High school, conducted by MacMurray College. Philosophy is rarely offered in high school, so the project was to ascertain if a college course in philosophy could be effectively taught in high school.

I was hired by MacMurray College to design the course as well as teach it. It was to be the equivalent of an introductory philosophy course in college, but within the context of a high school curriculum. I had help from President Louis W. Norris of MacMurray, who himself had taught philosophy in college. He had submitted the proposal to Lilly, and had his vision of what the pilot course should offer.

While we experimented as we went along, we gave the students a substantial feel for the usual introductory philosophy courses in college, with emphasis on ethics and logic. Since the class met every school day for an hour, which allowed for much more time than the course would have in college, we had time for lots of give-and-take discussion. The course was limited to "gifted" seniors, which was determined by four criteria: I.Q. scores, grades, reading proficiency, and teacher recommendation. But one year I offered the course to "gifted drifters" —those who had high I.Q. scores but

Pilot course in philosophy, Jacksonville (Illinois) High School, while a professor at MacMurray College, 1957.

low grades. We found that such students will likely perform according to their potential once they are sufficiently challenged.

We concluded from the three-year experiment that gifted high school students *can* handle a course in philosophy as well as first or second year college students. Eventually, we published a 45-page booklet on our findings, *Philosophy In High School,* which enjoyed a wide circulation. We suggested methods and resources for high schools that were interested in trying such a course. When the course was reported in the *New York Times,* we received scores of requests for more information from high schools across the country. The "gifted drifters" aspect of the experiment attracted special attention.

The Lilly grant enabled me to take the experiment to other high schools once I left MacMurray and Jacksonville. I offered the course at Triadelphia High School in Wheeling, West Virginia, while a professor at Bethany College, and at Denton High School in Denton, Texas, while on the faculty of Texas Woman's

82

University. After a decade with the course, I wrote a report on "Ten Years of High School Philosophy," which was published in *Educational Theory* in July, 1967.

I suggested to those who would offer such a course that the philosophers themselves should be read, not just books about them, and that the discussion method should be used more than the lecture method. Those were pioneer days in teaching philosophy in high school. While it is still rare, it is more common than back then. It was fun breaking new ground in education.

Along with the pilot course at Jacksonville High School, I was a professor of philosophy and religion at MacMurray College. This joint assignment opened up still another world for me. I lectured widely in schools, social clubs, and churches, not only on the experimental course, but also on subjects in general. By now I had a broader view of Christian fellowship and accepted guest preacher invitations from different denominations. This included an interim assignment at First Christian Church in nearby Winchester, Illinois, which lasted for several months.

When word of this circulated among Churches of Christ, it prompted an article by Professor J. W. Roberts of Abilene Christian College in the *Restoration Quarterly* on "Gone To the Christian Church!" It revealed just how far Leroy Garrett's apostasy had gone—all the way to the Christian Church.

Professor Roberts, an old friend, happened to be wrong, for I had not left Churches of Christ. By now I had resolved that I would never leave, not even if they kicked me out. While I loved my sisters and brothers in all denominations, I had a special love and a special mission for those in Churches of Christ. If it was a quarrel with my own church, it was a lover's quarrel. But I would nonetheless be a Christian-at-large, accepting all those as my sisters and brothers who, as Alexander Campbell put it, "hold to Christ as Head."

83

My transformation from a sectarian to an ecumenist came neither quickly nor easily. It was like Professor Cadbury's description of such change: "One usually yields his position one trench at a time." I began my retreat from legalism and sectarianism—gradually yielding my trenches—as I was exposed to more education, particularly at Princeton. Too, my study of the pioneers of the Restoration Movement, especially Alexander Campbell, served as a wake-up call that we in Churches of Christ had betrayed our own heritage. We were supposed to be a unity people, not factionalists. Our plea was to be "We are Christians only, but not the only Christians."

By 1957, the year I finished at Harvard and began a career as a college professor, I had been an editor among Churches of Christ for five years, a ministry I continued all through my teaching career. My writings during those first five years are reflective of the change I was undergoing. It was during this time that Carl Ketcherside, who was experiencing the same transformation, and I began working together. We became soul mates in what he called "a pilgrimage of joy." As we drew closer to Christ and became more grace-oriented—and more biblically responsible—we became less sectarian. I joined Carl in his insistence that "Wherever God has a child, I have a brother or sister."

Our newly-found freedom in Christ was revolutionary for both of us. It turned our lives in new directions and extended the reach of our ministry. We discovered, joyfully, that we had far more sisters and brothers in Christ than we realized. At the same time, it served to distance us from many in Churches of Christ who feared we were going too far. But they were our people, and we were committed to serving them, whatever the cost. We loved them too much to leave!

It was while at MacMurray that I had one of the strangest experiences of my life. Sherwood Eddy, a noted world missionary and writer, lived in Jacksonville with his wife, who was a trustee at the college. Arthur Ford, famed medium, was their friend. While on a visit to the Eddys, Ford agreed to a "sitting" (seance) for some of the Eddys' professional friends. I was invited. Since I was scheduled to give a commencement address at a high school that night and would be a bit late, Mrs. Eddy told me to enter by the back door and quietly take my place in the circle where a vacant chair would await me.

Ford was stretched out on a recliner with a napkin over his eyes, surrounded by a circle of some twelve people, all of whom were either professors, physicians, or clergy. Impressed by the circle of community leaders, I was nonetheless skeptical of it all and saw it as ridiculous. I was hardly seated with such thoughts before Ford nailed me with, "What is Leroy laughing about?"

Not being there for instructions at the beginning, I had to be whispered to by a professor friend sitting beside me that I was to respond to the medium. I learned later that the Eddys had given Ford no information about those in the circle, not even any names. Knowing them to be people of integrity, none of us questioned this, however tempting it might have been, considering Ford's performance that night.

Befuddled by his citing me so quickly, even calling my name, all I knew to do was to lie. I told him that I wasn't laughing—even if inwardly I suppose I was—but that I was amazed by it all. I was astounded by what followed. He made reference to the speech just given at the high school, and one I had made a few days before at a local church, expressing appreciation for all my good work.

Then came the zinger. He called our three-year old Phoebe by name, referred to her adoption, and told me

85

that she was an "old soul" with psychic power who could teach me a thing or two. He also said that "we" had arranged the adoption, a reference to departed spirits.

For some two hours, Ford did this sort of thing, all around the circle, giving details that no one in Jacksonville knew. For a minister in the circle he described the funeral of an old friend, including the Masonic lapel pen worn in his casket. He named friends and told the circumstances of their death. He even delivered messages from the dead, which impressed some of us as trivial, considering their presumed origin. One departed spirit wanted to commend one of our number for her work as organist at the Methodist Church; another urged a history professor not to grieve over the loss of a friend, for he was fine.

When someone afterwards complained to Ford that one would think that messages from the dead would concern weightier matters, he explained that "incarnates" are like ourselves in that they too enjoy small talk. But he made no effort to defend what was said during the seance. He rather insisted that he did not know what was said, for he was in a trance serving only as a medium between two worlds. It was spooky.

Arthur Ford was a Disciples of Christ minister before he became a medium. He wrote a book, *As Strange As It Seems,* that tells his story. In it he reveals how a Roman Catholic priest, a Frenchman, who lived on earth hundreds of years ago, drafted Ford to be a medium. Ford called him "Fletcher." That was what was going on that night, we were told. Fletcher had spirits around him in the world of the departed, and Ford had his circle on earth.

An admirer of Alexander Campbell, Ford claimed that the reformer was psychic and details instances in his book of such power, as he saw it. It is true that one cannot help but be impressed that Campbell—while in Scotland—"felt" that something was terribly wrong back home at the very time his young son Wycliffe drowned. Observing Campbell's unusual disquietude, a friend noted the time and date.

All those at the Eddys that night agreed that Ford's performance was remarkable. Some thought it supernatural—that we had actually communicated with departed spirits. None saw it as contrived. I saw it as an incredible demonstration of mind reading, assuring my friends, "Everything he said he got from us." But in time I changed my mind about what happened that incredible night.

Further study of "the spirit world" —as Alexander Campbell called it—and demonology in particular convinced me that we talked to demons that night in Jacksonville. I am now persuaded it was indeed miraculous, performed by Satan himself. Demons were doing missionary work for Satan. Campbell believed that demons are the spirits of wicked men who once lived on planet earth and who know their way around.

That we had talked to demons became further evident when Ford a few years later conducted a seance on TV for the controversial Bishop James Pike. Pike's son had committed suicide, and the bishop was eager to communicate with him. Ford provided the opportunity, and it was on nationwide TV.

At one point the bishop asked his son what they thought about Jesus "over there." He is known and respected, the son replied, but he is like one of us, not a savior or anything like that. After the seance the bishop assured the audience that it was for real—that things had been said known only to him and his son. A great night for Satan!

If I had that night at the Eddys to do over, I either would not have been present or I would have boldly affirmed my faith in Jesus as Lord. Those who have expertise about such things say that probably would have broken up the seance. Years later I read a report in a national journal from someone who had attended a

87

Ford séance. He said it caused his hair to stand on end! I know from personal experience what he meant.

When Perry Gresham, president of Bethany College, saw some of the things that I was writing about Alexander Campbell in my journal *Restoration Review*, he wrote and invited me to join his faculty as a professor of philosophy. Since my three-year Lilly project at the high school had concluded, I accepted, though I might have remained as a professor at MacMurray.

Shortly before we left MacMurray for Bethany, West Virginia, in the summer of 1960, we adopted our second child, less than a year old. We named him David Benjamin. He grew up as Benjy, around the house at least. He was a handsome lad, destined to attract attention in the Bethany community. He is now a seasoned schoolteacher living in Chillicothe, Missouri, and he is married to a teacher.

At Bethany I felt as if I had moved next door to Alexander Campbell, who founded the college in 1840. He even gave Bethany its name, which was at the time barely a village, and he lived there for 55 years, from 1811 till 1866. From that village, he sent out millions of copies of his own writings—journals, books, debates, hymnals. As the village postmaster with franking rights, he sent them all out postage free!

When heirs of the Restoration Movement visit Bethany, they sometimes exult, "This is where it all began!" which is only partly right. Priority in time has to go to Barton W. Stone and Cane Ridge in Kentucky, but priority in leadership belongs to Campbell and Bethany. It is what went forth from Bethany that gave the Movement its genius.

President Gresham, who loved the heritage that he was illustriously a part of, spoke often of how history had laid a heavy hand upon Bethany. And so it has.

Down the road from the college is "the Mansion" — earlier called "Bethany House" —the home of the Campbells. It is now registered as a national historic site. One can see the parlor where the young reformer took Margaret Brown, whose father had built the house, to be his wife in 1811, as well as the chair desk where he wrote many an essay and the bed in which he died. There is also the cabinet where he kept his wines.

In the yard is the Campbell study with its light from above—very much as it was when Campbell stood at his desk to read and write. Across the road is "God's Acre," the family cemetery that is sometimes called "the Westminster Abbey" of our heritage. Not only are the Campbells and their families buried there, but other such notables of the Movement as Robert Richardson, William Pendleton, Archibald McLean, and, only recently, Perry Gresham.

There is the college itself, which Campbell founded on his own farm in 1840. Old Main, the largest and oldest building, which was built after the order of Glasgow University back in Scotland, the university Campbell attended, is at the center of the campus. Now also a national historic site, Old Main was built in 1842 with money from Campbell himself, a loan the college trustees spent fifteen years in repaying.

Up the hill behind Old Main is Pendleton Heights, longtime home of Bethany presidents. Down the street from the college is the old Campbell church, where both Thomas and Alexander Campbell preached and where their funerals were held. It was built in 1827 as successor to the Brush Run Church, built in 1812, the old site of which is six miles from Bethany. Plans are currently underway to rebuild this old Restoration shrine, which was the first Church of Christ of the Campbell wing of the Movement.

While I basked in such history, my job was to teach philosophy, which I did in the same building where Campbell had taught. Ouida and I were often at

Professor of philosophy, Bethany College, 1960

Pendleton Heights where we were entertained, along with other faculty, by President Gresham and his wife Aleece. There were sometimes distinguished guests who served as resource persons for interesting conversation. These included Huston Smith, a specialist on world religions, and George Buttrick, one of America's great preachers.

Perry and I formed a lifelong friendship, and we shared the pain of the divisions within the Stone-Campbell heritage. We talked of ways to unite our fractured churches. Out of this concern came the Annual Unity Forum, which began at Bethany in 1966 and continued at various colleges for the next decade. These forums are further detailed in Chapter 13.

President Gresham not only lent his influence to this series of unity meetings, but he spoke at several of them.

In his inimitable way, he always wowed the audience with his tales of our founding pioneers, in a down-home, Will Rogers-like kind of appeal. It was disarming, even therapeutic, for our people in Churches of Christ who had never before heard a Christian Church minister. And these were unity meetings!

He and I also did some fun things on campus. Wearing straw hats and with canes in hand, we did a "soft shoe" on stage before the student body. It caught the students by surprise - - the college president and the professor of philosophy doing a fast foot step together!

As at MacMurray, while at Bethany I often spoke to various groups, especially to teachers' organizations, and preached at different churches. As mentioned above, I also continued my research in high school philosophy in nearby Wheeling, West Virginia. And it was at Bethany that I won my first professional honor, the Valley Forge Distinguished Educator's Award. It was for my pioneering work in teaching college courses to high school students.

There was a tragic figure around Bethany in those days, one for whom Ouida and I had compassion. He was a giant of a man, highly intelligent and fantastically interesting. He stood head and shoulders above those around him, and he had long hair and an abundant beard.

He was Julian Barclay, a great grandson of Alexander Campbell, and apparently schizophrenic. While he was presumed to be harmless, President Gresham cautioned the students not to take chances.

Some unruly boys did not take his advice. A number of them wrestled Julian to the ground and cut off his beard. To the boys' chagrin, Julian responded with Christlike submission—blessing them instead of cursing. I once wrote an article about Julian, describing him as one who was presumed to be crazy, but who was the most Christlike of all!

Julian supposed that he was Christ. When the college

choir sang the Hallelujah Chorus at Christmas and the audience was standing, Julian could be seen in the balcony seated. As he saw it, we were all singing to him. He would send us Christmas cards, signed by the Lord himself!

Once when he was a dinner guest in our home, Julian showed us the palms of his hands, explaining that sometimes one could see the scars of crucifixion. I could hardly realize that he was a great grandson of Alexander Campbell, and I recalled the rumor that there was a strain of insanity in the Campbell family. We've all heard that the line between insanity and genius may be a thin one.

The irony of it all was that Julian Barclay *was* Christlike—kind, loving, forgiving, nonresistant. He was presumably insane but much like Christ. The rest of us were sane but not as much like Christ!

Poor Julian. We tried to keep up with his doings long after we left Bethany. One year his old house burned, leaving him homeless. He became a migrant farm hand, his whereabouts unknown. After some years he was found dead on a bus. While he had no identification on him, it was at last determined who he was, and he came home to Bethany to be buried not far from his illustrious great-grandfather.

Julian Barclay epitomizes the tragedy that was the Campbells at Bethany. That little village has many sad stories to tell, including the heartache of Alexander Campbell. He lived to bury ten of his fourteen children, one being bright, ten-year old Wycliffe—the pride of his old age—the one destined to walk in his father's footsteps. He drowned while his father was in Europe in 1847. Six others were daughters, "all young mothers," as the reformer described them.

When I was back at Bethany to attend Restoration Forum XVIII in 2000, I once more visited God's Acre, this time to search out the grave of my friend Perry Gresham who passed on in 1994. I placed a flower on his tomb, only yards from that of Alexander Campbell. It was a modest tribute to one who, like his famous predecessor, was a pathfinder for Christian unity.

———— —— ———— ——

After five years of college teaching away from home, I was eager to return to Texas, so when an opportunity opened to teach philosophy at Texas Woman's University in Denton, I accepted. We moved in the summer of 1962. We are still here in Denton 41 years later.

Our move from West Virginia to Texas—1200 miles—was unique in the history of teachers moving cross-country. We packed our belongings in a 20-year old moving van I bought from a transit company in Wheeling. Ouida followed in the family car. Phoebe and Benjy had a great time riding in the truck with me. The van became a part of our family history. For some two years, we lent it to friends and leased it to businesses before finally selling it.

Later that same summer I flew back to the northeast for church appointments and to meet our third adopted child, who flew into New York from Germany. Our friend Richard E. Smith, then a teacher in Germany, assisted us in the adoption. We named him Philip Herbert Garrett, the middle name being his German name. He had spent his first six years of life in a Catholic orphanage, and the adoption agency advised us that he had problems.

We had difficulty bonding with Philip. He didn't blend in with the other children as we would have liked. But we got him raised with some degree of success, or so we thought. Soon after high school he was gone—on the fast track, unfortunately. We were suspicious that he was gay before he finally wrote and told us so. He said he loved us and wanted a home to come home to. We assured him that our love was unconditional and that he was welcome at home anytime under any condition.

93

In 1986, when we received word that he was dying of AIDS in a Washington, D.C. hospital, Ouida flew to be with him. It was a grim experience for her—sitting at his side wearing the mask required by the nurses—and communicating the best she could, sometimes in writing. A local Baptist preacher, who ministered to him during that time, told Ouida that during those dreadful days Philip found solace in the faith of his youth. He had been baptized into Christ at a Church of Christ youth camp as a teenager.

The situation being what it was, we had his body cremated and deposited in a Washington garden. The gay community in D.C. had a service for him, and we had a private service in Denton, conducted by family friend and minister George Massey, at Philip's request. He was 29.

It was a devastating blow. Ouida still says it is too sad to think about, to talk about, or to write about. But I sometimes talk about it, especially to parents who have the same problem. I tell them there is probably nothing they can do if a son or daughter is homosexual—except to keep on loving *unconditionally.* We cannot tell our children that we love them only *if* they are all that we want them to be. We must accept them on the same basis God has accepted us, as we are.

Those were the early days of the AIDS epidemic. When *Newsweek* ran a cover story in its August 10, 1987 issue on "The Face of Aids: One Year of the Epidemic," it published the pictures of 302 people who had died of AIDS the past year—mostly young men. Philip's picture was one of them. I wrote the magazine and told them that I thought our son would appreciate the attention that they had given the problem. They published my letter.

When a reporter from a Dallas newspaper saw my letter, he thought our story would make a suitable feature for his paper, if we would allow it. Since Ouida and I felt that it might help others to cope, we agreed to

94

an interview. After a time the reporter called back to say that his editor had rejected the story. Too hot to handle! That illustrates how sensitive the subject was back then.

Sometime later I was visiting a gay church as part of a series I was doing on "Visiting Other Churches." There was a chap there from a prominent Christian family in Denton, a family I knew well. He came up to me and said, "Leroy, don't tell my parents!" I wouldn't, of course, but it confirmed to me all the more that we have a problem that is not going to go away—and it is in the most exemplary of Christian families.

Chapter 11
Teaching All
Women & All Blacks

While some educators frown on separate colleges for women, claiming that women are better educated when integrated with men, others contend that when women have the classroom to themselves they achieve more. I joined the faculty of Texas Woman's University in the fall of 1962 with no opinion on that question, but in time I became convinced that there is a place for single-gender institutions—whether for men or women.

Women speak up more readily in a classroom they have to themselves, and in an all-women's college they have more opportunity for leadership positions. When it is their school, they rise to the occasion in running it. Whether it is the student government organization, the student newspaper, or discipline problems, they perform as well or better than men. And they are at least as loyal to their alma mater.

Early on I was involved in the affairs of the students beyond the courses I taught. I served as a class faculty sponsor, taking an entering class of freshmen and staying with them all four years. The dean asked me to address the incoming freshmen on how to do college. I spoke to their various clubs and societies—one made up of Catholic girls. I served as president of the local chapter of the American Association of University Professors, which watches out for the rights of faculty.

While I was not an official counselor, students often came to my office to talk about their problems, probably because they trusted me. Some had serious problems, such as being pregnant: "Shall I tell my parents?"

Answer, yes, and immediately. Some were lesbian, and I advised special counseling. I learned to be a good listener. I talked to them about being responsible for their own actions and not to blame others when they got into trouble.

I scored high when students evaluated the faculty. The second year I was there I won my second academic honor, the Outstanding Faculty Award, which was both decided by and conferred by the students. I seemed to get special billing. They thought a professor riding a bicycle to work was a big deal, so they put my picture in the student newspaper with my bicycle! They did write-ups about my travel, about having adopted children, about the speeches I gave.

Since philosophy was required of nursing students and library science majors, I had a high percentage of the student population in my classes. It was great fun stimulating them to think, and they soon learned that that was what philosophy is about. Philosophy is not only a love for wisdom—as the name implies—but it is a search for truth. And truth can sometimes be painful, especially truth about oneself.

I pointed out to them that the great truths that philosophy has turned up are often capsuled in a single line, such as Socrates' "The unexamined life is not worth living," or Francis Bacon's "Knowledge is power," or Descartes' "I think, therefore I am." The ancient Greek dictum "Know thyself" epitomized much of their thought as to what life is about. Spinoza's "intellectual love of God" points up where that Jewish thinker was going.

I told the young women that they could start with such aphorisms and build their own philosophy for living. We all have a philosophy, whether good or bad. I never hesitated to share my Christian faith, noting that a responsible faith can sustain the life of the mind.

It would be found amusing when I insisted that the educated woman not only knows how to entertain a

Looking in at my office in Old Main at Texas Woman's University as professor of philosophy, 1966.

man with feminine charm but also with ideas. To talk philosophy makes a date better than dates usually are!

One time in ethics class we were considering why right is right and why wrong is wrong. When I asked one of the students to name something she believed to be wrong, she answered that stealing is wrong. "Why?" I asked. "Because it's one of the Ten Commandments." I asked her if she would feel free to steal if it were not one of the Ten Commandments. She conceded that she wouldn't, that stealing would still be wrong.

Then I said, "Maybe stealing isn't wrong because the Bible says it is, but the Bible says it because it is wrong." We came to see that a thing is wrong when it is destructive of human dignity and when it hurts people unjustly. Statutory laws, such as the Ten Commandments, are based on a moral law written in human consciousness.

I was able to bring with me to TWU the Lilly project in high school philosophy that I conducted while at both MacMurray and Bethany. The money for it was depleted, but I persuaded the Denton Independent School District to allow me to continue the experimental course at Denton High School at its expense. Each school day I'd ride my bicycle from TWU to the high school to teach the one-hour blue-ribbon class. With the children of faculty of two universities in town as part of my special class, I had some of the sharpest students ever for the program.

I taught them as if they were college students. That was the point of the study: to see how well they could do it. I introduced them to Socrates, Plato, and Aristotle. We read Locke, Berkeley, and James. We did some logic, some ethics, some philosophy of religion. We argued the existence of God, pro and con. They loved it! I became convinced that the more we expect of students, the more diligently they will apply themselves.

Philosophy is also about making distinctions. It was always a ball when we discussed the difference between contrary statements and contradictions. We are often deceived when statements are only different (contrary), but not contradictory. One person says, "Mary is at the door," while another says, "Jane is at the door." These are contrary statements, but not contradictory, because Mary and Jane could both be at the door. For it to be a contradiction, the second person would have to say that Mary is *not* at the door. In contradictions, both statements can't be true, while contrary statements can be.

We observed that this helps in reading the Bible. We might suppose that when Mark says Jesus was a carpenter he contradicts Matthew who says Jesus was a carpenter's son. Contrary, yes, but not a contradiction, for both could be (and are) true. Similarly, Matthew has Jesus' resurrection appearances in Galilee and none in Judea, while Mark has them in Judea, and none in Galilee. Contrary—and perhaps confusing—but not necessarily a contradiction.

100

We made much of Voltaire's "I'll not argue with you until you define your terms," noting that philosophy is also a discipline that calls for definition of terms—especially emotive terms like "liberal," "conservative," "communist," "racist." That one spilled over into other classes. Other teachers let me know that in their classes my students were demanding even of them, "Define your terms!"

Besides all this classroom stuff, I looked for ways for the high school students to apply their philosophy to the real world. The local police chief allowed them to ride in squad cars on a late night run to get a taste of a different side of life. Parents had to sign a consent form to relieve the city of responsibility. From the dispatcher's desk, I listened in to what some of my students were witnessing alongside the police. Family disturbances, wrecks, burglary calls. One was in a police car that was in hot pursuit of a robber. They had unforgettable experiences.

When I pointed to the influence that fasting has had in the lives of such moral leaders as Jesus and Ghandi, the students wanted to try it for themselves and fast as a class project. Including the teacher! So, we did a three-day fast. No food, only water. The high school principal started getting calls from concerned parents wanting to know what was going on in that strange class! But the students were pleased with what they did, and they learned something from it.

One student in that high school project was Mike Gregory, who became a prominent attorney in the same city where he was born and grew up. He was interviewed a few years back by the local paper and was asked about his extensive educational experiences, including University of Texas Law School. He named my special course in philosophy at Denton High School as his most memorable experience. That made cheerful reading for an old teacher!

While serving as a faculty leader at TWU, I conspired with my counterpart at the University of North Texas, also in Denton, to invite Melvin Curry, president of Bishop College in Dallas (predominantly black), to address a joint session of our faculties. I figured our all-white faculties would do well to listen to a black college president talk about education in African American colleges. While we all had some African American students in our classes in those days, President Curry exposed us to problems and possibilities in the education of blacks that was an eye opener to most of us.

President Curry and I became friends. I visited with him at Bishop College, a new college to Dallas. He told me how he wanted Bishop to become a great college, not a great *black* college, but a great *college*. He had ambitious plans for years to come. He invited me to join his faculty as professor of philosophy and help him build that great college. Always one to reform the world, I was taken by the idea of what I might do in philosophy at an African American college.

So, in the fall of 1968, I joined the faculty of Bishop College, which turned out to be a mistake. The college had serious financial and academic problems, and faculty morale was low. Enrollment was in decline. I was fired after two years, along with a few others, because we were the last to be hired. The college survived only a few years longer, closed its doors, and reopened sometime later as Paul Quinn College, which moved in from another Texas town, still predominantly black.

A touching story grew out of that rather depressing experience, one that I found humbling. A black female faculty member, who had been at Bishop for some time, went to the administration and asked if she might give up her place on the faculty "for the sake of Dr. Garrett, who does so much for our students." It apparently was for real. She would give up her job and security so that I might keep mine—for the sake of the students!

The administration, of course, would not hear of such a thing anymore than I would. Nonetheless, I consider what that dear woman did as the ultimate compliment of my entire teaching career. In fact, I think the administration was pleased to get rid of me. They didn't like my support of the American Association of University Professors on their campus. Some administrations rightly fear an AAUP "censure," for it tells the academic world when a college maltreats its faculty or students.

And when the students were threatening a strike—for understandable reasons—I was accused of aiding and abetting them. My crime was no more than being a sympathetic listener. I urged reason and caution, but I listened to them. That may be why the students never called the strike, but they finally did get to express their grievances.

Later, when I applied for a position at another college, the president recommended I be hired, but the chancellor vetoed it, based on the report he had from Bishop. Hardly anything is more dreaded by some college administrations than a faculty member who might side with the students. Never mind that the college is supposed to be there for the sake of the students. And never mind what a faculty member might have to offer the students. The institutional system comes first! College or church, that is so often the rule.

James Russell Lowell said it well: "Truth forever on the scaffold, wrong forever on the throne." But we must believe, as he went on to say, "Yet that scaffold sways the future, and behind the dim unknown, standeth God within the shadow, keeping watch above his own."

I was blessed by my two years at Bishop College. One might call it some needed chastening. I did not realize how serious the problems were in African American education. I identified three problems in particular. All three exist in education generally, but they are compounded in an all-black environment. The first was the student's profound sense of inadequacy or feelings of inferiority, a resignation to the presumed fact that he or she simply can't do it.

103

The second acute problem is that the majority came from broken homes. These one-parent homes, nearly always matriarchal, have their own clusters of problems, including poverty, dependency, and absence of a male role model. The third was an inadequate educational background—coming as they did from poor, inefficient high schools. For the most part, they were not equipped to do college work.

I found it extremely difficult to motivate my students at Bishop as I had at other colleges. I questioned them as to why they were in college when they had so little interest in learning. Sometimes I walked from a classroom so downcast as to wonder if I really knew anything at all about teaching. But there was a small minority that was teachable. I solved my problem by giving my efforts to them—leaving the majority to go ahead and sleep through class if they chose, which is what a number of them did. Some of these were students who had worked all night. You can see we had problems.

During those years at Bishop I wrote several articles of a different kind for *Restoration Review,* my journal that succeeded *Bible Talk*—which I will tell more about in the next chapter. One was titled "Calling At the Back Door," which told the story of a retired black man who had been an educator for 40 years, including serving as principal of a Dallas high school with an integrated faculty. He was then serving as assistant to the president of Bishop College. Refined and dignified as he was, I described him as ambassadorial.

We became friends. He told me what it was like growing up as a black man in America in the 1920s, and what a task it was getting an education. He learned early on that when he went to a white man's house he must "call at the back door." Even after becoming a high school principal, he still called at the back door, even when the house was not as nice as his own or the people not as well educated or positioned as he.

When I asked what the answer was to that sort of thing, he told me a story. He said that when he called at one man's back door, the man protested, insisting that if he had come to visit him he should come in the front door—and the man called him Mister. That's the answer, he said. He noted that while things have changed and black people no longer literally call at the back door, they still "call at the back door" when it comes to pay, promotions, housing, and opportunities.

That was 1970. I wonder what that wise man would say now, if he were still living, about the black man's progress the past three decades. I noticed a reluctance around the college at that time to recognize any substantial progress for African Americans. When I protested—citing all the progress the civil rights movement had brought—they would tell me I wasn't black. They would remind me that when they worked at a job alongside white students from other colleges, doing the same work, the whites made more money.

Another article called "Black And White Together" told of a memorial service for Martin Luther King, Jr., held just three days after King's assassination at a black church in Dallas. Ouida and I sat with African American dignitaries and civic leaders, including the mayor of Dallas. What impressed me most was that great song "We Shall Overcome," which seemed to emerge spontaneously.

Black and white leaders were all now standing, singing that hymn over and over. I studied the audience—clergy, teachers, college presidents, city officials—as they all sang, *We shall overcome someday.* The phrase *Black and white together* was especially poignant, and it testified to the unity in that room that day.

I did another piece on "Complexion: Brown" in which I said that none of us is really white or black or red or yellow. God made us all brown—the universal color—only in varying shades, which is another way of saying we should all be color blind. When it comes to the way we accept and treat people, color must be beside the point. There should be no black people or white people in our judgments, just people.

By the time I left Bishop College, I was persuaded that there should be no black colleges, just as there should be no white colleges. Just colleges. Just as there should be neither white nor black churches. Just churches.

Bishop was my last full-time teaching position. For the next 25 years, off an on, I would serve as an adjunct (part-time) professor at three Dallas institutions. These were Richland College, part of the Dallas Community College System, where I taught from 1970-79; Dallas Christian College, which is associated with Independent Christian Churches, 1980-93; and I taught one year at University of Dallas, a Roman Catholic college, 1987-88, while at Dallas Christian.

This means I was doing adjunct teaching well past the usual age of retirement. I taught a summer course in ethics at Richland College, my last for them, at 80, which may have been a record in that category for that college.

This arrangement fit well with my other work. It helped support me financially and gave me time to be an editor and to travel widely among the churches. I could usually teach mid-week, leaving long weekends for other work.

Richland added to my widely diverse teaching experience. I had taught all women, all blacks, and gifted high school students. At Richland, I not only taught older adults, many of whom were professionals in various fields, but many Orientals. This was a challenge I relished, for my first love in teaching was to introduce philosophy to those unfamiliar with it or who even feared it. It was a course they were pleased to take because it looked good on their transcript, and the credits always transferred to other colleges.

A number of my students were airline attendants who could improve their status with some college credits. Then there were older folk who had missed college. With a community college in their neighborhood, they dared to take a few courses—even philosophy!

It was a challenge introducing such ones to philosophy by telling them about Socrates. Socrates *is* philosophy, I told them. I drew interesting parallels between Jesus and Socrates. Both gathered disciples. Both were controversial. Both were executed—one they crucified, the other they poisoned, and for similar reasons. As much as each impacted his world, neither left any writings. Plato wrote for Socrates; the evangelists wrote for Jesus. Then there was Plato's great student Aristotle, who said, "Great was Plato, but greater still is truth." Off we went. They took to it!

The Orientals were the most competitive I ever taught, and they were usually very bright. Most had graduate school in view—law or medicine or science—and philosophy served them well. But they had to score high; a C was unthinkable. I've always given frequent tests so a student knew at anytime where he or she stood. Orientals would usually drop the course—before the deadline—if there were a danger of making less than a B.

Dallas Christian College was special for me in that it had roots in our Movement. In addition to philosophy, I was privileged to teach Restoration history, using my own book, *The Stone-Campbell Movement*, as the text. I told them that I'd always heard that students should beware of taking a course from a professor who had written the text, but they were willing to give it a try.

I emphasized—as my book does—that ours is primarily a unity heritage. The principles unique to our plea were unity principles; the mottoes that capsuled those principles were unity mottoes; the founding documents were unity documents. The purpose of the

Movement was to "unite the Christians in all the sects," or as Barton W. Stone put it, "Let the unity of Christians be our polar star."

Those years at Dallas Christian reminded me of the advantages of a tiny college—such as I had enjoyed at Freed-Hardeman. With hardly more than a hundred students, most classes were small, and there was an *esprit de corps* that made college feel like a big family where everyone felt close to everyone else. The faculty was able and incredibly dedicated, teaching at a sacrifice in pay.

Mark Berrier was such a one. I first heard of him when I read his insightful essay on baptism in the *Christian Standard*. I wrote to him to commend him for such a liberating article. Then I met him and taught with him at Dallas Christian, and we became lifetime friends. He has been at the college over three decades, teaching Greek, Hebrew, and Biblical Studies. He has blessed hundreds of students—many of them now preachers—both by his teaching and his exemplary life. He epitomizes what can be special about a small college.

I taught a year at the University of Dallas, located across the highway from Texas Stadium, where the Dallas Cowboys do their thing. One of my students at Texas Woman's University had become a department head and needed temporary help. Knowing I was then in retirement, she drafted me to do a course in the history of education, which I had done at TWU, along with my courses in philosophy.

This was my first and only experience teaching in a Roman Catholic college, and I found its program excellent, its academic standing high, and its student body highly selective. It may well be the most academically demanding college in the Dallas-Ft. Worth area. One gets the impression that they go first class in everything they do, and it is expensive. I was impressed that they gave a four-year scholarship to one of our bright Church of Christ girls from Amarillo.

In 1968, the year I left TWU for Bishop College, Ouida and I opened a fast-food restaurant in our hometown of Denton, Texas. It was our first and only business venture, besides our home book business that we had in conjunction with our publications. Longtime church friend Ralph Hancock had teamed up with two of his friends, Ed Johnson and Rex Sanders, to open two chicken-to-go places in Dallas. Both places were selling fried chicken faster than they could cook it.

Ralph insisted that we start one in Denton, assuring me, "Leroy, the day you open it you can retire." When we were fortunate enough to get a key location in a shopping center, we decided to go for it, if we could finance it. I was in for a surprise when I went to my bank and spelled it all out to the president. "You say they have two places in Dallas?" he asked, and then added, "Let's drive over and sample the chicken."

There I was driving the president of the bank over to one of those chicken places. After trying the chicken, we drove back to the bank without much being said. As he got out of the car he said, "Come by in the morning and we'll make you the loan." That was the way of small town banks in those days. It is quite different with that same bank today, now that it is part of a conglomerate.

We called it Chick-A-Go-Go—the name of the Dallas operation, and we were their first franchisee. One of my older brothers, who needed a job, first managed it for us. It did so well that my brother left us after two years and started one of his own in a nearby town.

Ouida then became the manager. All this time I was teaching, preaching, and publishing as usual, but I worked in the "store" enough to learn to do what Ouida wanted me to do. We sometimes had four or five people behind the counter packaging orders with that many more in the kitchen frying the chicken. The customers were often lined up back to the doors.

Ouida was a successful manager, but she had one "shortcoming." She could hardly fire anyone. One dear lady who needed the job was all thumbs behind the counter, and when the customers lined up she got nervous. Ouida had to let her go. She cried, and Ouida cried!

After three years, we sold the business to the people who got us into it. We did well enough to provide some financial security for the rest of our lives. Besides, it was a great entrepreneurial experience. I took special delight in paying the bank back well ahead of time.

We learned that in business—as in all of life—success or failure is largely a matter of one's ability or inability to get along with others. Ouida's social skills, as well as her business acumen, had much to do with our success.

When the family was young, 1965. The children, left to right, are David Benjamin, Philip Herbert, and Phoebe Anna.

110

Chapter 12

Editor Of
Restoration Review

Whether I was a college professor, a preacher, or in business, I was always an editor. Counting the newsletter I now edit, I am going on 51 years, which may be a record within Stone-Campbell—even longer than that of David Lipscomb, who edited the *Gospel Advocate* for 47 years. I made my living as a professor, so I could serve as an editor at my own expense. My preaching has also been without charge in the sense that whatever I was paid I passed along to my publications.

Early on I resolved that I would never ask for donations for my journal. Since the subscription price is never enough to fund a publication, and since there was no advertising, donations were necessary. But still I would not ask. If what I wrote contributed substantially to the renewal of the church, it would be funded without my asking. If not, I would let it die with no regrets. With that as my rule, I have always had the money to pay the bills. The Lord provides!

After editing *BibleTalk* for six years, 1952-58, I started *Restoration Review* in the winter of 1959 and continued through 1992, 34 volumes in 34 years, with 200 pages to each volume. We issued most of those volumes in book form. The last 22 years were published in 11 volumes of 400 pages each, two volumes in each book. I wrote a preface for each bound volume and there was a table of contents.

Since I treated a particular theme throughout the two years, the book form had a title, giving it the appearance of a regular book. For example, volumes 26-

27, 1985-86, were issued as a hardcover book of 400 pages under the title *Adventures of the Early Church*, that being the theme for those two years. The last bound volume, 1991-92, had the title *What The Old Testament Means To Us* because I wrote on that subject in each of the 20 issues for those two years.

For the first five years, *Restoration Review* was published as a quarterly, 64 pages in each issue, 256 pages each year. That gave me space to get a lot said, and to provide room for numerous guest writers, some of whom were writers of reputation. In the first issue I published "Faith For The Space Age" by Donald H. Andrews, a professor of chemistry at Johns Hopkins University. He pled for "a chain reaction of the spirit to release in the world a new power of love," based on the marvels of the atom. He found "music of the spheres" in each atom, and just as there is a chain reaction in the atom, there can be a chain reaction of love.

Also in that first volume was "Have You Met Socrates?" by Harry and Bonaro Overstreet, noted authors and philosophers. They said Socrates re-complexified life in a world guilty of over-simplification by dogma, habit, preoccupation, institutionalization, and caution. A great person, they said, allows life to be complex because she is not afraid of complexity.

Arthur Schlesinger, Jr., a Harvard historian, did a piece on Alexander Campbell. He thought it significant that Campbell gave his attention to Acts and the epistles rather than to the gospels. He was also impressed that Campbell defined faith as belief in testimony, which ran counter to the popular Calvinism of the frontier.

Carl Ketcherside wrote on "Gospel and Doctrine," which was near the beginning of a long struggle we were to have within Churches of Christ over the vital distinction between those terms. Carl quoted Alexander Campbell at length to support his view that the gospel is the apostolic proclamation of good news to the world, while doctrine is the apostolic curriculum to be taught to those enrolled (by baptism) in the school of Christ.

In that first year I was saying the likes of "We must learn that fellowship comes first—then agreement on doctrine might follow. We have reversed the order. Can we not see that we will never be in fellowship if we wait until we see everything alike?" and "Fellowship is one thing, endorsement is something else. I may not endorse instruments of music in worship, but I can fellowship the brother who uses them." I cited some rather significant disagreements between Barton W. Stone and Alexander Campbell and noted that they didn't let such differences disrupt their fellowship.

In an essay I did on "My Dream of the Restored Church," I wrote "Unity is diverse by its very nature. It does not entail our seeing everything alike, but it implies togetherness despite differences. The primitive church was shockingly diverse, and yet it maintained 'the unity of the Spirit.'" I went on to say, "A church can have a thousand differences within it and still be united. It is not differences that cause division. It is the party spirit."

These ideas were new, even revolutionary, to most people in Churches of Christ. They would be the battleground for many years to come, the basis for my lover's quarrel with my own church.

Time was to show that our concern for the renewal of the church involved more than cultivating a broader view of unity and fellowship. To put it another way, if we were to be effective in attacking the scourge of division, we must emphasize spiritual values, particularly the ministry of the Holy Spirit in the life of the church. For decades to come, I stressed the great truth, drawn from Ephesians 4:3, that unity is not our doing, but the Spirit's gift to the church. We are to accept the gift!

The theme for the 1966 volume of *Restoration Review*, for example, was "Resources of Power." The basic resource of power for the believer, I observed, was the gift of the Holy Spirit, which was "the great promise," as Phillips renders it, on the day of Pentecost.

113

I noted that, while we in Churches of Christ have behaved all these years like those Paul found at Ephesus "who have not so much as heard whether there is a Holy Spirit," it is high time for us to lay claim to this resource of power that is rightly ours.

I put it this way in that 1966 volume: "It is clear that the Holy Spirit is bestowed as a heavenly gift upon all repentant and baptized souls. The Spirit is himself the gift, the great promise that God had long intended for both Jews and Gentiles, so that all men might come into communion with God through Christ." Commenting on Romans 8:26, I wrote of the "heavenly Guest" who is our constant companion, dwelling within us, who knows the language of heaven, and who intercedes for us "on those agonizing longings which never find words." I added: "What a thrill to think of the Comforter praying for us in a heavenly language that only God can understand!"

The Holy Spirit was a continuing theme in my journal. A 1985 essay on "The Baptism of the Holy Spirit: What Does It Mean?" drew special interest. I concluded that the baptism of the Spirit is the same as the gift of the Spirit, and that one is baptized of the Spirit when he receives the Spirit as a gift. I posited that being baptized of the Spirit, receiving the Spirit, being filled with the Spirit, drinking of the Spirit, and the Spirit being "given" or "poured out" all referred to the same thing. All are baptized of the Spirit when they believe in and obey Christ.

Even as recently as one of my 1997 newsletters, I wrote on "God's Birthday Gift to His Children," noting that we receive the Holy Spirit when we are born anew from above. I observed that, while Christ and his apostles were missionaries to the world, the Spirit is a missionary to the church. His mission is to conform us to the likeness of Christ, and this is what unites us.

In a 2001 newsletter, I asked "What Happened to Walter Scott's Fifth Finger?" I showed that while we in

Churches of Christ have followed a "five-finger exercise," we lost Scott's fifth finger along the way, which was the gift of the Holy Spirit. The way he counted his fingers, based on Acts 2:38, was faith, repentance, baptism, remission of sins, Holy Spirit. I concluded by saying: "We must once more become a Spirit-filled people, allowing the Spirit to transform us more and more into the image of Christ."

Grace was also a continuing theme from early on, as evident in that 1966 volume on resources of power. "Saved By Grace—And Only By Grace," I titled it. "The man never lived, except the Christ himself, who deserved to go to heaven," I avowed. It is not our good works that will get us there, certainly not by being good or sacrificial. It is only by God's grace through faith. While I found a contradiction between grace and works, I did not find one between grace and obedience, or between grace and baptism. Baptism is not a work that we do but the cultivation of grace. It is the "working of God," his way for us to respond to his grace.

I charged that we in Churches of Christ are seen by our neighbors, with some justification, as "a works church," not unlike the Roman Catholics; and we have not left the impression that we really believe in salvation by grace. As for harmonizing James' emphasis on works and Paul's on faith, I ventured: "We are saved *for* deeds, James is saying. We are not saved *by* deeds, Paul is saying."

It was a theme I've emphasized for a half century. In the last year of *Restoration Review,* in a series on what the Churches of Christ must do to be saved, I was still charging that "the Churches of Christ have a head knowledge of grace, but at the gut level we do not, generally, know the grace of God." In that piece I insisted that to be saved as a people we must boldly claim such passages as Ephesians 2:8 ("By grace are you saved through faith") as our own. It is only as we stand in the grace of God that we will be free from our

115

legalism and from the backwater of our sectarianism.

Related to the subject of grace is the believer's assurance of his salvation, so I also wrote on "Can We Know We Are Saved?" I pointed out that most of us in Churches of Christ are uncomfortable with the question *Are you saved?* All these years we have equivocated with such responses as "I hope so" or "If I am found faithful." I assured my readers, in the light of Scripture, that we can be sure of our salvation, trusting not in our own righteousness but in God's grace. We can be as sure as Paul was when he said, "I know whom I have believed, and I am fully persuaded...."

The 1967 *Restoration Review* provided an arena for some critical exchanges on the state of affairs in Churches of Christ. In 1966 Robert Meyers edited *Voices of Concern: Studies in Church of Christism*, a volume of essays critical of Churches of Christ by long-time leaders who had left. It was a kind of "Why I Left" survey of what is wrong in Churches of Christ, and it stirred up quite a controversy. I invited James D. Bales of Harding College to respond to some of the key essays, and I invited those he addressed to give a rejoinder. It was a series of candid exchanges that brought into focus issues that our people were having to face.

Bales charged that while the voices in *Voices of Concern* wanted to be free of fences erected by human traditions, they did not want to be bound by the fences the Lord has built. Robert Meyers, the editor, observed that thousands in Churches of Christ are profoundly disturbed by the aridity produced by authoritarianism. Referring to those who had left Churches of Christ, Meyers suggested that they might have stayed if they could have seen any semblance of unity in diversity in Churches of Christ. Bales denied that the Bible teaches unity in diversity.

Those responding to Bales' criticisms were among our brightest minds in those days: David R. Darnell,

Carl L. Etter, Logan J. Fox, Ralph V. Graham, Cecil Franklin, Pat Hardeman, Roy Key, J. P. Sanders, Charles E. Warren. That they had all left us was embarrassing enough. Why they left were reasons we in Churches of Christ were reluctant to consider. They left to escape sectarianism and legalism. Roy Key, a graduate of both Lipscomb and Pepperdine and a Churches of Christ minister for 20 years, who is now with the Disciples of Christ, probably spoke for them all when he said to Bales, "I conclude unequivocally that any view that rests on my 'rightness' —intellectually, ethically, legally—is destructive of the Gospel and is in reality a doctrine of self-righteousness."

I especially enjoyed doing the volumes for 1971-72 in which I developed the theme "The Restoration Mind." I posited that restoration is reformation and vice-versa, that we restore the primitive faith through a renewal or reformation of the church. It is renewal through a recovery of the ancient order. Like a wrecked Ford in a ditch that bears little resemblance to what its maker intended, I illustrated, the church can wander so far from what God intends as to bear little resemblance to his eternal purpose. But just as the wrecked car is still a Ford and can be restored, so the church is still the church and can be renewed. Restoration does not imply that the church ever ceased to exist, but that it is always in need of reformation.

In those same volumes, I did a ten-part series on "The Travel Letters of Alexander Campbell." I gained new insights into the reformer's mission and character by following him on his extensive travels both at home and abroad over some 40 years. We find him on a snow sled in the streets of Chicago when it was a small frontier town, in train wrecks, visiting with the President in Washington, and even in prison in Glasgow, Scotland.

One installment was on "Campbell Takes His Dying Wife To Nashville." He hoped in vain that the southern climate would restore her health. It was on this trip that

117

Margaret, his first wife, realizing that she would not get well, urged her husband to take Selina Bakewell as her successor, a dear friend of hers who had been caring for her five young daughters. A year after Margaret's death, Campbell married Selina.

Another is about his 94-day tour of New York in 1834 (he was sometimes away from home six months at a time!), which included much of eastern Virginia. In Richmond he met with a gathering of 17 Churches of Christ (1200 total members) that had been forced out of Baptist churches. It pleased Campbell that there was never an instance of his people forcing others out, not even when his people were the majority.

His letters reveal that he often visited other churches, as his schedule allowed. In Baltimore he visited a Jewish synagogue. In Philadelphia he spoke in a Universalist church, and in New York he addressed a society of skeptics in Tammany Hall. While in Philadelphia, he also spoke to an overflowing crowd at the Musical Fund Hall on Christian hope—for three-and-a-half hours!

On and on the themes in *Restoration Review* developed through the years. Like Campbell himself, who during his many travels gave the common people his very best stuff, not saving it for the elite, I laid before my rank and file readers the best that I could come up with. In 1975-76 it was "The Word Abused," in which I exposed how our leaders twist and warp the Scriptures in order to justify their sectarian practices.

In 1983-84 it was *The Doe of the Dawn,* in which I depicted God, in terms of Francis Thompson's famous poem, as "the Hound of Heaven" who out of sheer grace seeks sinful man. That is what makes Christianity distinct, not that we seek God—which is basic in all religions—but that God through Christ seeks *us.* I had such articles as "The Hope of History," "Deliver Us From Evil," and "None Of These Diseases."

One of my favorite themes was treated in 1985-86:

The Sense of Scripture: Studies in Interpretation, which grew out of my conviction that most of our problems—especially our sectarian exclusivism—are hermeneutical in nature. This theme was a call for reasonable and responsible interpretation of the Bible. I dealt with the myth of "the law of silence," the capstone argument against instrumental music and societies, noting that there is no such law. All that silence of a given subject proves is that the Bible is silent on that subject.

It was in that volume that I asked, "Do We Shoot Our Wounded?" an essay I would like to make required reading for all in Churches of Christ. I gave instances of how we abuse and reject our own people at a time when they need us the most, whether those going through a divorce or those having problems with their faith.

The most popular series I ever did was a 20-part study of "Visiting Other Churches," which began in January 1988 and continued for two years. After visiting every congregation of every denomination in my hometown of Denton, Texas, I wrote about my experiences. The reason my readers responded so positively, I think, was because it was not an exposure of other churches' errors—concerning which our people have heard enough—but an account of a friendly visit and what impressed me. It gave me a chance to give a short history of each denomination and what it believed.

I visited them all: Episcopalians, Seventh-Day Adventists, Quakers, Mormons, Roman Catholics, and even the Greek Orthodox and a church for gays and lesbians. It was my treatment of the last that was the most controversial, with some readers canceling their subscriptions. Some thought I was too accepting of gay and lesbian Christians. But I was only saying, without approving of their lifestyle, that since churches in general had turned them away, I was pleased that they have a church of their own—and that they worship Jesus Christ.

What impressed me the most from all my visits, as I

119

told my readers, was that we all have far more in common than we have differences—and we can unite upon what we have in common. That, by the way, was Alexander Campbell's conclusion at the end of the day. We unite upon what we hold in common—especially in the One we hold in common—and allow for differences otherwise. Campbell called this the "catholic rule" for unity.

At the end of the series, I answered the question of which denomination I would join should I leave the Churches of Christ. I first made it clear that I would never leave the Churches of Christ, never! But I could join the Salvation Army as an "adherent member," which the Army allows, and still belong to my own church. It would be a religion of ministering to the needy.

My visit with the Jehovah's Witnesses was the only uneasy experience. They wanted to know what I was doing there. If one visits, it is to be with a Witness. But I was sort of accepted when I convinced them that my purposes were friendly. "I'm visiting all churches, just to get better acquainted" got me off the hook, though they could hardly believe that I would include the despised Jehovah's Witnesses.

The Mormons may have been the friendliest. I was introduced by a Mormon friend who extolled me as "one who goes all over the world preaching the gospel." But in a Bible class I found them surprisingly ignorant of the Bible. The Quakers may have been the most endearing; "Quiet Rebels" they are, as I described them in my write-up. I have to confess to being a Quaker at heart to some degree.

By far the most surprising was my visit to the Roman Catholic Church, which on the occasion I was there turned into a charismatic service. We all praised the Lord together with uplifted hands. The visit I most appreciated was to the Greek Orthodox Church in Dallas, perhaps because they allowed me to stay over for a private family service and witness the baptism (thrice immersion) of a baby. I was impressed by how seriously they took it, and that it took them well over an hour. I quipped in my report of the visit that we in Churches of Christ do baptism in just a few minutes!

There was sometimes exciting drama in my articles, such as "High Adventure At Pat Boone's House" (1971). Bob Cannon, minister in Churches of Christ at the time, and I watched as Pat immersed several Jews "in the name of Yeshua the Messiah for the remission of sins" in his swimming pool. Bob and I agreed that it was a page right out of the book of Acts. Pat has had quite a witness for "Yeshua" among Jews all these years.

This was some years after Pat and Shirley were excommunicated by the Church of Christ where they had been longtime members. Pat nonetheless often in his public statements expresses appreciation for his background in Churches of Christ, where he was both a preacher and a song leader.

I was also a friend of Pat's parents, Archie and Margaret Boone in Nashville. They too were withdrawn from by the Church of Christ where Archie had served as an elder. This was because they, like son Pat, experienced speaking in tongues.

Often in my writings I vigorously opposed such oppressive treatment—shooting our wounded when they break from the party line. The time was when Pat and Shirley were in trouble with their faith, their finances, and their marriage. They had to turn to others for help.

The good news is that it would not have happened that way in many Churches of Christ today. We are moving from being people mostly of the head to being people of the heart also. We are becoming a more compassionate church.

One of my favorite articles was "The Professor And His Poodle" (1974). I was in Cleveland, Mississippi for house meetings with two young men who were professors at the local university. The elders of their congregation were unhappy that they had invited me, but agreed to the meetings so long as they were limited to the two families and a few area preachers who wanted to be present.

One would have thought that such a conciliatory spirit on the part of the professors would have made for peace, but on the Lord's Day when I was with them at their congregation we were all subjected to unmitigated abuse. Instead of lifting up Christ in his sermon, the preacher spent his time castigating the professors and me. Calling my name over and over, the preacher branded me as a heretic and false teacher in their midst. No one was to have anything to do with me, nor were they to read my writings, even though he quoted from them repeatedly.

The professors were berated and their motives impugned. It was incredibly cruel and rude—especially since they had gone out of their way to conduct the meetings peacefully. Two elders followed the preacher, giving their endorsement to the tirade. More abuse followed the service. I told the preacher afterwards that he was nonetheless my brother and that I loved him, and I apologized to the elders for being there—that I would not have been present had I known that the service would be about Leroy Garrett rather than Jesus Christ.

We had planned dinner out, but the two families opted for prayer and fasting instead. I was pleased that they took the persecution with grace and dignity—showing no malice toward their abusers. But one of the professors, a sensitive man, sat in his cushioned chair and quietly wept. Lisa, his poodle, climbed into his lap, cuddled in his arms, nestled her head under his chin, and at last licked the tears from his cheeks.

The scene remains to this day one of the most poignant I ever witnessed. I was moved to lament in my travel diary: "My God, has it come to this, that a man receives more compassion from a little dog than he does from his own brothers and sisters in an assembly of the saints!"

The rest of the story: One of the professors was Allen Dennis, who is now a professor at Troy State University in Alabama and author of the Preface to this volume. He left the Churches of Christ for many of the years since then. But now—after 27 years—he is a member of the Landmark Church of Christ in Montgomery, rejoicing in its spirituality and openness. I was invited to speak there in 2000 and was warmly introduced by Buddy Bell, the minister, who said gracious things about what I have done for Churches of Christ.

I think I saw tears in Allen's eyes once more—tears of joy this time. He has lived to see changes in Churches of Christ that he could not have dreamed of back in Cleveland, Mississippi in 1974. And, oh yes, he told me that one of those elders who did "the Sunday massacre" —as Allen came to call it—apologized to him some years later for what happened on that sad Sunday morning.

Those who sow in tears will reap in joy!

Editing *Restoration Review* on our first computer, 1987.

123

Chapter 13

My Unity-In-Diversity Heresy

It has been a puzzle to me all these years how anyone could question the principle of unity in diversity. Unity implies diversity—a union of things different—whether in marriage, a family, a picture, or in all of nature. If there is unity in anything at all, it has to be unity in diversity, for there is no other kind of unity. That is certainly the case in Christian unity, as the apostle Paul expressed it, "Now indeed there are many members, yet one body" (1 Corinthians 12:20).

It was nonetheless the case that as our unity efforts began to have effect, they were dubbed "the unity-in-diversity heresy," with the names Ketcherside-Garrett usually appended. Some years ago when Alan Highers, editor of *The Spiritual Sword*, was in my hometown to speak at the Annual Denton Lectures—which has long been faithful in exposing "the Ketcherside-Garrett unity-in-diversity heresy" —he called at our home. It was our first time to meet. Though editors of a different persuasion, we had a friendly visit. Concerning the lectures he was attending, he said, "Those fellows down there use 'Ketcherside-Garrett' as if it were one name!"

That was our sin; we believed in unity in diversity. At last, I decided that they could not possibly mean what they were saying. Perhaps they meant, I allowed, that we advocated a unity with too much diversity, or that we were too latitudinarian. So, in my writings I made it clear, as did Carl Ketcherside, that unity certainly has its parameters. We were not calling for unity "with anybody and everybody" —as we were accused—but only with those who are in Christ. Carl had a way of putting it: "Wherever God has a child, I have a brother or sister." We are in unity and fellowship with all God's children, wherever they are, but only with God's children, we stated over and over.

Moreover, we noted that the New Testament makes it clear that fellowship is sometimes impossible even among believers, such as "Reject a divisive man after the first and second admonition" (Titus 3:10) or when a brother becomes grossly immoral (1 Corinthians 5:9) or is disloyal to Christ (2 John 9-10). We conceded that yes, of course, unity has its limits, but nonetheless insisted that unity by its very nature is diverse and embraces all those who are faithfully following Christ according to such light as they have, in spite of differences.

These clarifications usually fell on deaf ears. The doctrine of unity in diversity remained a "heresy" and became the proverbial straw man that received continual castigation. But our critics condemned themselves, for whatever unity they have in their own party is unity in diversity in that they differ on numerous other issues. They allow for differences except on those issues that make up the party line. On the party issues, unity must be by conformity, whether millennial theories, instrumental music, marriage and divorce, or congregational cooperation.

The battle was ongoing, year after year. We were accused of "fellowshipping brothers in error." We retorted that there are no others to fellowship, for we are all in error on some things. One might be wrong about many things, we insisted, and still be right about Christ, and *he* is the ground of our unity and fellowship.

The nature of fellowship became the battleground. We showed from Scripture that fellowship is not about things—whether instruments or societies—but about people. Fellowship is a relationship between fellows who share a common life in Christ, which is what the Greek word means. If unity demands conformity of opinion or interpretation, then our Lord's prayer for the unity of all believers can never be realized, for we will never see everything alike. We can no more see everything alike than we can all look alike.

We were accused of approving of false doctrine and endorsing those who teach error, for "if you fellowship them you approve of what they teach and practice." This way of thinking has hung like an albatross about the neck of Churches of Christ, isolating us from other believers and locking us into a legalistic, sectarian mindset. If you call on a Christian Church brother to lead a prayer you are approving of instrumental music! If you do something with the denominations in town, you are endorsing denominationalism! Unhorsing such oppressive logic proved to be our most difficult task.

If such logic is valid, we pointed out, then we could not even be in fellowship with each other—yea, with no one at all, not even with our own wives or husbands. There couldn't be a single church on earth—unless it be made up of folk who approve of everything everyone does or believes! We showed from Scripture that fellowship has nothing to do with either approval or endorsement.

Paul did not approve of or endorse a lot of things about the church at Corinth—but he still called them the body of Christ and accepted them as his beloved sisters and brothers in whom the Holy Spirit resided. He disapproved of some of Peter's conduct—even rebuking him to his face publicly—but he still accepted him as his brother in the Lord. Such problems may put a strain upon the fellowship, but forbearing love preserves "the unity of the Spirit in the bond of peace." The call for forbearance is itself evidence of disapproval and differences. If unity were a matter of conformity, there would be nothing to forbear.

Behind all the disputation about unity and fellowship was a more seminal question, one that goes back to the struggles of our Restoration pioneers: "*Who is a Christian?*" Carl Ketcherside and I questioned what lay at the root of Church of Christism, the dogma that we are the true church and the only Christians. When we began this renewal effort, that mindset was alive and well among us. We were heretics because we taught that the body of Christ and the kingdom of God reaches far beyond what we call "the Church of Christ." Our sin was compounded when we pointed out that the Churches of Christ were a denomination not all that different from other denominations.

A related issue was the distinction we drew between the gospel and the apostles' doctrine—or between preaching and teaching. It was a difference made not only by our own Restoration pioneers, but by leading New Testament scholars—notably C. H. Dodd, who published a groundbreaking book on the distinction.

The distinction relates to unity and fellowship, in that it is the gospel—once believed and obeyed—that unites us in Christ and brings us into the fellowship of the Spirit. Or to use a metaphor, it is the gospel that matriculates us into the school of Christ, while it is the apostles' doctrine that is the curriculum in that school. Those matriculated in the school through faith and obedience will be diverse in that they are at different grade levels. Some will be but babes in Christ, others mature.

Some of our critics responded to this distinction in surprising ways. G. K. Wallace, in a debate with Carl Ketcherside, challenged him to preach awhile and then teach awhile, and to tell the audience when he switched gears! When I asked Yater Tant if he made no distinction at all between the terms, he said that preaching is when one stands and teaching is when one is seated! I pointed out that Philip the evangelist was seated when he *preached* to the Ethiopian eunuch while, according to Luke, Jesus was standing when he *taught* the multitudes. No, it is the *content* of what is said that makes the difference.

At last I decided that our detractors understood more than they were admitting. They were not yet ready to say so—in contrast to many in the present generation who seem willing to say so.

We drew heavily upon our Restoration pioneers to show that we were saying what they said. We pointed out that Alexander Campbell made the same distinction between gospel and doctrine long before C. H. Dodd or Ketcherside and Garrett. Campbell even insisted that one must recognize this distinction in order to understand the ancient order.

We also quoted Campbell to the effect that a Christian is one who believes in Christ, repents of one's sins, and obeys him in all things according to one's understanding. We showed that Barton Stone taught that unity should be based only upon loyalty to Christ. Both of them believed that there were Christians other than in what they had come to call the Church of Christ or Disciples of Christ. That, in fact, was the mission of their "new reformation": to unite the Christians in all the sects.

Along the way, we revived some of the old mottoes passed along by our forebears, charging that we have ignored their significance. While our pioneers insisted "We are Christians only, but not the only Christians," our people have been sectarian in claiming to be the only Christians. And while they said, "In essentials unity, in opinions liberty, in all things love," our opinions have been made into essentials. By multiplying the essentials, several sects have been spawned among Churches of Christ.

Since Carl and I were as sectarian as anyone else earlier in our ministry, how did it happen—I am sometimes asked—that we came to espouse such views as referred to above? Was there any defining moment that the change occurred?

As for Carl, he identifies a defining moment in his

autobiography, *Pilgrimage of Joy*, as coming in a little chapel in Belfast, Ireland in 1951. For the first time in his life, after baptizing thousands and being a leader in a Churches of Christ faction, he invited Jesus into his heart. Thus began his arduous journey out of factionalism. I was witness to his gradual transformation from what he called "a wing commander" in a sect to an envoy for peace and unity. As he grew closer to Christ, he became less a party man. He attributed it all to "the dynamic of love."

While my change was also gradual, it was less dramatic. My exposure in graduate studies to some of the leading biblical scholars of the world, whose intellectual grace lifted them above the pettiness of sectarianism, could not help but influence me in a different direction.

My study of our Restoration fathers also had a telling effect upon my own transformation. I came to see that our Stone-Campbell unity heritage was a different breed from what I had been taught in Churches of Christ. Somewhere along the way we in Churches of Christ became derailed and lost contact with our true heritage. I felt betrayed by my teachers in Churches of Christ. They taught me sectarianism, while Stone and Campbell taught me unity in Christ.

I also came to see the futility of our endless debates, which only fostered more divisions. Like Thomas Campbell, I became "sick and tired" of the whole sectarian mess, and at last I resolved to work for peace and unity among all the heirs of the Restoration tradition.

But when I finished my resident work at Harvard in 1951 and returned to Dallas, I had not yet shed all the shackles of sectarianism. While serving the Hampton Place Church of Christ in Dallas on a temporary assignment, I persuaded a dozen people or so to join me in starting a congregation that would practice mutual ministry and eschew the professional ministry system.

130

This eventually became Wynnewood Chapel, which we called "A Congregation of the Restoration Movement." It would play a leading role in "the unity-in-diversity heresy" for the next two decades.

With some justification, Wynnewood Chapel was labeled from the outset as a faction. I would live to regret that it started the way it did. It was largely a walkout from another congregation, which was quite contrary to what I would later teach. In spite of this factional origin, the Lord worked in it for good, for Wynnewood became the catalyst for scores of unity meetings.

Wynnewood not only practiced mutual ministry—which allowed every qualified male member to address the congregation—but we vigorously opposed what we called "the pastor system" as it was practiced by other Churches of Christ. We challenged other congregations to defend their practice. We sponsored a debate on the issue between Carl Ketcherside and Flavil Colley in 1954, which stirred up considerable controversy.

We did not limit our crusade against error to Churches of Christ. We prepared a pamphlet that kindly exposed Billy Graham's failure to preach what Peter preached on the day of Pentecost in Acts 2 and handed them out by the hundreds at the Graham crusade in the Cotton Bowl in Dallas in 1954. It was so effectively done that the Graham people hurriedly announced over the speakers that "unauthorized literature" was being distributed, and the people were urged not to accept it. With that kind of advertising, we soon ran out of pamphlets!

The Wynnewood brethren may not have always been wise in their opposition to what they conceived to be wrong, but they were always eminently Christian. And they did not make the things they opposed terms of fellowship. We never drew the line on other believers, and we were always at peace among ourselves.

In our pursuit of both peace and truth, we became

131

With Carl Ketcherside, first unity meeting, Wynnewood Chapel, Dallas, 1955.

increasingly concerned over divisions among Christians, particularly within the Restoration Movement. We were soon encouraging brethren of different persuasions to meet with us for prayer and study.

The first gatherings—beginning in 1955—consisted only of Carl Ketcherside and me, along with the precious few who would accept our invitation. J. D. Phillips, of the set-order-of-worship Churches of Christ (based on Acts 2:42), and Ervin Waters, of the one-cup (for Communion) Churches of Christ, were among our first participants.

Ervin Waters was the champion debater for the one-cup churches and their "hatchet man," as he described himself. He attended with some trepidation. He brought several brethren along with him at the outset to make sure his tracks were covered—having to do with the likes of us! Time proved him to be one of the greatest influences of our unity efforts. His inestimable contribution, made through numerous unity meetings for years to come, is a story within itself. It all started at Wynnewood Chapel in Dallas.

There were others who dropped in for some sessions during those early years, such as Pat Hardeman, Arnold Hardin, Bryan Vinson. Some who came to scorn remained to pray. For years to come the hardest part was to bring people together. They didn't want to have that much fellowship with each other. It eventually became less difficult, and today such gatherings have become politically correct for many.

The unity meetings at Wynnewood Chapel in the 1950s and 1960s were followed by more ambitious efforts—particularly the Annual Unity Forum, a series that continued for a decade, 1966-1975. While Perry Gresham, president of Bethany College, and I initiated them, we were joined by such able leaders as Ferrell Walters of the Disciples, Charles Gresham of the Independent Christian Churches, and Thomas Langford of Churches of Christ.

All but two of the series of unity forums were held on college campuses. The order was: Bethany College in West Virginia (1966); Milligan College in Tennessee (1967); Southeastern Christian College in Kentucky (1968); West Islip Church of Christ in New York (1969); Lubbock Christian College in Texas (1970); Atlanta Christian College in Georgia (1971); Blaney Avenue Church of Christ in Cupertino, California (1972); University of Tulsa (1973); Scarritt College in Nashville (1974); and Bethany College (1975).

Unlike the earlier Wynnewood meetings, these were better attended and there was a greater representation of Restoration churches. At the first Bethany gathering, for instance, there were six different segments represented, counting Churches of Christ sub-groups. These included from the Disciples of Christ: A. Dale Fiers, executive director of the International Convention; A.

133

T. DeGroot, professor at TCU; Lawrence V. Kirkpatrick, general secretary of the World Convention of Churches of Christ; as well as President Gresham.

From the Independent Christian Churches: James DeForest Murch, noted writer and lecturer; W. F. Lown, president of Manhattan Christian College; Seth Wilson, professor at Ozark Bible College; Richard Phillips, professor at Lincoln Seminary; and Henry Webb, professor at Milligan College.

From Churches of Christ: Carroll Ellis, professor at David Lipscomb College; David Stewart of Sweet Publishing; W. F. Cawyer of Herald of Truth in Abilene, Texas; Tom Olbricht of State College, Pennsylvania; Gene Shelburne and Tom Langford of the non-Sunday School Churches of Christ; Laverne Houtz, president of Southeastern Christian College (premillennial); as well as Carl Ketcherside and myself.

The only major group missing was the conservative, non-institutional Churches of Christ. Since they were our severest critics we made special effort—to no avail—to include them. In time a number of them either took part in some of our unity meetings or wrote for our journals. These included Charles Holt, Arnold Hardin, Edward Fudge, Clyde Goff, Lloyd Moyer, and Ron Compton. Some of these were also branded heretics and were rejected by their party for their expanded views of grace and fellowship—some having to suffer maltreatment.

The Bethany affair was historic. It was the first time in our history that such a diverse group of our divided Restoration family gathered to talk and pray about unity in Christ. The most important thing about it was that it happened at all. Brethren who had long been isolated from one another and suspicious of each other greeted one another in love—and they studied and prayed together for the first time.

There were memorable moments, such as when we gathered for a meal in the front yard of the Campbell

With Perry Gresham, president of Bethany College, First Annual Unity Forum, Bethany College, 1966.

Mansion alongside Alexander Campbell's famous octagonal study. We opened up the old Campbell church that dates back to 1827 for our Lord's day service. We declared our oneness by breaking bread together. We closed by singing the old hymn composed by M. C. Kurfees (Churches of Christ) and A. C. Hopkins (Christian Churches), who were themselves seeking unity for their people in Louisville, Kentucky, part of which reads:

> *How blest and how joyous will be the glad day,*
> *When heart beats to heart in the work of the Lord;*
> *When Christians united shall swell the grand lay,*
> *Divisions all ended, triumphant His word!*

As the service closed, someone suggested that we take "the spirit of Bethany" back to our churches—that if we could be one at the fount of our heritage we could be one everywhere. I would later describe the gathering

135

at the old Campbell church as "one of the Movement's finest hours."

These unity forums were often groundbreaking. At Cupertino in 1972, we had a Roman Catholic priest on the program. He surprised us by admitting there was no pope in the New Testament, and by predicting that by 2001 there might not be a pope at all! He also ventured that someday we will all be one with but one creed— *Jesus is Lord!* It must have been the first time ever that a Roman Catholic priest received a standing ovation in a Church of Christ.

In Tulsa in 1973, three women on the program exposed us to a different perspective on the role of women. At Lubbock in 1970, we heard the spell-binding oratory of Ervin Waters as he described his "Odyssey of Division" —pledging that he would never again "draw his sword and spill fratricidal blood on the polemical platform."

It was also at Lubbock that Perry Gresham spun stories about our old pioneers, to the delight of the west Texas ranchers. It was the first time they'd ever heard a Christian Church preacher. In Nashville in 1974, Robert O. Fife told us that while we might not be able to work together on everything, we could surely work together on some things.

At Cupertino in 1972, Everett Ferguson of Abilene Christian lectured on theological foundations for unity. At Milligan in 1967, Dean E. Walker, president of the college, cautioned us that "renewal of the church" must be Spirit-renewal, not self-renewal. Howard E. Short, editor of *The Christian* and a historian, pointed out that our history reveals that each of our factions has presumed to be the true church.

On and on it went—ten years of the Annual Unity Forum. Other such efforts were going on at the same time. The Hartford Forum in Hartford, Illinois began in 1957 and continued annually until 1972, involving hundreds from all segments of our heritage. These forums provided more opportunity for the rank and file to get involved and were largely discussion sessions, with no holds barred.

There were scores of other unity efforts all across the country—with others besides Carl and me initiating them. Carl had some of his own, without me, while I conducted a long series of "Mini-meetings" in which I brought the unity plea into people's homes and hotel suites, as well as churches and small study groups.

The Annual Unity Forum was a forerunner to the Restoration Forum, which began in 1984 at Ozark Christian College and continues until now on an annual basis. While it resembles the earlier Forum in both purpose and format, it is usually limited to Churches of Christ and Christian Churches. It draws larger numbers and is more generally accepted, which is reflective of the progress that has been made.

Restoration Forum XX, held in Lubbock, Texas in 2002—which I attended—was historic in nature. Things happened that we could not have anticipated back at Wynnewood Chapel in the 1950s. The Forum opened on a Sunday evening at the Broadway Church of Christ with a Communion service attended by upwards of 900—from all three wings of our heritage. For the first time the Forum had invited the Disciples of Christ to participate. Royce Money, president of ACU (Churches of Christ) and Bob Wetzel, president of Emmanuel School of Religion (Christian Churches) spoke on "The Restoration Dream: The Spirit of Unity." The singing and fellowship were breathtaking. I told Royce Money that evening that I had been waiting a half-century for such an occasion!

The Forum continued at the Quaker Avenue Church of Christ with the theme "With One Heart and Mouth," drawn from Romans 15:6, with over 300 participants from all three churches. Two unusual things took place. There was a video presentation on "Honor Roll of Unity," conducted by Doug Foster of ACU and

Victor Knowles, editor of *One Body*. It recognized those, living and dead, who helped to bring us where we are today—pioneers in unity. I was pleased to see those honored that I not only knew but had worked with in building bridges: Perry Gresham of the Disciples of Christ; Seth Wilson, Charles Gresham, and Don DeWelt of Christian Churches; Carl Ketcherside and Tom Langford of Churches of Christ. They were gracious to include me—displaying a picture of me when I was young, one that Ouida had not seen before!

If all that were not historic enough, the Forum closed by inviting all to sign a "Covenant of Unity," pledging "To be part of the answer to our Lord's prayer for unity among believers in Christ" and "To turn away from any kind of divisive or factious spirit which is not characteristic of the spirit of Christ."

It was awesome to see 302 people—of diverse backgrounds—lined up to sign a pledge to be peacemakers amidst our divided people. When all this started 50 years ago, we did well to gather a handful of daring souls who ventured to shake hands and get acquainted; now I was witness to hundreds pledging themselves to do something about our tragic divisions. Wow!

These unity meetings through the decades are a reflection of my own transformation, and they serve to define my own pilgrimage—from sectarianism to freedom. Moreover, they epitomize what I want for Churches of Christ. In these unity meetings we were indeed united—accepting each other even as Christ accepted us. Differences were honestly discussed in brotherly love, and we saw that we could differ without rejecting each other—and without anyone having to compromise any truth or approve of any error.

They became a microcosm of what we envisioned for our people. Even if we remained in separate groups, we could be at peace—loving and accepting each other as equals in Christ—and finding at least some things to do together. The unity meetings were who I was, my alter ego. They were the essence of unity in diversity—my heresy!

If there was one defining moment, it may have been in 1957 when Carl Ketcherside and I had a debate on instrumental music with Seth Wilson and Don DeWelt, both of Ozark Christian College, in Nowata, Oklahoma. Some weeks before the debate I wrote to Carl and told him that I thought this should be a different kind of debate. We should make it clear that Seth and Don are our brothers in Christ as much as we are to each other. We might differ on the issue under discussion, but that would not keep us from loving and accepting each other as brothers in Christ. We don't have to agree on instrumental music to be united in Christ!

Carl never answered that letter, but to my surprise he began his part of the debate by reading it aloud—giving it wholehearted approval. The atmosphere of the debate completely changed. We discussed differences without rancor, condemnation, or competition, but in brotherly love.

On that occasion, we publicly stated what Churches of Christ had never said before—we can differ on such issues as instrumental music and still be a united people. For the next three decades—until Carl's death in 1989—that was our message. We unite on the Center who is Christ; we allow for differences in the margins.

But long before Carl's passing we began to be listened to. The "unity-in-diversity heresy" became increasingly less heretical!

Chapter 14
High Adventures Abroad

Mark Twain in his *Innocents Abroad* said, "Travel is fatal to prejudice, bigotry, and narrow-mindedness." That has proven to be true in my case, or at least I can say that I am less prejudiced and more open-minded as a result of my extensive travels. It is one more reason that I can give for my transformation from a sectarian outlook to a more ecumenical one, an important part of my pilgrimage of freedom.

My travels abroad were not as a tourist, but to do things with the peoples of various cultures. I walked their back streets, visited in their homes, dined at their tables, taught in their schools, preached in their churches, and talked to their officials. I was a guest of the head of state in Taiwan, the pope of the Armenian Church, a bishop of the Russian Orthodox Church in Moscow, an archbishop of the Roman Catholic Church in Latvia, a renowned theologian in Glasgow, and Mother Teresa's nurses in Calcutta. I was even an overnight guest in a Buddhist temple.

I've assembled with believers in Westminster Abbey in London and in an Orthodox Cathedral in Moscow, as well as in a hotel suite in Beijing and a bamboo hut with a dirt floor in Thailand. I've preached in a military camp in Korea, in a house church in Tokyo, in a school in the Philippines, and in historic churches in Australia and New Zealand. I even spoke at the Assembly Hall in Taiwan at the invitation of the Speaker of the House!

I made every effort to be with the people themselves, whatever the country—to live like they lived. I opted to stay in homes rather than hotels. When I did stay in hotels, I usually avoided their dining rooms and went out into the streets—particularly in Asian countries—to eat with the people at their sidewalk stands, sometimes at risk to my health. In a seaside restaurant in Taipei I asked the waiter what an average native would likely order should he come in, and I ordered it. It attracted some attention that a visiting American would eat such food! My rule was if they could eat it, I could eat it. I was blessed in never being ill in all my travels abroad.

I say that I ate what they ate—but I recall one potential exception. Ouida and I were startled when we saw a cat butchered and laid out for sale at the Quinping Market in Canton, China, head and all. When we doubled back, it had been sold, but thankfully not to our hosts! It illustrates the difference in cultures.

I have seen unbelievable squalor and poverty as well as extravagant opulence, often in the same city. It was so in India. I have at hand a letter I wrote to Ouida from Calcutta in 1963 in which I revealed how distressed I was that families were sleeping on the sidewalk in front of my hotel. I described to her the injustice of it all, that some of us have so much, while others have so little. Some die on the sidewalks. That was part of Mother Teresa's ministry. She would pick up the diseased and dying off the streets and give them care and dignity during their last days.

———————————

My first major journey abroad in 1963 turned out to be my first and only trip around the world. My ticket read "Dallas to Dallas." In between were 12 nations and such cities as Tokyo, Taipei, Hong Kong, Saigon, Bangkok, New Delhi, Beirut, Jerusalem, Cairo, Athens, Paris, Heidelberg, London, Glasgow, New York—in that order. I swam in the Mediterranean in Beirut, floated in the Dead Sea in the wilderness of Judea, and waded in the River Jordan. I saw the Suez Canal and the

Red Sea from the air and took hikes alongside the Nile, the Seine, and the Thames.

I visited renowned museums in Jerusalem, Cairo, Paris, and London, and lingered at such elegant structures as the pyramids in Egypt, the Taj Mahal in India, the Mosque of Omar in Jerusalem, the Acropolis and Parthenon in Athens, the Eiffel Tower in Paris, and Westminster Abbey in London.

This trip was made possible by a Fulbright grant from the U.S. State Department to study Chinese culture and civilization in what we then called Free China (Taiwan). I was part of a team of 22 professors from as many American universities. The idea was that once we were exposed to China in this way, we would share the experience with our students back home. It called for six weeks of concentrated study at Tunghai University in Taichung, Taiwan.

We heard lectures on every aspect of Chinese culture, including the culinary arts, by the most eminent scholars, mostly Chinese, some of whom had come from mainland China with Chiang Kai-shek. They not only had to leave their university posts when the Communists took over, but their homes as well, sometimes leaving elegant art collections. One such displaced scholar complained to me that American presidents were naive about Communism, that they needed to wake up to its evil intentions. I hope that professor lived until President Reagan, whom he would have loved for his "Evil Empire" rhetoric.

We were taken all over the island and spent several days at the opulent Grande Hotel in Taipei the capital. We wined and dined with the great and near great. At one party, sponsored by the U.S. Ambassador to Taiwan, we were seated twelve to a table with diplomats, politicians, military brass, scientists, and educators. The Chinese tradition is to have a dish for each person at the table, with the dishes served one at a time. Each dish is toasted by lifting a glass of wine and saying "To the

143

dish." Each time we drank, the waiters refilled the glasses. Not used to alcohol, I had to fake it long before dish twelve!

While at the capital the 22 professors, along with Ambassador Wright, had audience with President Chiang Kai-shek. The protocol was the same as if we were heads of state. Four of us, including me, were asked to speak to the president for the group on different subjects. I was asked to make some reference to Madame Chiang, who could not be present because of illness, but I had to prepare my own short speech. Along with expressing regrets for the Madame's absence, I referred to her American education and noted that we claimed her as partly American, which appeared to delight the president. There was nothing profound about the meeting, but we did get to meet and shake hands with a head of state.

In Taipei I made contact with a native preacher, Jordan Wen, whom I had befriended in America, and through him I spoke to several of our Restoration groups—divided even in Asia. In Taichung we had no mission of any kind. In search of some Christian gathering in that Buddhist city, I started walking the downtown streets early one Sunday morning.

After some time I heard a familiar tune emanating from a store front, *All for Jesus, All for Jesus*—in Chinese, of course. They turned out to be "just Christians," and I was impressed that they had two services: one for unbelievers, with instrumental music; and one for believers, the singing a cappella. I attended both. The latter service was only for "baptized believers," by which they meant immersed believers. I was questioned before being invited. Unlike the service for outsiders, we sat in a square with the Lord's table at the center, about 30 of us. No preaching as in the other service. They spoke words of encouragement to each other—brothers and sisters alike. A few knew enough English that I could understand fairly well.

I had a distinct advantage over the other professors in that I had brought along names and addresses of parents of my Taiwanese students at Texas Woman's University, who had informed their parents of my visit. They would pick me up in a rented limousine (few had cars, not even the wealthy as these were) and take me to upscale restaurants, to the envy of the other professors. This was another way I got to be with the people, usually leaders in the community. Some were native Taiwanese, to be distinguished from the Chinese from the mainline who had largely taken over Taiwan.

I got the lowdown on Chiang Kai-shek, whom the natives saw not only as an intruder but also as a murderer. One Taiwanese host pointed to a stadium we were driving by and revealed that many Taiwanese had been executed there for not being "politically correct" in the eyes of the invading Chinese.

My stay in Taiwan not only gave me a broader view of the world, but also a better understanding of the complexity of both human nature and international problems. I found it interesting, for instance, that Taiwan talked about invading mainland China and restoring "one China," when everyone—including themselves—knew it would never happen. That the mainland might invade Taiwan was more of a possibility. But they had to preserve their hope.

It better informed me of the "Oriental mind," which we in the West little understand. For years to follow I shared with my students my experiences among the Chinese, reminding them that the Orient had an advanced civilization before the West was born. This is what the Fulbright grant was intended to accomplish—to make us Americans less provincial.

It also gave me a larger view of the church's diversity. Asian Christians are very different from us, and yet, not so different. They too nurture that hope that is never found in a Buddhist temple, a Hindu mosque, or a Shinto shrine. When they sing *All For Jesus* they mean

145

just what we mean. To move in that part of the Christian world and encounter all its diversity firsthand makes our differences—the ones we divide over—seem so petty.

I had to hurry home to get back to work, but in the two weeks or so that was left of the summer, I saw the Taj Mahal in Agra, India, the pyramids in Cairo, Egypt, and the Parthenon in Athens, Greece. In Jerusalem I happened upon Professor Jack Lewis of Harding College, an old classmate at both Abilene and Harvard, with whom I walked through Hezekiah's tunnel that was dug back in 700 B.C. and is referred to in the Bible. In Bethlehem, I visited the Church of the Nativity and in Bethany I descended into the tomb of Lazarus.

Since the Dead Sea Scrolls were part of my Ph.D. studies at Harvard, I made it a point to visit the caves where they were found alongside the Dead Sea, placed there by the Qumran sect of Jews—probably Essenes—sometime around 70 A.D. In Jerusalem itself I did a lot of walking, enjoying the usual "holy" sites. From the Garden of Gethsemane one can look across the Kidron valley and see the Mosque of Omar, which stands where Solomon's temple once stood on Mt. Moriah.

I did lots of walking in Paris and London, taking buses when wanting rest. In Paris I got to see *Mona Lisa* at the Louvre and the site where the historic Bastille once stood. In Westminster Abbey in London I saw a sign I've never forgotten. It was an invitation to prayers for Christian unity held in that chapel. I asked myself if I had ever seen or heard any such announcement in our churches back home. And *we* are the ones who are supposed to be praying for unity!

In Glasgow, Scotland, I visited a Church of Christ that practiced mutual ministry and had a visit with Professor William Barclay of Glasgow University. Among other things, we talked about Christian unity. Of the twelve nations that I visited, Scotland was my favorite.

In 1974 I was invited by the World Convention of Churches of Christ to take part in a conference of the secretaries of the World Confessional Families in Geneva, Switzerland. These secretaries, representing many denominations, had been carrying on bilateral talks about how unity might be realized between their communions, and they were meeting to evaluate their work. The Lutherans were talking with the Orthodox, the Congregationalists with the Presbyterians, and the Disciples of Christ with the Catholics, to name a few.

From the Stone-Campbell tradition were W. B. Blakemore, Allan Lee, and Paul Crow from the Disciples of Christ; Robert O. Fife from the Christian Churches; and I from Churches of Christ. It was an elite gathering of clergy, including bishops, archbishops, metropolitans, canons, protopresbyters, theologians, agency secretaries, and professors—some with colorful sacerdotal robes.

While most major Protestant denominations were represented, I was especially impressed by the presence of both Russian and Greek Orthodox prelates, an Anglican bishop, and a representative of the pope. There was even a Quaker and a Seventh Day Adventist. They were all ecumenical—prayerfully concerned about divisions among Christians. They were students and practitioners of unity, eager to share their findings.

Bishop John Howe of the Church of England served as moderator. When I told him I had read in the American press that he was the probable choice for the next Archbishop of Canterbury, he modestly insisted that I must not believe what I read in the American papers. It didn't happen.

This was my first experience with high-level clergy in an ecumenical conclave. I was interested to see how they would behave toward each other. They did very well indeed. I was impressed with their intellectual grace,

147

their piety, and their sense of urgency for Christian unity. Their mission was "reconciled diversity" —a term they often used and one that I came to appreciate. They would have been sympathetic with my own role as a "unity-in-diversity" heretic.

They pointed out that reconciled diversity acknowledges that the things that unite us are greater than those that separate us. That we will differ is evident enough. The question is whether or not we are willing to yield to the Spirit in such a way that our differences will give way to reconciliation—reconciled diversity.

In a private conversation with the Anglican bishop, I quoted Thomas Campbell's great line, "The Church of Christ upon earth is essentially, intentionally, and constitutionally one," noting that to Campbell the church *is* one—that by its very nature it cannot be other than one. He responded with "Campbell is right. It is a contradiction to speak of a divided church." In this context they conceded that the unity of the church is a given—it is real—but it isn't realized. And that is their mission: to lead the church to accept the Spirit's gift and thus "preserve the unity of the Spirit in the bond of peace." To realize what is real!

The Geneva conference was a super experience for me but humbling. It gave me pause that these ecumenical officials had given their lives to the study and implementation of Christian unity—and they took their mission very seriously. While I sometimes thought they were overdoing it and making it harder than it is, they caused me to understand better that division among Christians is a complex problem, one that calls for painstaking research—just as any other serious social evil.

I resolved to return home by way of Ireland and Scotland, so as to do some research in "Campbell country." I wanted to see the remnants of the old Glasgow University that Thomas Campbell attended from 1783-86, and the place where stood the old

Bridewell Prison on Duke Street, where Alexander Campbell was incarcerated in 1847. In Ireland I wanted to visit those humble places made famous as part of Campbell lore—Ballymena, Market Hill, Richhill, Ahorey.

An unexpected blessing was flying to London with W. B. Blakemore, dean of the Disciples Divinity House, University of Chicago, a true ecumenist and a true liberal of the old Chicago school. He had been a mainstay at the conference. He was impressed with the unity meetings we were then having among the Stone-Campbell churches, and he invited us to have one at his place—an invitation that we never got around to accepting. He was a scholar and a gentleman, now long gone to his reward. I prized my time with him, a highlight of my trip.

From London I made my way to Glasgow by train, mainly because I wanted to see rural England and rustic Scotland other than from the air. I met interesting people on the train. Watergate had just ended at home, allowing one cordial Englishman to say, "Because of the agony of the American people, we are glad it is over." Another, with whom I was talking religion, pointed to the lovely white Anglican chapels with their steeples that appeared in every village we passed. He then said, "When I was a boy those churches were comfortably filled each Sunday—with as may as 100 to 150 even in the villages—and the rector was taken good care of." He added with pathos, "But now the rector has to speak to as few as three or four old people and having a hard time of it financially." It has not improved all that much since then.

I stopped off in Leicester, staying at a bed and breakfast so as to be with the people. The oldsters told me of the air raids during World War II. They learned which was a Nazi plane by the sound of the motor. They cautioned me not to go to Ireland due to the violent unrest there between Catholics and Protestants.

Since Ouida was safe at home, I ventured on toward Ireland in spite of the supposed danger, but to Scotland first. In Glasgow I was a guest in the home of Professor William Arthur, whom I knew when he was a visiting professor at Bethany. He was an elder of the Coplaw Church of Christ— "Associated," akin to Disciples— where I attended services the only Sunday I was in Scotland. The same night I was with Dan Mitchell of the Castlemilk Church of Christ—American, non-instrumental—which was having a hard time surviving.

I also visited with brethren of a third kind of Church of Christ, commonly referred to as Old Paths—Scottish, non-instrumental but also mutual ministry. I was told that if I spoke in their church, some would walk out since I had attended an Associated church. It made me feel at home. You are loved and accepted only when you belong to the right party!

Jack Paton, a young Scot, showed me the old campus of Glasgow University, now in ruins, where Thomas Campbell studied. It was there that he learned the Scottish "Common Sense" approach to learning from his old teacher, the acclaimed Thomas Reid, which he brought to America and applied to the study of the Bible. When I saw the old site of the prison where Alexander Campbell spent almost a fortnight, I thought of those dear sisters who competed with each other in making his stay more comfortable, furnishing his bare cell with amenities. I suspect the old hero enjoyed all that attention!

In Edinburgh, the capital, I met with several of our American preachers who were serving churches and/or doing graduate work at the famous university of the same name. I was impressed by their openness—and by their fertile, growing minds. Some of them are now leading Churches of Christ in new directions. Andrew Gardiner, a native Scot and an American-sponsored missionary, showed me both tourist attractions and old Restoration sites.

150

He drove me by the old home of John Knox that dates back to the 17th century. Methinks I could hear "the thundering Scot" preaching repentance to Queen Mary Stuart. He showed me the townhouse where Alexander Campbell lectured, and the site where once stood a tabernacle where preached James and Robert Haldane, restorationists of Scotland who influenced the Campbells.

I was especially pleased to see an old Sandemanian church that was still being used. Its sign read "Meeting Place, Church of Christ, Commonly Called Glasites or Sandemanians." It gave the hours of assembly and cited Acts 2:42 as the order of worship. This persuasion found its way to America and influenced those churches ministered to by J. D. Phillips (referred to in Chapter 11).

Despite all the warnings, I was hardly prepared for what I found in Ireland. I took a ship from Ardrossen, Scotland to Belfast in North Ireland. It was my first "sea" voyage, though only across the North Channel of the Irish Sea and only for five hours. I no more than set foot in Belfast before I realized I was in a besieged country. British troops patrolled the streets with Tommy guns. Some streets were barricaded. To enter a hotel, I had to check my bag outside at an improvised booth and submit to a body search. It was that way all over northern Ireland. But I had the advantage of being just about the only tourist around. I had it to myself!

I took a bus from Belfast to Armaugh, where I hoped to spend the night at a hotel before proceeding the next day to Ahorey—the village/church where the Campbells lived before migrating to America. I was virtually alone in Armaugh, even at the town square. No hotel was in sight. It was a week before Christmas; I noticed a Yuletide celebration for children going on at a church across the square, which happened to be Baptist. They received me warmly and sent word to the pastor that an American visitor was at the church who needed to find a hotel.

Jim Armstrong, who was a policeman in that small city before he became a minister, was a take-charge kind of guy who graciously managed my evening. While most hotels had been bombed out or closed down, he found one that would both house and dine me. He turned me over to a parishioner to make sure I got there and invited me to come back after dinner for an adult Christmas party.

The walk to the hotel was eerie. The streets were well lighted but deserted. My guide and I made our way around barricades. Not a soul did I see on a main street in early evening and not a car was in sight. A pall of uneasiness overwhelmed us. The entrance to the small hotel was right on the sidewalk. I couldn't believe my eyes when my host began knocking on the hotel door. Knock at the door of a hotel?

We were checked out through the peephole and allowed entrance. It turned out that there was a holiday party going on in the hotel—lots of people and lots of noise. The Irish know how to frolic. I could only conclude that they all got there the same way I did—by walking some distance. After faring well on typical Irish cuisine, I returned to the church for the party, making my way alone this time. Unbeknownst to me I was in for the most forbidding night of my life.

At the party, Pastor Armstrong kept introducing me as "Mr. Garrett, a believer." A believer! I was not used to being introduced that way—but in that setting it had special meaning. That church, along with all believers in that besieged town, was caught up in a world of cruel disbelief and violence. A believer could be trusted, hopefully. The people all had kin or friends who had been killed or maimed by "the troubles." Most every night there was gunfire. They learned to live with fear, they told me.

After the party, the pastor took me for a walk—about the town he had once walked as a police officer. He

152

showed me one bombed-out building after another. On one corner was a miniature "Ground Zero." Jim told me that on that site there were once "as nice stores as you would find anywhere." One store was once a haberdashery. It was now in ruins; the owner, a Protestant, had been killed by a Catholic mob. The minister took me to a hilltop and beckoned me to look over his lighted but benighted town. That is when he told me his belief that it wasn't their people that were destroying each other, but that it was Communist-inspired.

At one corner we stood by a fire station where several British soldiers had been killed by snipers from the rooftops. As we stood there together in a well-lighted area, with not a person in sight, the pastor said to me, "People would say we are fools to be out here like this, but I am not afraid." He added, "We're being watched, that's for sure." I asked him where the soldiers were. He said they were in the recesses—that it was too dangerous for them to be exposed.

As my eyes scanned the rooftops of the four- to five-story buildings surrounding us—whence gunfire might erupt at anytime—I had a feeling that I never had before. I was uneasy about my safety; but since the Lord had brought me to such a place with such a devoted Christian, I had peace about it all. While I felt we had no business being in such a frightening place, there was something about it that seemed appropriate. It was something that, for my own soul's sake, I needed to experience.

It was a grim night in Ireland. Isaiah's lament appeared relevant: "Your country is desolate. Your cities are burned with fire. Strangers devour your land in your presence." It was traumatizing. I felt it all night long.

The next morning, Dr. Alfred R. Scott, pastor of the Ahorey Presbyterian Church, took me to see his church, where Thomas Campbell was pastor before he migrated to America in 1807. The village of Ahorey, some 10

153

miles from Armaugh, is much the way it was when the Campbells were there. The congregation is aware of its Campbellite heritage. A stained glass window honors Alexander Campbell, appropriately depicting an open Bible. A bell tower memorializes Thomas Campbell, describing him as a former pastor and founder of the Christian Church in America.

Dr. Scott insisted I stand in the old Campbell pulpit and say a word; he would serve as the congregation. I chose to read Psalms 46, which begins with "God is our refuge and strength, a very present help in trouble." From the pulpit I reminded my host that Thomas Campbell read that same psalm one Sunday when his church was overrun by soldiers during a time of unrest.

My host graciously showed me the places I wanted to see: Richhill, where the Campbells conducted a school in a building that still stands; Market Hill, where young Campbell attended school; Hamilton Bawn, where the family lived for a time, walking to Ahorey for church.

Mrs. Scott prepared a tasty boiled Irish dinner, giving her version of the Campbells along the way. Thomas was her favorite—being the sweet, compassionate soul that he was—but she didn't like Alexander, who was austere and unyielding. I told her a few tender stories from Alexander's life, particularly how he would follow his grieving, inconsolable wife to "God's Acre" where their beloved Wycliffe had recently been interred, and whisper in her ear, "My dear, they are not here," and gently lead her back to the house. My hostess, impressed with a side of Alexander Campbell that she had not heard before, at last conceded, "Maybe he wasn't so bad after all!"

I was witness to a bruised Ireland all the way to Dublin and then to Shannon. There I boarded a giant Irish Airlines jet for home.

In 1983, I took a month's journey to Japan and Thailand. In Japan I visited several of our churches and helped celebrate the 100th anniversary of Charles E. Garst's coming to Japan as our first missionary in 1883. The celebration was held at the elegant Aoyama Wedding Hall, and I realized I was in Japan when we dined on raw fish while sitting on the floor around low tables. Garst preached and built churches for fifteen years before his death in 1898. With missionary Harold Sims as my interpreter, I spoke on our common heritage that began in America but found its way to Japan.

My hosts in Japan were Moto and Yorika Nomura, native missionaries longtime supported by American churches. Yorika taught me the excellence of Japanese cuisine by what she placed on the table. Being in their home was a highlight of the trip. I especially enjoyed their showing me places that American visitors do not usually see, including interesting shops.

Moto accompanied me to Ibaraki Christian College, then not as closely related to Churches of Christ as it once was, where I spoke in chapel. I relished visiting in a number of homes, seeing firsthand how the people live and something of how they think. I was impressed by their attractive homes—small and sparsely furnished—except for artistic appointments. Beds were on the floor. Tea is inevitable, no matter the hour: the hospitality overwhelming. The visitor, of course, removes his shoes and dons house slippers.

Next to the Garst celebration, our most significant event was a unity meeting at the old Ochanomizu Church of Christ in Tokyo. Several missionaries of our divided witness in Japan were present. I addressed the group twice on our heritage as a unity people. We dined and talked and prayed together with such a spirit of love and acceptance that some were heard to say that our people in Japan had been waiting a hundred years for that day.

155

After a week in Japan I had to hurry on to Thailand where I taught for three weeks at Chiangmai Bible Institute in Chiangmai, some 500 miles north of Bangkok. It was conducted by Christian Church missionaries. I took twenty students through the book of Romans, again through an interpreter. By now I had come to see advantages to teaching through an interpreter. The teacher is forced to hone his syntax and to keep his ideas simple. The students benefit in that it helps them to learn English as well as the subject at hand.

I conned my interpreter, Ahtapa Seenlee, a native Thai, into letting me go with him one weekend to his home, which was in a Lisu tribal village north of Chiangmai near the Laos border. These villages were made up, in part, of refugees from China, Cambodia, and Laos. Some of them, including Ahtapa's parents, were Christians. We made the trip of some three hours on a motor bike over both bad roads and no roads. On the way, Ahtapa bought a dressed chicken. With its legs tied, he draped the naked chicken over the handlebar of the bike. To this day, one of my memories of Thailand is that dangling chicken doing all sorts of gyrations as we bumped our way along the rough terrain.

We joined his parents in their rice paddy, helping with the harvest. As I carried bundles of sheaves on my shoulder, I sang "Bringing in the Sheaves," written by one of our pioneer preachers, Knowles Shaw. Ahtapa soon joined me, to the curiosity of the parents who knew no English. Ahtapa was still singing Shaw's old hymn as we bumped our way back to Chiangmai the next day!

The Seenlees' home was a bamboo hut with a dirt floor. That evening, now joined by a daughter, we dined on "that chicken" and rice, along with green sprouts from the garden and roasted corn on the cob for dessert. The meal was followed by Bible study, all on the dirt floor. With Ahtapa interpreting, I taught as simply as

156

possible some basic biblical themes: the beatitudes, the golden text, the golden rule, the greatest commandment. That night we all bedded down on the floor of the sizable one-room hut, with a curtain or two serving as partitions.

They were poor, but they didn't appear aware of it. They were thankful to have food and shelter, and to have work to do. It was all they ever knew. But I thought of their lovely teenage daughter. Would she have any chance of an education? There must have been fifty children in that village, but no school for them. While the missionaries do some schooling in these numerous villages, they can't get to them all.

Alone early on Sunday morning, I walked the village, made up mostly of bamboo huts, some of them on stilts several feet above ground, providing both protection and a place for animals. Small shrines were in trees or on poles, containing doll-like gods, where the spirits of their ancestors were believed to dwell. Animism, with its multiplicity of gods, is basically ancestor worship.

Exposure to such paganism made our small gathering of believers in the Seenlee home all the more meaningful. I talked to them in simple terms about the hope of the gospel, with Ahtapa translating into their tribal tongue. We sang, prayed, and "broke rice" together, which is the only bread they know. The way they cooked it—sticky and cake-like—it could be passed from hand to hand and broken. A memorable Communion!

In Chiangmai, I was a guest in the home of Jerry and Pam Headen, Christian Church missionaries, while teaching at the Bible Institute. Chiangmai is something of a capital for missionaries of our tradition. At some gatherings, I was with as many as twenty families. I was privileged to be in the home of longtime Disciples of Christ missionaries Allen and Joan Eubanks, who work with Payup University, which I also visited. From the Christian Churches were David and Delores Filbeck, who were involved mostly in translation work.

I happened upon Ken Dobson, to whom I had taught philosophy in high school back in Jacksonville, Illinois, 25 years before. He was now a Presbyterian missionary. We went together to McLean Institute, a school for lepers. We were impressed that a medical missionary a century before would travel for months on an elephant's back to reach this isolated area—and then build a leper's colony. McLean had persuaded the government to let him use a small island that was not inhabited because it was believed to be demonized by a white elephant. He invited the despised lepers to come to the island, build their own homes, learn a trade, and live freely. It has become an island of hope for lepers and their families—an educational enterprise of reputation.

I had a great time with my Thai students, studying Romans. Three hours each day we traced the major themes of the book. I had them memorize the key passages. I would quote them in English and they would respond in Thai. On the last day of class, they bade me farewell by standing and quoting in unison those awesome lines from Paul in Romans 11:33: "Oh, the depth of the riches both of the wisdom and knowledge of God! How unsearchable are His judgments and His ways past finding out!"

It was one of my finest moments as a professor.

———————————

My visit to El Salvador in 1984 was one of triumph and tragedy: triumph in that it began as one of the most interesting and fruitful of all my travel experiences and tragedy in that I was called home due to the death of our four-year old granddaughter. Due to some problems our daughter Phoebe was having at the time, Ouida and I were keeping her little Christi much of the time. But on this particular Sunday afternoon in June, she was at the farm of her paternal grandparents some ten miles from our home. Ouida, still caring for her mother as well as

158

for Christi, was getting some needed rest. She received an emergency call that Christi was missing.

By the time Ouida arrived at the farm, the sheriff had found Christi's body in a small pond. It was too late to revive her. The sheriff found little footprints leading into the pond. It was presumed that she had followed a dog into the water.

It was late that Sunday night before Ouida was able to reach me in the home of Andrew and Kathy Fuller in San Salvador. It was the saddest news I ever received.

Christi and I were pals. I took her with me on errands about town. We spent lots of time at the city parks. We played chase about the house to her utter delight, and she never tired of riding me piggy-back. We even "shaved" together, with Christi—her face overwhelmed with lather—enjoying herself in the mirror. My favorite memory is the interest she took when I would playfully embrace Ouida in the kitchen. She watched with delight, and if I broke the embrace sooner than she thought appropriate, she would protest by urging my arm back into an embrace!

I had been in San Salvador only two days when Ouida's call came, but they had been unusually interesting and enjoyable. My host, Andrew Fuller, worked for the U.S. Embassy. He gave me a tour of the facility and filled me in on its operation in a country amidst civil war, as El Salvador then was. From the Embassy's roof, we had an excellent view of the city and the mountains surrounding it. In those mountains lurked 12,000 Communist guerrillas—a continual threat to the city. We visited a Salvadorian army training camp. Andrew sadly observed that a high percentage of the young men we saw in training would likely die in the ongoing conflict.

On Sunday I taught a class of eager-to-learn adults and addressed the assembly of the Union Church of San Salvador on the grace of God. It is an independent church made up of English-speaking Salvadorians and

159

Americans. It has an impressive edifice of Spanish architecture, walled–in as most everything in San Salvador seemed to be. A short distance behind the church was a volcanic mountain, which could be seen from the window behind the pulpit. I told them that it was my first time to preach at the foot of a volcano, but that I had been in more dangerous situations! Present that Sunday was a group of dentists and physicians from Tennessee who were on their way to a mission station to do works of mercy. We had a delightful visit following the service.

In the afternoon, I was part of a large gathering of Embassy families in a luxurious home with a walled-in backyard of gardens and pool. They not only wined and dined me, but also briefed me on our country's mission in troubled Central America. I got to talk with military, political, and diplomatic figures—and a woman reporter. She admitted that the press is often "left wing" and biased against U.S. policy in that part of the world.

While we were visiting, a little child fell into the pool in the garden but was, of course, immediately rescued. It was about the time that Christi was in trouble back home. I am not much for omens and premonitions, but I was made to wonder when something even more impressive happened later that evening. I was visiting in the home of a longtime missionary to those parts—one who had a different view of the problems in Central America than the Embassy people. The only thing that will bring peace is the gospel of Christ, he insisted, and he took heart that so many thousands of people were turning to Christ.

As the missionary and I visited on into the evening, he talked about how God loves children, referring in part to the thousands of little ones who have to suffer grave injustices in Central America because of the sins of their fathers. He kept on impressing upon me God's *special* love for his little ones, and how he gloriously receives them into heaven—as if preparing me for the

160

night ahead. All this time Ouida was trying to reach me. The beloved missionary would have insisted—had he known what was going on—that while the news was sad for me, it was not for Christi.

Back home at Christi's funeral, our son Ben read lines from one of William Barclay's prayers: "Make us to be sure that in perfect wisdom, perfect love, and perfect power Thou art working ever for the best." He read on: "Help us to face life with grace and gallantry; and help us to find courage to go on in the memory that the best tribute we can pay a loved one is not a tribute of tears, but the constant memory that another has been added to the unseen cloud of witnesses who compass us about."

On the Lord's day after the funeral, our congregation sang to Ouida her favorite hymn, one she sometimes sings to me:

To love someone more dearly every day,
To help a wandering child to find his way,
To ponder o'er a noble thought and pray,
And smile when evening falls, And smile
      when evening falls.
This is my task.

To follow truth as blind men long for light,
To do my best from dawn of day till night,
To keep myself fit for his holy sight,
And answer when he calls, And answer when
      he calls.
This is my task.

And then my Savior by and by to meet,
When faith hath made her task on earth complete,
And lay my homage at the Master's feet,
Within the jasper walls, Within the jasper walls.
This crowns my task.

As her sisters and brothers in the Lord sang to her out of caring hearts, Ouida—like her Lord—quietly wept. It is a precious memory.

A few months later, Ouida had a very realistic dream about Christi—and she is not one to dream such dreams. In the dream Christi came to her in a park and took her hand. They played for a time in the park and on the swings. Her caretaker or guardian angel, who was waiting patiently in the distance, finally said, "Christi, it is time for us to go." Christi responded at once and hurried away, as if eager to go with her caretaker.

In relating the dream to me, Ouida said it was as real as if she were actually with Christi—and it was of great comfort to her that Christi was happy to go away with her guardian angel. Then she said, "A strange thing: Christi was bigger."

Then I said, "She would be, wouldn't she? She's three months older."

Chapter 15

More Adventures Abroad, Now With Ouida

For the ten years leading up to 1992, Ouida was not free to join me on my trips abroad since she was caring for her mother. During my earlier journeys, the children were still at home. She was, however, sometimes with me on shorter, domestic ventures, and it was a blessing to all involved when she was around. As I've often told her, she's like Coke in that things go better when she's along. And those who know me best say I behave better when she is along.

While caring for Mother Pitts was a labor of love—considering the gracious soul she was—it was nonetheless both confining and arduous, especially in her last years when she was a virtual invalid. When she could no longer manage the stairs, even with help, we gave her our master bedroom with its private bath, with Ouida serving as caretaker. Often Ouida would call me from my study to help her lift her mother, who had a way of falling in the most inopportune places.

Even before Mother Pitts passed on, I gave notice to the readers of *Restoration Review* in 1988 (when I was in India) that it was my last extended trip abroad without Ouida. The main reason was that she was missing what had become so much a part of my latter years—an expanding fellowship with the church around the world. I was uniquely blessed with soul-expanding experiences that helped to define who I was, and I wanted her in on them. I resolved that there would be no more until she could join me.

That last 1988 venture without her illustrates what I

mean. First I was in the Philippines teaching at a seminary and traveling with Wycliffe Bible translators. I went on to India, where I stayed in an orphanage and taught missionaries, then to Singapore to visit with still more Christian workers, and finally to New Zealand to address churches and help celebrate the Campbell Bicentennial at the World Convention of Churches of Christ. It was 45 days of incredible exposure to people and events of which most people never even dream—too much for Ouida to miss.

I might have chosen a less auspicious destination for Ouida's maiden journey abroad than China. I had not yet been there myself, for it had long been a closed society to most people. In 1993 we were invited by Christian Church missionaries to join other couples in making contact with people in China who had expressed interest in the Christian faith. Radio missionaries in Hong Kong had gathered names of interested parties all over China. Our mission team would travel to the various provinces, search out these prospects, and, if possible, bring them to the Lord.

I will admit to having some doubt about the prospects for such a mission, but I saw it as an opportune time to see China and to be with still more dedicated Christians. Any good we might do would be a bonus.

There was one part of the mission that disturbed Ouida to the point of near revolt. We were to smuggle Bibles into China! She was as eager for the Chinese to have Bibles as anyone else, but she didn't want to be a smuggler. We could be arrested and put in prison. After all, this was communist China. They treated people that way all the time. Besides, it was against the law. She didn't want to do it.

In Hong Kong, where we had gathered to plan our conspiracy, the missionaries, led by Danny Thurston, assured us that we would be all right. If we were caught, they would do no more than confiscate our "contraband." China at that time was seeking the 2000 Olympics, we were reminded, and it didn't want any kind of international incident. Besides, the missionaries knew how to pack the Bibles in our luggage so the x-ray devices would be less likely to detect them.

They were actually New Testaments in modern Chinese—greatly cherished by Christians in China. If we sixteen people did no more than take several hundred New Testaments into China, that alone would justify our mission. Ouida at last consented to join the conspiracy. It would have been the irony of ironies if Ouida had been arrested as a smuggler.

It so happened that on the day we were to fly to Beijing, a fierce typhoon swept through Hong Kong. From our lofty hotel room it was a sight to behold. Businesses closed, the streets were deserted, and debris was blowing wildly. Since we had food stashed away in our luggage, we were prepared for such contingencies as typhoons or expensive restaurants. Allowing for the tea that Oriental hotels always have in their rooms, we fared quite well. Believe it, there's nothing like eating peanut butter and cheese with Ouida during a raging typhoon in a high-rise hotel halfway around the world!

The typhoon had sufficiently disturbed airport routine that once we were in Beijing we were waved through customs without a single bag being inspected. Some of our group insisted that the Lord used the storm to aid our smuggling enterprise. That is not exactly my theology.

It turned out that our "contraband" of New Testaments—each couple had about sixty—was a significant part of our mission, especially while we were in Beijing. We passed them along to lay missionaries who were in China ostensibly to teach English, but were using the opportunity to share the gospel. They were delighted to have the Chinese Testaments to pass along to their students. But I was reminded where we were when I offered a pack of several Testaments to a British

165

teacher at a gathering of believers at a hotel. She cautiously looked both ways before hurriedly taking them and slipping them into her bag. We handed several to people on the streets—strictly taboo of course.

Before taking off to our assigned provinces, we got in some sightseeing. We had often seen the Great Wall on TV, but it was something else to see it firsthand and to walk it. When one sees how it snakes its way through the mountains as far as the eye can reach—and ponders its antiquity—it easily qualifies as one of the wonders of the world. But Ouida thought it ironic to lunch at a Kentucky Fried Chicken alongside the Great Wall!

Tiananmen Square was dear to us because of the struggle for freedom that had occurred there. Back in the bus, I prophesied to our group that one day tourists would visit the Square and see a memorial dedicated to those who died there back in 1989 for the cause of democracy. The optimists agreed with me!

We also saw the People's Palace and the Forbidden City. The latter is a complex of several palaces, built by fourteen emperors, dating back to 1640. While it was elegant, it reminded us of the absolute rule of the emperors of ancient Cathay (some of whom were both wise and benevolent).

I took with me the name and address of a Chinese Christian pastor who had been imprisoned for twenty-one years for being unwilling to place his church under the aegis of the communist government. Allen Yan was now free, and I was hopeful of interviewing him. Our Chinese adviser cautioned me that it might be a problem for Allen if I, a Westerner, contacted him. So he called and arranged the interview at our hotel.

Fluent in English, Allen told me his story. When he told authorities that he could not place his little "flock of Christians," which is what they called themselves, under a government bureau because they believed that only Jesus Christ is the head of the church, he was imprisoned. He said they freed him after two decades because he had grown too old to work. And this is the China that wants the Olympics! We saw the banners everywhere: "Beijing 2000 Olympics." Nonetheless, as Allen assured us, there are thousands of underground churches in China and millions of believers, besides the state-sponsored churches.

While we were still in Beijing, Ouida came down with a respiratory infection that occasionally afflicts her. Since the antibiotic she brought with her didn't help, we summoned a doctor from a hospital that caters to foreigners. She came to our hotel room with a nurse in tow and a cache of medicines, loaded for bear. Since she was thoroughly Chinese, I asked if she was going to use acupuncture. She was delighted with the suggestion, as if she had not thought of it, and proceeded to do needles on Ouida. She also gave her a sulfur drug, assuring us that she would be well by morning. We had our doubts, but sure enough Ouida was ready to travel by the next day. We never knew whether it was due to the acupuncture or the sulfur drug or both. Ouida was so impressed that she has tried to duplicate the same drug in this country, but to no avail.

We were assigned Hainan province, now known to Americans for the 2001 spy plane incident. We flew into Haikou, the capital, with Daisy, a Chinese Christian girl who served as both our interpreter and guide. Ouida was so impressed by what happened to us there that she wrote an essay for our newsletter titled "In A Quaint Chinese Village." She not only said it was the experience of a lifetime, but named one day as "the most unusual day we had ever spent."

One prospect we were to track down was a taxi driver whose only contact with Christianity was a deceased Christian grandmother whose memory he revered. He assured us that he would be ostracized and unable to find work should he become a Christian. But he arranged for us to visit a nearby village where he had grown up and still had relatives. We could preach to

167

them. It was a communist compound of some 300 families who farmed a common plot of land within walking distance. We were hosted by two brothers whose father had fought with Chiang Kai-shek against the communists and was then in Taiwan.

Villagers gathered in the brothers' home and I talked with them about how God has revealed himself both in Nature and in a Person. Daisy translated into Mandarin; then one of the brothers translated into the village tongue. Ouida wondered what the people finally heard, and what it would mean to people who worshipped idols and ancestors. They filed in and out, probably as much out of curiosity as out of interest. Children, well fed and clothed, gaped at us between their school classes. We were as much a curiosity as if we had come from another planet. We were the first Westerners the village had ever seen.

The brothers served us their best cuisine: spinach soup, turnip greens, tough chicken wings, and Pabst Blue Ribbon beer. On this occasion, rice was served as a dessert. During the meal, the brothers told us of some of the oppression they suffered under a communist regime. The government owns the land and parcels out a small plot to each family. There is little chance to improve one's lot in life, although some of the children go away to college and a freer life.

Ouida was hardly prepared for what she saw in the Chinese markets, such as cooks preparing chicken entrails. Some stalls offered snails, worms, giant flies, and even a butchered cat with the heart still beating. She was dismayed by the lack of hygiene in the villages. In places outside Beijing, we were the only Westerners in sight. It was Ouida's first culture shock.

But in the cities, we witnessed luxury that would rival any in the world—such as the luxurious Swan Hotel in Canton. The cities bustled with businesses, and skyscrapers were going up everywhere. Because of its turn toward the free market, China is changing for the

168

better in spite of its communist leadership. But the pollution was so bad that we decided to come home early lest Ouida become ill again. But we first took time for Ouida to stock up on Chinese silk!

China served well in initiating Ouida as a world traveler.

———— —— ————

Ouida was now conditioned for even a longer journey and one even farther from home. In 1994 we spent forty-eight days on an exciting journey to Australia and New Zealand. We were guests of the Australian committee of the World Convention of Churches of Christ. They planned our itinerary, which included teaching at two of their colleges and preaching at numerous churches, and arranged for us to be escorted by a consummate Aussie—the gentlemanly Ken Masterton who became a dear friend. Ken, a bachelor, has since been a guest in our home.

Over several days, Ken drove us from Melbourne, Victoria, our port of entry, to Adelaide in South Australia. In Ballarat, we visited Sovereign Hill, an old gold rush town (1851), and Dawson Church of Christ, an historic church. On the way to Horsham, we saw Halls Gap in the Grampies Mountain, a tourist attraction; and in Horsham, we visited another Church of Christ where Harvey Clark ministered. At Pioneer Village, Ken showed us an old school where he had taught as a young man.

In Adelaide we were guests in the home of Ken and Erma Dawson, and had tea (in Australia this means a meal!) with David and Heather Brooker. Both families are leaders of Churches of Christ in Australia. There are some 400 congregations of this denomination there. While they are of the Stone-Campbell heritage, they are to be distinguished from any of the three branches of the Movement in the United States. They have their own history and uniqueness.

169

I was honored to speak on "The Old Paths" at the historic Grote Street Church of Christ in Adelaide, which is the mother church of all the Australian Churches of Christ, founded by Scottish brethren in 1844. We also visited Point Sturt Church of Christ (1855) on the southern coast, though there is no longer a regular assembly. Next door live Graham and Edna Yelland, who watch after the historic chapel. Graham at that time had lived seventy-six years in the same house, which might be a record!

In Goolwa, we had an appointment in the library with a historian named Barry Griffin, who gave lectures on Eliza Davies, early explorer (the first white woman into the Outback) and pioneer educator. I first discovered her in her autobiography that I came upon in the TCU library. When I saw it had a chapter on "Life in Bethany," I brought it home to see what she had to do with our heritage. Ouida also read the book, which was the beginning of her consummate interest in Eliza Davies. Mr. Griffin was aware of Davies' connection with Churches of Christ, but his interest was confined to her other endeavors, especially as a pioneer explorer.

Ouida was pleased that on several occasions in formal settings she could tell leaders of Churches of Christ in Australia about one of their own pioneers—going back to the 1850s when Davies brought Alexander Campbell's writings to Australia. She had been to Australia as early as the 1830s, when she joined Captain Charles Sturt, a pioneer explorer, in an exploration of the Murray River, which took them where the white man had not yet been.

Ouida told how Davies, then a Baptist, heard Campbell preach in her native Scotland, and was so impressed that she resolved to join his reformation movement. She followed him to America and spent some two years at his home in Bethany; the Campbells described her as "a ministering angel," helping to tend their sick and bury their dead. She became a dedicated

"Campbellite," esteeming Campbell as the greatest man she ever knew. After serving for a time in Midway, Kentucky, she returned to Australia, taking with her a trunkload of Campbell's writings which she effectively used to promote his cause in New South Wales, a land that was still little more than a British prison colony.

Having read her autobiography to each other over and over, we had become well acquainted with Eliza Davies. She became a virtual member of our family. Ouida, greatly admiring her sacrificial devotion, adopted her as a kind of older sister. Part of our mission to Australia was to search out places where Davies conducted schools—especially one she named "Hurricane Hill" near Kiama, about 100 miles south of Sydney.

Ron Brooker, then president of the World Convention of Churches of Christ, and his wife Dot, who hosted us in New South Wales, drove us to Kiama in search of contact. Once the town librarian heard our request, she summoned the town's old history buff to see if he could help us. When Ouida gave what sketchy details she had of where Eliza once had her hut school, the old buff said he knew exactly where it was, and that he would take us there.

It was something of a spiritual experience to "see" Eliza and the hut where she had conducted a school for uncouth ragamuffins, transforming them into decent citizens in spite of incredible obstacles and hardship. The hut, of course, had disappeared over a century before (we were standing in a cow pasture), but we were nonetheless with Ms. Eliza. We felt her presence. It was an appropriate place to thank God for her beautiful life. What a compelling person she was: Alexander Campbell's ministering angel when he needed her the most! (Oh, yes, Eliza Davies was also among the women who ministered to the old reformer when he was in prison in Scotland!)

We did some "tourist-y" things with Ron and Dot—

171

such as touring Sydney, the harbor, and the elegant Opera House. They also drove us to Canberra, the nation's capital, where we saw the Parliament, the most magnificent building in Australia. We attended a conference at the sizable Wollongong Church of Christ in New South Wales where I spoke, by request, about the Boston Church of Christ (now International Church of Christ), which was creating some confusion among them. My portrayal of that controversial movement was probably more balanced than they expected.

I was especially pleased to visit two of the three Churches of Christ colleges in Australia. In Mulgrave, near Melbourne, I spoke in chapel and taught classes at the Churches of Christ Theological College. Graeme Chapman was our host. He and his wife Eileen, now our dear friends, have also visited us in America. I talked to Graeme's classes on Restoration history and addressed the faculty on the Lord's Prayer. We also visited Carlingford Theological College near Sydney, where I lectured on principles of the Stone-Campbell heritage. Principal Keith Farmer, also active in the World Convention, and his wife Margaret hosted us in their lovely home.

A fun thing happened at Carlingford. In my lectures, I had referred to the neglect of Barton W. Stone, who really preceded Alexander Campbell, noting that it is always Campbell's picture that we have on our walls— which was the case at that college. Afterwards, at lunch, there came a coterie of students parading through the cafeteria hoisting a large framed picture of Barton W. Stone!

Ken Masterton flew with us to Tasmania, the island-state south of the mainland. Aussies insist that maps of their country that leave off Tasmania, as they often do, are incomplete. We drove the eastern coast from Launcester to Bicheno, where I addressed Churches of Christ ministers and their wives at the church's Sea View Camp, and on to Howrah where we were guests in the home of Ray and Gwen Morfew. I spoke on "The Transforming Friendship of Jesus" at the Howrah Church of Christ. At the southern tip of the island, we attended a musical at the Hobart City Church of Christ and went atop Mt. Wellington, which provides a panoramic view of that part of the island. We were in the home of the minister, Clinton Wardell, for tea.

After a busy 40 days in Australia, we flew to Christchurch on the south island of New Zealand. We walked Victoria Square and Cathedral Square, and lingered in the elegant old Cathedral for some time. Ouida likes to browse in the stores of such quaint cities. We were again blessed as guests in the home of World Convention people—this time that of Ray and Marge Blampeid. Ray loves Alexander Campbell, and he regaled me with questions about the old hero.

We rented a Toyota with a view of circling a large part of the south island, where much of New Zealand's mountain beauty lies. Once in the Alps, Ouida was so intimidated by the hairpin curves and deep gorges that she turned the driving over to me. It appeared that no one was in those mountains but us. While awed by all the beauty, we were fearful of the one-way bridges that were also used by the railway. The motorist at either end of the bridge was to await his turn; Ouida's lament "Suppose one meets a train about halfway?" was laid before a hotel clerk, who told us he'd never heard of an accident on those bridges. They are so dangerous that they are safe!

We spent nights in towns that we'd never heard of before, such as Hokitika and Haas. We took time to see the renowned Fox glacier. It is quite a challenge to get close enough to touch it. Ouida balked, opting to see it from a respectable distance. I was determined to lay hands on it, which I was able to do with considerable effort, along with a few other daring souls. I was most impressed by its magnitude, a mountain of ice that moves, and forever it both freezes and melts. A river of

173

icy water continually flows from its underbelly.

On our way to Dunedin on the southeast coast, we were held up nearly six hours by a landslide that blocked the narrow road, and we had to spend the night in Wanaka. At Dunedin we were in the home of still another World Convention family, David Coulter, a physician, and his wife Ann. On the Lord's day, I addressed the St. Andrews Street Church of Christ on "Things We Surely Believe." The Scottish pioneers who planted our first churches in Australia had first been in New Zealand. The St. Andrews Street Church of Christ dates back to 1847.

Both the Australian and New Zealand churches have suffered through the same issues that divided us in America—but without division. While for a time there were both instrumental and non-instrumental churches, they eventually all became instrumental, with no particular problem. That is because they had editor-bishops of a different spirit than ours in the States. We found both the Aussies and the New Zealanders perplexed that we Americans have so many divisions. We fell in love with our dear sisters and brothers in both countries. They blessed us richly. The more we traveled, the larger the community of faith became to us.

By the time we drove back to Christchurch, we decided that New Zealand is not so small after all (both islands are about the size of California). We took a small plane to Auckland on the north island where we boarded a big jet for Los Angeles. Ouida was now a bona fide world traveler. She found a world of difference between China and Down Under. She preferred the latter to the former by far.

———————

By now Ouida was telling me that she had been abroad enough, and that from now on she would be content to see more of our own country. But I had one more big outing in mind—something strictly tourist, a real vacation—such as a trip to England on the Queen Elizabeth II.

Ouida was so impressed with our six-day voyage to London in 1997 that she wrote "On The Queen Elizabeth II" for our newsletter. She was awed by the immensity of the old lady: three football-fields long, 13 stories high, room for 1850 passengers and 1000 crew. It had three large, elegant restaurants, a library, a theatre, four swimming pools, a gym, casino, spa, boutique, and shops. We heard lectures on Shakespeare and British royalty (the lecturer thought the monarchy was in jeopardy). There were even computer classes.

It was a luxurious hotel at sea. We dined sumptuously. But my favorite thing was to jog on the top deck and watch the sunrise. With so much ocean about us for so long, I pondered that ominous line in Rev. 21:1, "And the sea shall be no more." I got up early on our last day to see the old girl dock at Southampton, with several tugboats helping out. Quite a show!

We had a week in London. We stayed at the historic Grovesnor Hotel in the heart of central London, which was within walking distance of renowned places, including Buckingham Palace and Westminster Abbey. We took in much of London by riding buses and the Underground. We rode buses to the end of the line! Ouida enjoyed Harrod's so much that we went there twice. We took in the British Museum, Trafalgar Square and the National Gallery, St. Martin in the Fields, Picadilly Circus, and the tombs in the bowels of Westminster Abbey. We did a luncheon cruise on the Thames, which makes for a panoramic view of London, and, of course, witnessed the Changing of the Guard at Buckingham Palace (which was not all that big a deal to me).

We were up early on Sunday, August 31 to attend service at Westminster Abbey before flying home, our own assemblies being too far away. At breakfast, we learned of the death of Princess Diana in Paris only a few hours earlier. On the walk to the Abbey, we could sense the pall that fell over London. Of course there were prayers for her at the service.

The bus to Heathrow airport went by Princess Di's palatial home. Already there was a mound of flowers. There was quiet on the bus, some of us pondering the brevity of life, even for the rich and famous; and we were reminded that the young die, too.

———————

If Canada qualifies as "abroad," I got in one more trip with Ouida. In 1998, in company with A. C. and Ruth Oliver of Lubbock, we flew to Halifax, Nova Scotia where I spoke for the Maritime Christian Fellowship summer camp. We afterwards drove over much of Nova Scotia, staying at unique bed-and-breakfasts, viewing seascapes, shopping in interesting towns, and visiting historic churches. But as always in our travels, it is loved ones in Christ who interest us most. In Mill Valley, Nova Scotia, we were guests in the home of Jack and Joan Mackey, longtime leaders of the church in that area.

A highlight of the trip was crossing the North-umberlin Straits on a ferry to Prince Edward Island. In Murry River, P.E.I., we were in the home of Cliff and Norma Herring. Members of the extended Herring family were readers of my journals almost from the beginning. It was a joy to meet those with whom we had long corresponded. We visited the nearby Murry River Church of Christ.

Dr. Mack Beck, our host in historic Charlottetown, along with his wife Shirley, drove us by Cross Roads Christian Church, one of the oldest Restoration churches in the world, dating back to 1810. One is to remember that our Canadian churches did not start from American influence but rather Scottish; and the Scots were in Canada as early as the Campbells were in America.

176

In Charlottetown, we visited the Provincial House where the Confederation, that eventually became Canada, was formed. We crammed in a hurried visit to Maritime Christian College, conducted by Christian Churches. Especially fun for Ouida was to see the Green Gables in Cavendish.

Back in Truro, Nova Scotia, we were guests of Jane Herring and her mother Rhoda Oneil. We met with the Glenwood Christian Church, where Victor McCullough ministers. Before we left for home, Victor took us to historic River John, where we saw one of our oldest church buildings in Canada, no longer used as a church.

While Ouida is not as inclined towards world wanderings as I, these journeys abroad gave her, as they did me, a broader view of both the world and the church. We came to see first-hand how people of all nations cope with problems similar to our own: that life is not easy for any of us and very difficult for many. It is troubling that some people have so little, often through no fault of their own, while others have so much, usually through the circumstance of birth. Extensive travel forces a believer to face up to the implications of "the church in the world," the world for which our Lord died.

In 1995 I was back to traveling abroad without Ouida, but these trips were comparatively brief. I was part of a study seminar on the Orthodox churches—particularly Russian and Armenian—conducted by the World Council of Churches. It was led by Joan Campbell, Disciples of Christ, who was the executive director of the American-based National Council of Churches. Albert Pennybacker, one-time pastor of the University Christian Church on the campus of TCU and a director of the NCC, was also along. But the seminar was made up mostly of Presbyterians; I was the first from Churches of Christ ever to take part in these ongoing seminar trips.

Beside lectures by Bruce Rigdon, a scholar on Orthodoxy, we visited churches and clergy in Moscow and St. Petersburg in Russia, Yerevan in Armenia, and Riga in Latvia. I was impressed with the antiquity of it all. Russian Orthodoxy has a 1,000-year history. Some of its churches date back hundreds of years. Both Greek and Armenian churches trace their origin to the first century, the former insisting that their churches have spoken Greek since the days of the apostle Paul! We visited churches—still standing—that date back to the fifth century.

I was also impressed by the severe, decimating persecution they have suffered under Soviet communism. There were 160 million Orthodox in Russia when the Communist revolution began in 1917. Seventy years later, there were 60 million. They went from 180 bishops to *two*. The bishops were either murdered or disappeared into the Soviet gulag.

Armenians suffered similarly, not only from the Communists but from the Armenian genocide, perpetrated by Turkey during World War I. This tragedy is little known by the rest of the world due to the political influence of Turkey, which denies it ever happened. The Martyrs Memorial in Yerevan informs one about the deportation of a million Armenians from Turkey, including women and children, most of whom died of thirst and starvation in the desert. It was a calculated genocide, one reason being because they were Christians.

I heard stories of the women who kept the Orthodox faith alive during those dreadful times, in Russia and Armenia alike. Atheistic communism may have shut down churches and seminaries throughout the Soviet Union, but it couldn't extinguish the flame of faith that burned in millions of Christian homes.

We visited the famous Trinity-St. Sergius Monastery in ancient Zagorsk, Russia and we were briefed by the inspector of the Moscow Theological Seminary. Our trip was timed so that we could be at the Church of Annunciation—the Orthodox Cathedral in Moscow—for its Easter service. It was conducted by Patriarch Alexis, primate of all Russia, and was televised, an example of the freedom the church enjoys since the fall of communism. The service was still going on when we left at 3 A.M. The Orthodox take Easter seriously, and the liturgy with all its colorful symbolism is overwhelming.

Since our group was part of the World Council of Churches, we were given special treatment, which even included the hospitality of Karekin I, catholicos (pope) of all Armenians. He housed our party in the monastery of what they call Holy Etchmiadzin, the Vatican of the Armenians, located a few miles from Yerevan, the capital. We had dinner with him on several occasions, and he shared with us some of the problems his people face, such as poverty and the devastation of recent earthquakes.

He also was distressed that, since the dissolution of the Soviet Union, there was an incredible influx of sects into Armenia that treated Orthodox Christians as if they were pagans. He had no problem with the old-line Protestant churches that have long been in Armenia.

There are interesting similarities between the Orthodox churches and Churches of Christ. Not only are we both a cappella in our singing, but we both have (or have had) such a view of ourselves as being exclusively the church that we have trouble relating to other Christians. The Orthodox never took part in the World Council of Churches—just as Churches of Christ generally do not—until they were assured that they could be a part without recognizing other churches as equal.

We are both also strict constructionists in

interpreting the Bible. For example, an Orthodox priest cannot remarry should his wife die, for 1 Timothy 3:2 says the bishop must be "the husband of one wife," which they take to mean "married only once," which is perhaps the right interpretation.

This trip to Eastern Europe filled a void in my ecumenical experiences in that I had never before had close contact with Orthodox churches. I was impressed with their devotion to what they call "the liturgy" and by the authoritative role they give to the great ecumenical councils rather than to the Roman church. They see the pope in Rome as a usurper. He can be the bishop of Rome well enough—one bishop among many—but not *the* ruler over the entire church.

I made still another trip to Eastern Europe in 1999 with Dr. Joseph Jones of Michigan, this time to Ukraine. A memorable feature of this trip is that one leg of it, from Detroit to Amsterdam, was the roughest flight that either Joe or I had ever encountered. It was so intense that we were all confined to our seats, and dinner was long delayed. Joe accused me of peacefully sleeping through it all, but I was well aware of our rough ride.

Joe and I were to teach at Crimean Christian College and give lectures at the Crimean State Industrial-Pedagogical Institute, both in Simferople, Ukraine. It was a gathering of scholars from all over Eastern Europe. Arranged by George Carrilet, long-time Christian Church missionary in that area and our host, I lectured on "World Peace Through A Global Ethic," the thesis of which was that world peace can come only through a peace between the religions of the world, which can come through an ethic they all hold in common. Even when world religions disagree over dogma, they can work together for peace through a common philanthropic morality. It was well received.

I also addressed the Christian Church in Simferople.

We found the brethren thankful for their freedom from 70 years of Soviet oppression and encouraged by an emerging democracy. One brother told me, "Back then we had one state-owned filling station in this city, and we lined up for gas. Now we have seven privately-owned stations." The farmers now work their own land, but since they were regimented for two generations, the transition to freedom has had its difficulties.

Joe and I were joined by Epi Stephan Bilak, longtime Churches of Christ missionary to Ukraine, who was also on the program. Epi arranged for us to visit his mission congregation, the Old Park Church of Christ in Ternopil, Ukraine. I addressed the congregation on the great truths of 2 Chronicles 7:14. We met and came to love many beautiful sisters and brothers.

The trip allowed us some time in Lausanne, Switzerland, Epi's base of operation; Worms, Germany, where we visited Martin Luther memorials; Kiev, the capital of Ukraine; and Lviv, an educational center. We found missionary activity progressing throughout Ukraine.

Epi, a native Ukrainian, taught me to say Ukraine, not *the* Ukraine: "You don't say *the* England or *the* Germany, do you?" he chided me. The good news is that the future augurs well for the community of faith in Ukraine, a nation excited over its newly found freedom.

Chapter 16

Discovering My Stone-Campbell Heritage

In his classes at Freed-Hardeman College in 1940, N. B. Hardeman took us through M. M. Davis' small volume on *How the Disciples Began and Grew*—a responsible text for its size—but it made no lasting impression on me. A picture of Alexander Campbell graced the wall of Hardeman's classroom. He quipped one day about a Baptist debater accusing him of "straining out a gnat and swallowing *A. Campbell*" as he pointed to the reformer's likeness on the wall.

Even though Hardeman also included some Restoration history in his *Hardeman's Tabernacle Sermons*, I don't think he was much of a Campbellite or terribly conscious of our heritage. Nor were the other teachers. There was no emphasis on Restoration history, and I doubt if any of us preacher boys left Freed-Hardeman with any particular knowledge or appreciation of our pioneers.

It was not all that different at Abilene Christian College. But at least one of my professors, Homer Hailey—who afterwards did a master's thesis at Southern Methodist University on Restoration history—had an appreciation for our heritage.

In those days in Churches of Christ, we were anti-historical in reference to the nature of the church. Stone and Campbell did not really matter all that much. We were the restored New Testament church in the 20th century, so the intervening centuries weren't all that relevant. Since "the pattern" or "the blueprint" for the true Church is in the New Testament, and we had faithfully followed that pattern or blueprint and had "restored" the true church, no history had any particular significance except the first century.

We believed that the true apostolic church went into apostasy and ceased to exist for 1500 years or more. Martin Luther made progress in reforming the church, but what was needed was a restoration of primitive Christianity. This is what Alexander Campbell did; he went beyond Luther's reformation by an appeal to "the ancient order of things," the pattern for the church as revealed in the New Testament, and thus restored the true church in the early 19th century. We, in Churches of Christ, were that restored church.

Once these premises were accepted, it logically followed that we were the only true church. All others were sects or denominations—and we must be the only true Christians.

I still had this mindset when I graduated from Abilene Christian College in 1942 and began graduate work at Southern Methodist, while teaching at Richardson High School. Even when I did my master's thesis on "The Educational Philosophy of Alexander Campbell," it was Campbell the educator that interested me—not Campbell the reformer. I was ignorant at the time of the true nature of my Stone-Campbell heritage.

But my study of Campbell at SMU was an important beginning. The library had a complete (original) set of Campbell's 40-volume *The Millennial Harbinger.* It was the first time I had seen them all lined up on a library shelf. By the time I was a professor at Bethany College, I would have an original set of my own. While my first venture into Campbell was to ascertain his views on education, it was the beginning of a lifetime study.

The further I got into Campbell and other Restoration pioneers, the more my mind changed as to the real nature of my heritage. But the change was gradual, stretching over two decades. I eventually came

184

to see that I had been misled. It was a rude awakening when I at last realized that Stone and Campbell neither believed nor taught what was unique to us in Churches of Christ. When I came to see that we had, in fact, betrayed our heritage, it became my mission to set the record straight. What the Stone-Campbell movement was really about—as I came to see it, over against what we actually were in Churches of Christ—became the basis of my lover's quarrel with my own church.

When I became an editor, I drew heavily on our pioneers in my charges against Churches of Christ. In the 1953 *Bible Talk,* I quoted at length from Alexander Campbell to support my views on the distinction between preaching and teaching and between gospel and doctrine—which was critical to my opposition to the modern pastor system. The reformer insisted that this was not "a mere speculative distinction," but was "appreciated and fully understood in the apostolic ministry." To make Christ known to a lost world is to preach, he allowed; to disciple those who accept the gospel is to teach.

Campbell scored the practice of hiring men to make sermons as "a relic of popery." He even said, "To employ men to preach the gospel to a Christian congregation is a satire upon that congregation which employs them." He allowed that preachers should be supported for doing evangelist work, which he distinguished from "preaching to a church," and that elders should care for the established congregation. He said what I was getting myself into trouble for saying.

Campbell sometimes made these points indirectly, from his own personal ministry. In one article, for instance, I showed how Campbell disclaimed being an evangelist. While he did sometimes preach and baptize, his work was mostly that of a reformer and a teacher among the churches. In a series on "The Travel Letters of Alexander Campbell" (*Restoration Review,* 1972), I noted a peculiarity that a casual reader might miss. In all his travels and hundreds of presentations, he never referred to what he did as preaching. He taught, lectured, discoursed—and even gave "disquisitions" — but he never preached! This distinction was intentional on his part. He was a teacher, not a preacher. He held that, to understand what he called "the ancient order," it was necessary to make this distinction.

In the same volume I pointed to other areas in which Churches of Christ are at variance with Campbell. One essay was titled "Which Of Our Sects Would Campbell Join?" —which was a question put to me by Louis Cochran, noted Disciples of Christ novelist and historian, in a public meeting in Murfreesboro, Tennessee. When I turned the question back to Louis himself to answer, he said Campbell would join the Churches of Christ since he was opposed to instrumental music. His wife Bess, a historian in her own right, disagreed with her husband, insisting that Campbell would not join any of our churches because of all our divisions. He would start over and do what he did before, she ventured.

I gave Bess some support by noting that once when Campbell was in New York City he found three churches of his persuasion that were so divided they would not break bread together. For some time, he moved among all three, but wouldn't identify with any until they effected a union, which they eventually did. But I went on to say that, whatever Campbell might think of us in Churches of Christ today, we would not accept *him*—if for no other reason than he believed there were Christians in the sects. We would also reject him because he helped start and served as president of the Movement's first missionary society, and because he did not believe that baptism is absolutely essential to salvation.

I frequently editorialized about the wide gulf that stood between Campbell and the Churches of Christ—especially when the latter sought claim on him. A case in point was the 20th Annual Lectureship of the Memphis School of Preaching (1985), which was in honor of Restoration pioneers—particularly Thomas and Alexander Campbell. One speaker, Billy Bland, extolled the Campbells. The next speaker, Goebel Music, spoke on "False Witnesses: Stopping the Mouth of the 'Christians in the Sects' Teaching." In an editorial titled "The Campbell Myth," I suggested that Bland and Music should get together; Bland was extolling men that Music branded as false witnesses in that the Campbells vigorously defended the thesis of "Christians in the sects." In fact, Alexander Campbell claimed that proposition as the basis of his unity efforts, for if there are no Christians in the sects, then there would be no Christians to unite.

I explained that the "Campbell Myth" is the mindset that presumes that we are the true heirs of Campbell when, in fact, we brand as heretics those who teach what he taught. I wrote, "It is one thing to call Rubel Shelly and Leroy Garrett names, but something else to add *Alexander Campbell* to the list of heretics. They do not want to put us in such elegant company." I pointed out that it would hardly do for the Memphis Lectureship to eulogize Campbell in one session and to disfellowship him in the next!

I observed in separate essays that Campbell used two unique metaphors to describe his own pilgrimage from sectarianism to freedom in Christ. In the first, he likened himself to the Indian's tree: "I was once so straight," he wrote in 1825, "that, like the Indian's tree I leaned a little the other way." He went on to say, "I was so strict a separatist that I would neither pray nor sing praises with any one who was not as perfect as I supposed myself." He concluded with, "I persisted in this course until I discovered the mistake and saw that on the principle embraced by my conduct there never could be a congregation or church upon the earth."

In the other essay, "Alexander Campbell: A Speckled

187

Bird," I told of the metaphor that he borrowed from John Newton, who said, "I became so speckled that no specie would own me." Like Newton, in his search for truth wherever it might be found, Campbell said that whenever he found a pretty feather in another bird, he would pluck it and place it in his own plumage, until finally—as Newton put it— "I began to think that I had become the prettiest bird among them."

Campbell turned this rich metaphor into a two-edged sword. While we are to accept truth wherever we find it, even when it makes us different from others and we have to stand alone, we must guard against supposing we have a monopoly on truth. Inspired by Campbell's thought, I concluded the article with "May God make us a flock of speckled birds. There is a place for honest differences. I accept a man as my brother— not because his plumage is precisely the same as mine— but because he is in Christ. It isn't a pecking order I'm calling for, but some feather pulling."

I found especially liberating Campbell's view on what might be called "the principle of available light" — not only in reference to legalism and sectarianism, but also in the judgment we make on those who have never heard the gospel. Campbell did not adjudge the multiplied millions of unbelievers to be necessarily lost. Their salvation depends on the response they make to such light as they have.

In a 1988 essay on "Why Luther Could Not Be Saved As A Roman Catholic (And Why His Parents Could Be)," I told of an imaginary conversation that Campbell created between Martin Luther and a monk named Erastian. He has the monk ask Luther if it is true that he believes his parents are in heaven. Luther responds that yes, he believes his parents—and grandparents as well—are in heaven, "for Saxony cannot boast of more devout Catholics than they." Erastian then complains, "In the name of St. Peter and St. Paul, why have you raised all this fuss in Germany and throughout the world? Do you expect anything better than to go to heaven when you die?" Luther conceded that he expects nothing greater than heaven.

The monk now wants to know why, if Luther's parents could be saved in the Roman church, why couldn't he, and presses the point: "How dare you separate from the church in which your parents were saved?" Campbell has the reformer answer, "Because my parents were pious members of that church, which I could not possibly be." When Erastian wants to know why not, Luther answers, "Because I have been favored with more light than they."

Campbell goes on to make the point that one's responsibility is determined by such light as he has. He has Luther say of his parents, "They lived in conformity to all they knew, and died in the church; I live in conformity to what I know, and have left the church." He goes on to say, "No man can be justified today by living in accordance with the knowledge that he had yesterday," and concludes with "I must obey the light which God has given me."

In this mock exchange, Campbell draws distinctions that frequently appear in his writings, including the Lunenburg Letter, such as the difference between willful ignorance, which he found criminal, and unwillful ignorance, which he deemed excusable. Even an angel might be honestly mistaken, he allowed, while noting that many a sincere man has been wrong. It is insincerity of heart that is culpable before God—when one blatantly rejects such light as is available to him.

Campbell would have appreciated M. Scott Peck's definition of human evil as "militant ignorance." Campbell thus distinguished between unbelievers (those who have never heard, through no fault of their own) and disbelievers (those who hear but reject). He observed that it is always the disbelievers who are condemned in the Bible, never the unbelievers. In his debate with Robert Owen, an atheist, he put it this way:

> The man born blind will not be condemned for
> not seeing, nor the deaf for not hearing. The man
> who never heard the gospel, cannot disobey it; and
> he, through any physical impossibility, is prevented
> from any ordinance, is no transgressor. It is only
> he who knows, and has the power to do, his
> Master's will that shall be punished for
> disobedience.

In all my gleanings through the years in the
marketplace of ideas, I find this concept of available
light—posited by Alexander Campbell—as liberating as
any I ever found. It was expressed by the apostle Paul as
"It is required of a person according to what he has, not
according to what he has not" (2 Corinthians 8:12).
Moralists have described it as "Ability is the measure of
responsibility." While it is applicable to all of life, it is
one of the most neglected of ethical principles. We in
Churches of Christ appear oblivious to this principle—
particularly in our judgment that those who have not
heard the gospel will be lost.

I often reminded my students that true judgment of
academic work is not how students perform, but how
they *should* perform—each according to ability. It is
both a liberating and awesome principle that we will be
judged—not by what we don't know and can't know—
but by what we can know and should know.

I probably surprised my Churches of Christ readers
by a 1987 editorial on "Our First Church of Christ Was
A Baptist Church." I showed that the Brush Run
Church—the first of the Campbell churches (1812) —
was affiliated with the Redstone Baptist Association as
long as it existed. While it called itself a Church of Christ
and had its differences with the Baptists, it nonetheless
considered itself a Baptist church. In fact, the Campbells
sought denominational affiliation for all their earlier
churches. The second church at Wellsburg became part
of the Mahoning Baptist Association. It was not until

190

1831 that the Campbell churches, then called "Reformed Baptists," dissolved the Association and became Disciples of Christ.

It may have also surprised my readers to learn that the Brush Run church did not at the time have a single immersed member, including the Campbells. "Was it truly a Church of Christ?" I asked. What an illustration of the principle of available light! Later, when Alexander Campbell gained further light by an extensive study of the nature of baptism, he was immersed, along with several other Brush Run members, including his wife and parents. But Campbell did not believe that he became a Christian only when he was immersed. He was himself an illustration of his own definition of a Christian: "A Christian is one who believes that Jesus Christ is the Son of God, repents of his sins, and obeys him in all things according to his understanding."

It may have proved equally disconcerting to many of my readers, who glory in not being a denomination while labeling all others as such, to learn that Alexander Campbell had no qualms about using "denomination" in reference to his own church. He readily conceded that what he had started was a denomination. While it would spook our people today to refer to Churches of Christ as "our denomination," it was no problem for Campbell. He now and again referred to "We, as a denomination" and "other denominations." He even, finally, referred to his work as "the necessity of starting a new denomination," though it was not his intention at the outset.

He was only recognizing that his people had become a distinct religious society, clearly distinguishable from others. It was a *sect* that he would not have his people be. The clear-cut distinction he drew between a denomination and a sect is one his followers have not appreciated. When he was accused in the Rice debate of starting another sect, he replied, "You'll never make a sect of us because we are catholics." He spoke of

191

wearing a catholic name, serving a catholic table, practicing a catholic baptism. In time, he adopted "a catholic rule" for unity—claiming that Christians can unite on the universal/catholic truths they hold in common.

It was this principle of the catholicity of the church that I came to emphasize as the remedy for the parochialism and sectarianism of my own church. It was an affirmation that wherever God has children, we have sisters and brothers. I not only called Alexander Campbell as a witness to this, but other of the Restoration pioneers—particularly Thomas Campbell. In his *Declaration and Address,* the Movement's founding document, Thomas Campbell pled for the unity of all believers on the basis of a catholic or universal faith.

In the 1969 *Restoration Review,* I published a four-part study of that impressive document, which the late W. W. Sweet, a dean among American church historians, hailed as "one of the great documents of the American church." I published Thomas Campbell's picture on the front cover of the first issue, along with the quotation that serves as the theme of the document. It read, "The Church of Christ upon earth is essentially, intentionally, and constitutionally one, consisting of all those in every place that profess their faith in Christ and obedience to him in all things according to the scriptures, and that manifest the same by their tempers and conduct."

I consider that the most important quotation from our heritage outside the Bible. In affirming the essential unity and catholicity of the church, it defines what our heritage is about. It is to be noted that in 1809, when Campbell affirmed the existence of "the Church of Christ upon earth," he did not yet have a single congregation that would bear that name. Where was the Church of Christ upon earth that by its very nature was one? His answer was that wherever "in every place" there are those who believe in and obey Jesus Christ, there is the church. That defines who we are—or should be—as a people, and that is why Alexander Campbell would affirm that "We are catholics."

That quotation, the first proposition of the "Declaration" part of the document, also defines the nature of unity. Like Paul's complaint, "Is Christ divided?" Campbell affirms that the church *is* one—essentially, intentionally, constitutionally one—and cannot be other than one. Unity is therefore a gift of the Spirit that is to be claimed by the church. As Ronald Osborn put it to a later generation, "Unity is real, but it isn't realized."

I went on in that four-part series to show that the essence of the Campbell plea was that "private opinions are not to be made the basis of Christian communion," but "only those things that are expressly enjoined in the word of God." This became the basis of the slogan that eventually emerged: "In essentials, unity; in opinions, liberty; in all things, love." The Campbells clearly identified the essentials as only what is expressly enjoined in Scripture. All else is opinion.

There is a practical side to the document: "Since we will be united in heaven, why can we not be united on earth?" Thomas Campbell asked. He observed that divisions are always over matters of which the kingdom of God does not consist. And he had a select verse, one that epitomized his plea for unity: "Receive one another, even as Christ has received you, to the glory of God." He referred to this passage again and again in the *Declaration and Address*. When we accept others only on the basis of their conformity to our dogmas, it is to the glory of our party; but when we receive one another on the same basis that Christ received us—with all our errors and hang-ups—it is to the glory of God.

In my lectures among the churches on our heritage, I often suggested that we make that passage, Romans 15:7, drawn from our founding document, our "Scripture of identification." Let that be who we are: a people who accept others on the same grounds that Christ received us. None of us was perfect and all of us were wrong about some things when Christ received us. And in doing so we glorify God—not some party or church!

———————

While my emphasis in teaching about our heritage was on the Campbells, I gave considerable attention to other pioneers, certainly to Barton W. Stone, who holds priority over the Campbells, in time if not in significance. In 1976 I did a *Restoration Review* essay on "The Noblest Act In Barton Stone's Life," which had to do with his role in the union of the Stone and Campbell movements in Lexington, Kentucky in 1832 and which qualifies in my mind as the greatest event in our history. It gave the Movement the impetus that was essential to its survival. Without Stone, it would not have happened. As his life drew to a close, he looked back and named that occasion "the noblest act of my life."

In order to persuade his own churches to accept the union with the Campbell people, Stone published in that same year of 1832 "An Address to the Churches of Christ," which I wrote about in a 1992 essay. In that letter, he warned of the danger of making unwritten creeds tests of communion, they being more insidious than written ones. In that warning he was reading the future of Churches of Christ. Our unwritten creeds have done us far more mischief than written ones.

Stone also deemed the gift of the Holy Spirit as more important than baptism. The Holy Spirit was writ large in his ministry. A favorite sermon was "The Four Unities," three of which—head union, book union, water union—he named as false unities. The only true unity is when the Spirit dwells in the hearts of believers, which he called "fire unity."

It was in that letter that he gave us one of our great

mottoes, "Let the unity of Christians be our polar star," which was inspired by the Lord's prayer for unity in John 17. If the church, as the old ship Zion, is to succeed in reaching a lost world for Christ, it must keep its eye on the polar star. That great one-liner, which gets to the heart of Stone's ministry, is appropriately inscribed in marble under his likeness on a cenotaph that stands in the garden of the Disciples of Christ Historical Society in Nashville.

I could not write about Stone and our great hour at Lexington without also telling about Raccoon John Smith, which I did in the likes of "They Called Him Raccoon" (1976) and "Learning From A Backwoods Preacher" (1980). Raccoon was the keynote speaker at the Lexington meeting. He assured the two groups that had gathered that "While there is but one faith, there may be a thousand opinions; and hence if Christians are ever to be one, they must be one in faith, and not in opinions."

He concluded his momentous speech with "Let us then, my brethren, be no longer Campbellites or Stoneites, New Lights or Old Lights, or any other kind of lights; but let us all come to the Bible, and to the Bible alone, as the only book in the world that can give us the only light we need."

Stone took Raccoon's hand—agreeing with him as to the basis of unity—which one historian described as "the handshake that shook the frontier." The two groups, now uniting, broke bread together the next day. Raccoon, representing the Campbell churches, and Samuel Rogers, of the Stone group, rode horseback among scores of churches for three years, declaring that they were now one people.

Raccoon became one of my favorites, and since I talked about him with such enthusiasm, Jim Bevis, then director of a summer youth program among Restoration

195

Portraying Raccoon John Smith, Restoration Forum XVIII, in Old Campbell Church, Bethany, 2000.

churches, insisted that I do a portrayal of Raccoon before a thousand youth in their 1976 retreat in Gatlinburg, Tennessee. Wearing a raccoon cap and a Prince Albert coat, and with cane in hand, I walked in from a side door—unannounced and unexpected — disrupting the proceedings: "I'm Raccoon John Smith from the boondocks of southern Kentucky," I began. Since his story is filled with both pathos and humor, the kids got a bang out of it, and they probably learned more of Restoration history than they would have in several formal lectures.

Jim had me do "Raccoon" again when he was minister to the Brookvalley Church of Christ in Atlanta. Again dressed for the part, I walked in on the startled congregation, interrupted the preacher, and told them my story of tragedy and triumph—including what I had to say at the Lexington unity meeting back in 1832. It proved to be an effective way to interest a church in its history.

Since then I have done "Raccoon" a dozen times or so at both colleges and churches, including the

Restoration Forum at Bethany College in 2000. The old Campbell church was opened for the occasion, and I tailored the drama for that historic setting. It was, after all, Raccoon's first "visit" to Bethany, and he felt a little uneasy in such a sophisticated environment. "Raccoon" told them about his first visit with Alexander Campbell, who said Smith was the only man he knew that a college education would have ruined! We had great fun. The forum especially got a bang out of Raccoon saying that Alexander Campbell never used a small word when a big one would do!

———————————

Not to neglect any of the so-called "big four" of our heritage, I not only wrote about the two Campbells and Barton W. Stone, but also Walter Scott, our greatest evangelist. He joins the other three in being remembered on that memorial at the Historical Society in Nashville, which appropriately recalls his five-finger exercise: Faith, Repentance, Baptism, Remission of Sins, and Gift of the Holy Spirit.

I agree with W. E. Garrison, the late eminent Disciples historian, who asserted that except for the evangelism of Walter Scott—who early on baptized thousands—there would never have been what we call Disciples of Christ or Churches of Christ. I also believe that his five-finger device still has relevance today, based as it was on what Peter says in Acts 2:38 and accompanied as it was by the preaching of the Cross.

In 1976, I did an essay on Scott titled "The Golden Oracle of the Movement." This was wrongly worded, for he was the *Voice* of the Golden Oracle, not the Oracle itself—which to Scott was the proclamation that Jesus was the Christ. In his preaching, he effectively joined Peter's confession that Jesus is the Christ, the Son of God (Mt. 16:18) —which to Scott was the Golden Oracle or the premier truth to be believed—to Peter's command in Acts 2:38 on how to respond once one

197

believes. The five-finger exercise, therefore, was no legalistic device of "steps to salvation," but a means of responding to the gospel.

I frequently reminded my readers of the emphasis Scott placed on the gift of the Holy Spirit, his fifth finger, explicitly promised in Acts 2:38, I pointed out that while we have clung to Acts 2:38 we somehow lost sight of the promise of the Spirit. As recently as 2001 I asked in a newsletter, *What Happened to Walter Scott's Fifth Finger?* "We amputated Scott's fifth finger," I charged, "and thus reduced the Holy Spirit to little more than words on a page."

———————

I published three 32-page monographs on lesser-known pioneers. In 1961 I did *The Role of Robert Richardson in the Restoration Movement.* Dr. Richardson (1806-1876) is known mainly for his *Memoirs of Alexander Campbell,* the starting point for any serious study of our heritage. He was also one of the first professors of Bethany College, the physician for the Campbell family and the Bethany community, and an associate editor for Campbell's *Millennial Harbinger.*

In 1855 Richardson published an 88-page study of *The Principles and Objects of the Religious Reformation, Urged by A. Campbell and Others, Briefly Stated and Explained.* Campbell himself hailed it as "a well proportioned miniature view in a lucid and chaste style, and is worthy of himself and the cause." It was widely read, going through three editions. It deserved the reprinting that New Leaf Books gave it in 2000, for it captures for this generation in concise terms the genius of the Campbell plea. You will notice that Richardson called the Movement a reformation, not a restoration.

In this study he made the crucial point, so needed in our time, that the Movement's position was that faith is personal, not doctrinal, and that this is the only basis of unity. We unite upon our common faith that Jesus is

Lord, not on faith in various doctrinal systems.

But I found his most important contribution to be his teaching on the ministry of the Holy Spirit in the life of the Christian, a subject generally neglected by the leaders of the first generation. In a treatise on "The Office of the Holy Spirit," he not only held that every believer receives the Spirit as a gift of grace when he is baptized, but is led, taught, and comforted by the Spirit's indwelling. He equated the baptism of the Spirit with the receiving of the Spirit, and he never held that "the Spirit operates only through the Word," a position commonly held by his peers. When Campbell was to argue that premise in public debate, Richardson sought to dissuade him, to no avail.

Also in 1961 I covered *The Role of David King in the Restoration Movement,* which alerted readers to the impact the Movement had in Great Britain. By the time Alexander Campbell visited England in 1847, there were 80 congregations with 2,300 members. These churches grew out of 18th-century reform efforts that were independent of American influence. Starting in 1833, when they were introduced to Campbell's writings, they became identified with his movement. There was even a *British Millennial Harbinger* that published Campbell's writings for about 16 months.

David King (1819-1894) was the leading influence among these churches. As a powerful evangelist who took the gospel to remote areas of England as well as the major cities, he started many of the churches that welcomed Campbell in 1847. He taught the churches to practice a "mutual ministry," leaving preachers to serve as evangelists in the field. It created a problem during the first half of the 20th century when Churches of Christ missionaries from America sought to impose the one-man minister system on them. The British brethren saw their practice as more in keeping with both biblical teaching and the Campbell heritage, vouchsafed to them by David King.

199

I was eager to do a monograph on John T. Johnson (1788-1856), which I did in 1962—not only because his impressive work as "the evangelist of Kentucky" was largely unknown, but also because he illustrates the caliber of men attracted to the Movement. A scion of a prominent political family, his brother having served as vice-president under Martin Van Buren—and he himself in Congress—he was destined for a significant career in law and politics. At the urging of Alexander Campbell, he gave all this up to become an evangelist.

In time, Campbell was to write of him, "The great secret of Brother Johnson's great success, is his evident sincerity, honesty, and great earnestness—gifts of transcendent value." He wrote of his "good sense and clear perception of the gospel facts, precepts, and promises" and his "clear and emphatic expression of them in a familiar and intelligible style." He was even impressed with the earnestness with which Johnson gave thanks at the table!

Campbell's reference to Johnson preaching the gospel in terms of facts, precepts (commands), and promises points up the simplicity of pioneer preaching. Counting on three fingers, they would identify three facts of the gospel (death, burial, resurrection), three commands in response to the gospel (faith, repentance, baptism), and three promises of the gospel (remission of sins, gift of the Spirit, eternal life). It had great effect. Too bad we have become smarter than that!

Johnson averaged baptizing fifty people every month for twenty-five years! It was the likes of him that accounts for the great growth of our people during the mid-19th century, the one time in our history that we grew faster than the population, percentage-wise.

———————————

All these writings, and many more—enough to fill several large volumes—were reflective of long years of study, some of them traumatic. What I wrote not only came to define my own heritage in Stone-Campbell, but to affect my relationship with Churches of Christ. I became convinced that we had betrayed our heritage, in that we were not a unity-minded people as were our forebears. Our sectarian isolation from other Christians and our absolutist claim of being the only true church were inimical to what our pioneers believed. Our editor-bishops had, in fact, deceived us with reference to who we are really supposed to be as a people.

In my zeal to effect change, I became *persona non grata* in my own church. When it was suggested, not always in friendly terms, that I might leave the Churches of Christ, I answered in the tradition of Raccoon John Smith, who, when his Baptist brethren insisted he "leave and join the Campbellites," responded with a smile, "I love you too much to leave."

I had a quarrel with my own Churches of Christ, but it was a lover's quarrel. I would never leave—never, no matter what. But I would work for change, redemptive change. There was always a growing number who would listen. I came to call them part of "the remnant church." Together we would make a difference.

Chapter 17
My Magnum Opus –
& Doors It Opened

Among those who were giving me a sympathetic hearing was the late Don DeWelt, founder of College Press. At the outset, that publishing house served primarily Independent Christian Churches, but it eventually came to have a much broader outreach. Don, who became a trusted friend, had a passion for our heritage. In time, he republished scores of books from our earlier history that had long been out of print. These included all forty volumes of Campbell's *Millennial Harbinger* and his *Christian Baptist*. Don was a doer, as much as any man I ever knew. When he and an idea got together, which happened frequently, things happened.

When we roomed together during a retreat at French Lick, Indiana in 1976, Don had one of his ideas. If I would write a history of our heritage, he would publish it. When I cautioned him that it would likely run several hundred pages, his response was that we should go for it.

Four years later, College Press published *The Stone-Campbell Movement: An Anecdotal History of Three Churches*. The title itself reflected a significant change in that it was the first time any historian among us had identified our heritage as the Stone-Campbell movement. Mine was not a history of the Restoration Movement—as Churches of Christ and Christian Church historians have always identified their work. Nor was it a history of the Disciples of Christ.

While it told the story of all three of these churches, its title reflected what it truly was. It was the history of a movement within the church at large: the Barton W. Stone-Alexander Campbell movement "to unite the Christians in all the sects."

I don't know how much my book had to do with it, but it is remarkable how in the past twenty years our people in all three churches have begun to use "Stone-Campbell" to define who we are. Previously, virtually everything was "Restoration." We now have "The Stone-Campbell Dialogue," "The Stone-Campbell Journal," "The Stone-Campbell Encyclopedia," and all sorts of "Stone-Campbell" references in books, journals, and lectureships. While "Restoration Movement" was once practically synonymous with "Churches of Christ," we have begun to find our identity in Stone-Campbell. It is an important mid-course correction.

In fact, that is one thesis of my book—that we were born a unity movement, not a restoration movement, and that our pioneers were reformers leading "a new reformation," as Campbell preferred to put it.

My history was not a "house job," in terms of identifying any one of the three churches as the true heirs of Stone-Campbell. It did not favor Disciples of Christ, Christian Churches, or Churches of Christ. Sometimes it was critical of all three, implying that none of them had been faithful to the principles of Stone and Campbell. To his credit, Don DeWelt stood by me when some of the old guard in his own Christian Churches "took off like a Roman candle," as he put it, when they read proof pages of what I had written. They didn't like what I said about their role in the separation of Independent Christian Churches from the Disciples of Christ.

But I didn't fare any better with some folks in the Disciples of Christ or Churches of Christ. I had a story to tell, and I told it as objectively as I could, allowing the facts to speak for themselves—and letting the chips fall where they would. I wrote for the person in the pew. I wanted the ordinary member in all three churches, or

First published by College Press
in 1981; revised in 1994.

any outsider, to see what "the Movement" was about.

That is what I called it throughout its 739 pages—
"the Movement." It was a unity movement. I told of its
European background, its beginnings in America, its
rapid growth, its principles, its mottoes, its heroes,
heretics and defectors, its quarrels and divisions, its
strengths and weaknesses, and its potential for the 21st
century. I included what had not been done before—a
chapter on each of the three churches that grew out of
the Movement, and a chapter on their relationship to
one another.

I feared the book might have a hard time of it
financially. It would not be embraced by any of the three
churches as its own history. As for my own Churches of
Christ, we have not been all that enthusiastic about our
heritage as to be interested in a 739-page history book,
particularly one with me as the author. So, I was uneasy
when College Press cranked out 2,000 copies for the
first printing. But my fears were unwarranted. They
soon sold, especially among Churches of Christ, and
another 2,000 were printed. By 1994 we had done so

205

well that I rewrote large parts of it, bringing it up-to-date. We published a "Second Edition, Completely Revised and Expanded." It has continued to do well, far beyond expectations—six printings in all and almost 14,000 copies sold.

While the book has been used either as a text or required reading in many of our colleges, I am especially pleased that numerous churches have placed it in their libraries and used it in classes. Most gratifying is that it has been read by thousands of the rank and file in the churches, the ones I had in mind as I wrote it. It has been reassuring to receive many letters from members of Churches of Christ who rejoice over a heritage they did not realize they had.

Some have found it liberating to learn that they have a unity heritage rather than a sectarian one, and they are hopeful that we can get back on track and be what our pioneers intended. Some have "discovered the truth about who we really are" and have repudiated their sectarianism. It was exciting that a history book could do that for people.

Dr. Phil Davis, a pediatrician from Bakersfield, California and a member of Christian Churches, was persuaded that if our preachers in Churches of Christ could be properly exposed to the beauty of their unity heritage in Stone-Campbell it would help to bring about better relations between our churches. He thought my history book might do that. He made an unusual proposal to College Press. He would provide a free copy of *The Stone-Campbell Movement* to every Churches of Christ preacher who would agree to read it within a year.

Thus, College Press sent a two-fold card to every minister among us that it had on its extensive mailing list. One card explained the terms of the offer of the free book. The minister only needed to indicate by his signature that he would read the book by the agreed time and return the tear-off portion to College Press. It may have surprised Dr. Davis and College Press, as it did me, that 2,000 preachers returned their signed pledges. How unusual for one to buy a history book for 2,000 preachers—and have them sign a pledge to read it!

The doctor's generosity may well have contributed substantially to the improved relationship between Christian Churches and Churches of Christ in the two decades following. Time was when we would hardly speak to each other—if we knew one another at all—but these days we enjoy fellowship in various venues. The annual Restoration Forum, the Stone-Campbell Dialogue, *The Stone-Campbell Journal*, and the *Stone-Campbell Encyclopedia* are examples of a greater participation in such efforts by Churches of Christ. Other venues are the World Convention of Churches of Christ and the Disciples of Christ Historical Society. All three churches work together in these ministries. Equally important is that this spirit of mutual acceptance is spreading among our churches. Even college lectureships are in on it. All this was only a dream twenty years ago.

———————————

The years of research leading up to the publication of my *magnum opus* and the immediate years that followed were times of change in my ministry. I had long given some emphasis to Stone-Campbell history in my writing and lecturing, but my in-depth research deepened my appreciation of the riches of our heritage. Too, the history book opened doors formerly closed to me. I began to lecture widely in schools and churches on our Stone-Campbell heritage. As I saw it, my mission was to tell our people who they really are—or who they were supposed to be.

It was an ideal entree to my larger goal: to help rescue our people in Churches of Christ from a debilitating sectarianism. I wanted to encourage them to become a part of the church universal and to enjoy fellowship with countless sisters and brothers they never

207

realized they had. Our heritage has the dynamic resources for the realization of these goals.

Since so many of our people seem to agree with Henry Ford that "History is bunk," I found a way to make a study of our heritage a biblical study, as well as historical. One can teach the Bible by teaching history! That is certainly the case in our history in Stone-Campbell. Our pioneers conducted "an experiment in freedom" —as Ronald Osborn put it—in studying, interpreting, and even translating the Bible for themselves. To study Stone and Campbell is to study biblical interpretation—not in some ivory tower, but in the arena of a frontier, out on the growing edge where ideas had to compete for men's minds.

My favorite theme was "Our Heritage in Scripture and History," which gave me considerable latitude. I told stories of how our pioneers struggled over the meaning of certain Scriptures and how particular passages led them to renounce sectarianism and launch a reformation. I related this to the experience of earlier reformers such as Luther and Wesley. I showed how the mottoes our pioneers used, such as Stone's "Let the unity of Christians be our polar star," were inspired by the Bible.

I pointed out that our Movement's great founding documents, such as *The Last Will and Testament of the Springfield Presbytery*, were pleas to abandon sects and creeds and rely only on Biblical authority. The principles they forged amidst the fires of controversy were grounded in Scripture. They were "a Bible people" who insisted that Christ was their only creed and the Bible their only book. They built churches "on the Bible alone." If printer's ink ran in their veins—considering all the papers they published—it was the Bible they wrote (and argued) about.

This kind of teaching, drawn from our reform-minded pioneers, carried its risks. None of the three churches of the Movement showed much real enthusiasm for what our pioneers stood for. If the Christian Churches and Churches of Christ were to some degree in the throes of legalism and sectarianism, the Disciples were either apathetic about their heritage or turned off by the claims of "Restorationism." I, therefore, had a problem marketing my wares, especially in the earlier years of this mission.

There was, however, "the remnant" in all three churches that provided open doors. A reformer doesn't have to find the remnant—it will find him. Many in all three churches helped circulate my writings, and they provided me a hearing in various venues.

Early on I found meaningful contacts in both the Disciples of Christ Historical Society (DCHS) and the World Convention of Churches of Christ (WCCC). While both were founded by Disciples of Christ, through the years they have increasingly served Christian Churches and Churches of Christ as well. It has been said at the DCHS, with some justification, that "The Disciples support it the most and use it the least, while the Churches of Christ use it the most and support it the least."

But that is not true in my case, for I have both used it and supported it. By 1968 I was a Life Member, and in the 1970s it was my research center for the writing of my *magnum opus*. In the 1990s, I began serving on the Board of Trustees. Two of the founders and longtime leaders, Claude E. Spencer and Eva Jean Wrather, were personal friends. I was a guest in their homes and a beneficiary of their grasp of our common heritage.

Claude would identify pen names in Campbell's journals, and Eva Jean, a lifetime Campbell scholar, would answer my questions about the reformer. When I asked her about the "Two Campbell" theory commonly advocated by recent Campbell scholars—that the "Early" Campbell was sectarian, the "Later" Campbell

Lecturing on David Lipscomb at Avalon House (old home of David Lipscomb) on campus of Lipscomb University, Nashville, at dinner of board of trustees of Disciples of Christ Historical Society, 1997.

ecumenical—she said, "It is a myth." I agree with her. In fact, some of Campbell's best work on unity was in his earlier years—his *Christian Baptist* days. He himself considered it his best work. Once he left his native Ireland and came to America, he was never again sectarian.

But Eva Jean took me by surprise at lunch one day when she told me that Walter Scott and not Alexander Campbell should be the hero of Churches of Christ. This was because if we have a legalistic forebear, it would be Walter Scott. A neat way to tell me we were sectarian! That may have been her right, having grown up in Churches of Christ, her father serving as an elder in a Nashville congregation. But this time I disagreed with Eva Jean. Both Campbell and Scott can be our heroes, and neither was sectarian or legalistic, in my view.

In more recent years on the DCHS board, I have served with Howard Short and Lester McAllister—both noted Disciples historians—who have helped me delve deeper into our past. Still more recently, there have been Paul Blowers, Christian Church historian (Emmanuel School of Religion) and Douglas Foster, Churches of Christ historian (ACU), who offer fresh perspectives. Some twenty others from all three churches have come on and gone off the board during my tenure—all have broadened my vision of our heritage and what we can become as a people.

We not only do DCHS business together, but we do history together (including lecturing to each other!), and we have lots of fun at our dinners. One year we dined at Avalon House on the campus of Lipscomb University—the historic home of David Lipscomb, the founder. I was asked to tell the story of "Uncle Dave" right there in his own house, where in his old age he would be found nodding in a front porch chair with an open Bible—*upside down*—on his lap!

In 2000, Peter Morgan, who is sort of our board pastor as well as president of DCHS (and one of my former students in philosophy at Bethany College!), asked me to take part in a video presentation designed to advertise the DCHS among the churches. My role in the video was to walk around the cenotaph that stands in front of the library as a memorial to our four

Cenotaph in garden of Disciples of Christ Historical Society, Nashville.

founding pioneers, and say a word about each.

I have used that same entree in schools and churches all across the country. Since hardly anyone knows what a "cenotaph" is, I get to define that term first of all. Then I introduce "the big four" in their right order. Barton Stone is first since he has precedence in time, then Thomas Campbell, Alexander Campbell, and our great evangelist Walter Scott. The likeness of each is etched in stone, along with an identifying quotation. It is a good way to do our history—especially when one has but "one shot," maybe no more than thirty or forty minutes—to tell our people who they are.

———————

As for the World Convention, I have attended most of its gatherings, held every four years, since 1980 in Mexico City. I served on its executive committee for several years. At first, I was virtually the only one from Churches of Christ, and there were but few from Christian Churches. That has changed in recent years, with substantial numbers from those churches joining Disciples from all over the world in a joyous fellowship. There are usually upwards of two thousand or so in attendance.

At the 1988 convention in Auckland, New Zealand, we celebrated the 200th anniversary of the birth of Alexander Campbell. Allan Lee, then the WCCC executive secretary, asked me to lead a study on the old reformer that ran for several sessions. We had some great discussions. I met dedicated Campbellites from various countries, including Australia where Campbell's influence goes back to the 1840s. The Aussies are especially dedicated to the idea of a world fellowship of Stone-Campbell people. It was the executive committee of the WCCC in Australia that sponsored Ouida's and my tour of that country in 1994, visiting churches and colleges in four states.

For the 1992 convention in Long Beach, California,

Allan asked me to prepare the Bible Study Breakfast Guide, a twenty-four-page booklet that served as the discussion resource for the breakfast sessions. We called it "God's Dominion From Sea to Sea" —the Convention theme. It also ran in the *Christian Standard* in serial form. Among the things I said we could do to promote God's reign in the church was: "By being true to the Scriptures and to our heritage by having a passion for unity, for it is only in the oneness of all Christians that God's dominion will be fully manifest."

At the 1996 WCCC in Calgary, Alberta, led by general secretaries Lyndsay and Lorraine Jacobs, I gave a lecture that served as a different approach to who we are as a people. It was titled "Our Heritage At Its Best." I presented our heritage from the perspective of four quadruples, an outline that was easy to follow: four founding slogans, four founding documents, four founding events, and four founding pioneers.

I figured that, if our people had knowledge of those quadruples, they would have a grasp of their heritage at its best. I emphasized that the quadruples were all about unity. The WCCC afterwards issued it in tract form, and I have sent out hundreds of copies as a summary of the Stone-Campbell heritage.

———————

I also served on the board of the European Evangelistic Society (EES), which sponsors the Institute of Christian Origins in Tuebingen, Germany. It invites scholars from all wings of Stone-Campbell to teach and do research at one of the great learning centers of the world. The EES also conducts the annual Dean E. Walker Memorial Lecture, usually as part of the North American Christian Convention (NACC).

I gave this lecture at the 1991 NACC on "A Preface to Alexander Campbell." It was a different kind of study of the reformer in that I "introduced" him by what he

213

revealed of himself in the prefaces he wrote for his many publications—fifty-odd in number. I revealed some little-known facts about the old hero—such as his being "Alexander Campbell, P.M." in that he served as postmaster in Bethany. With his franking privilege, he posted over a period of four decades upwards of four million pieces of mail of his own writings free of charge!

———————————

Over the years I served numerous colleges of all three churches in various ways. Beside serving as adjunct professor at Dallas Christian College, which I have already chronicled, on two occasions I taught the "January term" at Emmanuel School of Religion in Johnson City, Tennessee on "The Literature of the Disciples of Christ." The class ran all morning for two weeks. I had in-service ministers as well as regular students. My own history of Stone-Campbell was part of the required reading. We had a great time getting into the nitty-gritty of the issues, with no holds barred, and I made some lasting friendships.

Equally exciting was the hospitality of the Emmanuel faculty. It was a distinct honor to visit with the renowned Dean E. Walker, Toyozo Nakarai, and Joe Dampier—longtime respected senior faculty. When Professor Nakarai and I dined at a Chinese restaurant (the mix of Japanese-Chinese culture did not go unnoticed), he told me something of his life as a Buddhist back in Japan long before World War II and how he came to be a Christian.

He was serving a Disciples missionary as a translator and was fascinated by the story of Moses and the burning bush that was not consumed. He asked the minister how he explained it. When the minister said he had no explanation, that he accepted it by faith, it set young Toyozo, who was studying to become a Buddhist priest, on a course that eventually led to faith in Christ. He explained that that kind of faith is radically different

214

from both Japanese and Buddhist thinking.

He also told me how, even as a longtime U.S. citizen, he suffered rejection in the 1940s as a Japanese—even by some in the church. He was such a joy to know—exemplary in both piety and scholarship. Though a Hebrew scholar, it was his devotional book, *An Elder's Prayers,* that most impressed me.

It was something special to return to Emmanuel in 1999 to receive their highest honor: The James A. Garfield Award was "For Noteworthy Service to The Church." I like the way they put that—simply "The Church." On that occasion, I gave the Commencement address for the graduating class on "The Spiritual Side of Our Heritage," in which I showed that our pioneers were heirs of Presbyterian piety as well as sons of the Enlightenment. It too was afterwards published in the *Christian Standard.*

Something happened during that program that rudely broke with tradition. Being the formal affair that it was, we were all in academic regalia. But it was a warm day in late May and the air-conditioner had gone out. When it was time for me to address the class, to the surprise of my hosts, I shed my Harvard doctoral robe and proceeded to give my lecture in short-sleeves!

The students loved it, applauding my boldness. President Robert Wetzel, always charming, was equal to the occasion. He told them that they were not to get any ideas about disrobing, for while I might get by with it, they wouldn't!

Ouida, who was present for the elegant affair, later explained to President Wetzel, unbeknownst to me, that I once had sunstroke and that my physician had warned me about getting too hot. I think I would have been forgiven anyway, but the president was even more forgiving when he realized that I had acted, not simply for personal comfort, but out of necessity.

Time would fail me if I told of all the interesting experiences I had among the colleges. Of the thirty-three colleges associated with the Christian Churches, I have lectured at twenty of them, usually in reference to Stone-Campbell history. When I did the B. D. Phillips Lectures at both Lincoln Christian College and Johnson Bible College, I was reminded of my own acquaintance with the inimitable B. D. Phillips.

Son of the pioneer preacher Thomas W. Phillips, author of the influential *The Church of Christ*, the late Ben Phillips was a renowned Campbellite in his own right, and one of the most interesting men I ever met. A man of wealth, he gave liberally to Stone-Campbell causes, to all three churches, and especially to the colleges—not only to Bethany and Milligan, and Lincoln and Johnson, but to Pepperdine as well. He paid for numerous handsome libraries across the land, including the elegant one in Nashville that is the Disciples of Christ Historical Society. Emmanuel School of Religion has as fine a facility as any seminary in the country; Ben Phillips wrote the check. He put his money where his heart was. I've known few men who loved our heritage as he did. And he takes his place as one of its heroes.

In 1961, as a professor at Bethany, I was a guest in Mr. Phillips' expansive home in Butler, Pennsylvania, where I had gone to speak at the First Christian Church. It was so spacious that we sat awhile in one living room and then in another. When we dined in the smaller dining room—just the two of us since Mr. Phillips was still a widower at the time—there were two servers, one for each of us! When I was escorted to my room, we must have passed eight or ten other rooms before reaching mine. It was the only time that I was a guest in the home of the very rich.

Being quite conservative, Mr. Phillips never seemed

216

to get what he wanted from the colleges. Perry Gresham, president of Bethany College who spent lots of time "nurturing" him, told me that Mr. Phillips wanted him to make a sectarian college out of Bethany. A son-in-law of Mr. Phillips who advised him on his philanthropy, in whose home I was also a guest, had to tell him frankly "You can't get what you want out of these colleges with money." That son-in-law said something to me that I found surprising— "It is more difficult to give money away responsibly than it is to make it."

Mr. Phillips was as crusty as he was rich. He despised Phillips University—even when it bore his family name—presumably because it became so liberal, betraying the family's confidence, as he saw it. At a conference at Bethany, he wouldn't allow his picture to be taken with a representative from that school! And when I told an audience that Mr. Phillips said that he would not give "a thin dime" to a "liberal" cause, he corrected me from the floor: "That isn't what I said," he bellowed, "I said I would not give a plug nickel"!

———————

Among the Disciples colleges, I had meaningful contact only with Bethany and Texas Christian University. I was frequently at TCU—using its library and visiting with faculty. The late A. T. DeGroot, noted Disciples historian, invited me to meet with his classes and tell them about Churches of Christ. We became longtime friends. In those early years, he took part in our unity meetings at Wynnewood Chapel in Dallas.

Since he had made a careful study of the divisions within Stone-Campbell, I asked him during my last visit with him in 1992, shortly before his death, if the cause for our divisions could be succinctly stated. His answer, "It had to be only one way." In those few words he answered a troubling question. When leaders emerged who insisted that it could be only one way about the way

217

we sing or the way we do mission work, it led to division. It isn't necessarily either/or, he was saying, and it might be both/and.

———————————

I had no entree at all with Churches of Christ colleges in those earlier years. In the 1960s and 1970s, when Carl Ketcherside and I occasionally attended the ACU Lectures, we were not unlike the proverbial skunk at a garden party. But there were always some who were pleased to see us, and we had clandestine sessions with a few students and faculty.

Nonetheless, *Restoration Review* circulated somewhat among Churches of Christ colleges, and there were friends on several campuses—students and faculty alike. I would occasionally hear from students who had discovered my journal in the library, and librarians would sometimes write for replacement copies, explaining that the regular copies were missing. When one librarian continued to write for replacement copies, I wrote her that she might place a sign in that section of the library, *Thou shalt not steal!*   But I was otherwise off-limits. The only exception was when Carl and I both took part in the 1974 Preachers' Workshop at Abilene Christian, which allowed for discussion of controversial issues. In spite of its popularity, it was cancelled after a few years.

That didn't substantially change until the 1990s. When I was lecturing at the Westwood Christian Foundation in 1993, housed in the Westwood Christian Church in Los Angeles, the Restoration History Faculty Colloquium of Pepperdine University presented me its Distinguished Christian Service Award. The handsome plaque honored me as an "Enthusiastic Promoter of Unity and Openness In The Stone-Campbell Movement." Jerry Rushford, professor at Pepperdine, presented the award at the dinner they had for me at the Westwood church. Richard Hughes and Norvel and

218

With Norvel Young, chancellor of Pepperdine University, on occasion of the university's Distinguished Christian Service Award to Leroy Garrett, Westwood Christian Church, Los Angeles, 1993.

Helen Young were also present

Three years later, I was invited to take part in the Pepperdine Lectureship. I joined Tom Olbricht and Douglas Foster in reviewing Richard Hughes' *Reviving the Ancient Faith: A History of Churches of Christ* (1996). In three sessions of critical analysis we gave the book high marks, though we all had criticisms to offer— as reviewers always do, however excellent the book. I disagreed with Richard's "Two Campbells" thesis— which makes Campbell a sectarian in his *Christian Baptist* days and an ecumenist later in life.

I asked for the reference in the *Christian Baptist* where Campbell was ever sectarian, which Richard had defined as one who presumes his people to be the only true church. The fact is that some of Campbell's most eloquent ecumenical statements—as well as his severest repudiation of sectarianism—were in his earlier years. But I couldn't object too much to Richard's book. After

219

all, he talked about me in it and included my picture! Besides, he is a great guy whose painstaking research into our past has been a blessing to Churches of Christ—especially when it exposes our underbelly.

In 2000, I was invited to be on the program of the 82nd Annual Bible Lectureship at Abilene Christian University. I spoke on "Four Restoration Principles for the 21st Century," which was part of the Restoration Heritage Series. I was surprised—I think the audience was as well—when Professor Douglas Foster presented me, on behalf of ACU's Center for Restoration Studies, The Award of Excellence. The plaque reads in part, "For outstanding contributions to the field of Restoration History in teaching, publishing, mentoring."

I hope I received the honor with the same grace with which it was tendered. But the unexpected series of events, including simply being invited to be on the program, led me to say to the audience, "You're surprised, aren't you? It just shows what can happen if one lives long enough!"

If there is any victory reflected in these honors, it goes to Pepperdine and ACU for showing openness to the diversity and dissent that only a few years ago was not evident. That it was "politically" possible for them to do so also reflects an encouraging change in Churches of Christ. This openness came at the same time ACU apologized to the African-American community for its racist policies of decades past, all auguring well for the Churches of Christ of the future. If nothing more, it indicates that we have at last begun to overcome our obscurantism and sectarianism. It also shows that we are becoming more introspective—an imperative for renewal.

———— ——— ————

This is not to say that I think our colleges will play a substantial role in the renewal of Churches of Christ— except as they follow the churches. Understandably, institutions tend to act out of self-preservation. They may follow in the wake of change, and even have a positive influence, but they will not often initiate change. Reformers rise out of the church itself. Such is true with us today. Our "change agents," as they are sometimes called in derision, those who say and do the things that encourage change, are usually in the congregations.

Our reformers, in the main, are not the scholars and professors in the universities, but preachers, elders, and the rank and file in the pews. The churches themselves will effect their needed changes, not the universities. There are encouraging exceptions to this rule—such as a medley of liberating books issuing from the ACU Press and the openness and boldness of the Pepperdine lectureships.

It is what I have called the *avant garde* Churches of Christ and "the remnant" in all our churches that have made my own ministry possible. We are all indebted to the likes of: the Bering Drive Church of Christ in Houston; the Burke Road Church of Christ in Pasadena (Texas); the Brookvalley Church of Christ in Atlanta; the Central Church of Christ in Irving (Texas), now named Plymouth Park; the Lake Highlands Church of Christ in Dallas; the Westchester Church of Christ in Los Angeles, especially when Harold Thomas was minister there; the University Church of Christ in Conway (Arkansas); and the Liberty Street Church of Christ in Trenton, New Jersey.

The list could be extended. These are the ones I know best. Surprisingly, it was from our right wing, the non-Sunday School churches, that substantial leadership came, especially the Quaker Avenue Church of Christ in Lubbock and the Farmers Branch Church of Christ in Farmers Branch, Texas. Also, there were numerous "walk out" churches, as I called them, who dropped the name Church of Christ—the Broad Street Chapel in Cleburne (Texas) and Random Road Chapel in Arkansas

221

City (Kansas). Some of these did not long survive, but they made their contribution by their struggle for freedom in Christ.

When Mac Lynn published *Churches of Christ in the United States* in 1991, he identified thirty-six churches as "E" congregations—meaning "ecumenical" or "more progressive." But even then, there were more than that, and there are many more today that have moved in that direction. Most of the churches listed above have been out front leading the way since the 1950s and 1960s. In the past generation, hundreds of other churches have followed their lead.

I salute these churches. They have been heroes in the struggle. In recent years, I have been invited to numerous of our "mainline" churches that wouldn't have dreamed of having me in their pulpit a few years back. Occasionally I am introduced as one who, thirty and forty years ago, was saying what they are now saying, and even treated as a hero. I sometimes hear, "Had it not been for you and Carl Ketcherside...."

This would not have happened except for those up-front churches and that blessed remnant that had a way of turning up most everywhere. It also helps when one can live on into his 80s—and live to see some of the fruit of his efforts!

I sometimes had opportunity to represent the Stone-Campbell tradition at leading institutions of other churches. In 1975 I took part in a Baptist/Church of Christ Dialogue at Baylor University, sponsored by the Graduate Fellowship Seminar. Dr. C. W. Christian and Dr. James Leo Garrett (with whom I had studied at Harvard, but no kin) represented the Baptists. Since our two churches for generations had come together only to debate, we were aware that we were making history. I reminded them that we had started out together, for Alexander Campbell was once a Baptist and resolved to remain one so long as he could be free. He always regretted the separation, and on his deathbed he wept with joy at the news that the Disciples and Baptists were in a unity meeting. Moreover, the first Campbell churches belonged to Baptist associations and our people were first called "Reformed Baptists." I think they were surprised to hear all that!

We discussed baptism. Both sides were embarrassed that in our recent history we have often re-immersed those who go from one church to the other. I pointed out that it was not that way in the beginning. Even though thousands of Baptists came into the Stone-Campbell movement, they were never re-immersed. We had fun together. They took it with a smile when I told them—and I wanted the Church of Christ people present to hear it—that I loved and accepted them as brothers in the Lord, not because they were Baptists but because we were in Christ together.

Another exciting visit was in 1983 with the Presbyterians at Union Seminary in Richmond, Virginia. At the recommendation of two Christian Church students in the seminary—Larry Toney and Chris Davis—I was invited to speak for the Restoration tradition at their Week of Prayer for Christian Unity. My subject was "What I Desire for Christian Unity," which afterwards appeared in *Theology Today*, published by Princeton Seminary. Bishops from both the Greek Orthodox Church and the Roman Catholic Church had addressed the seminary that same week. My discourse may have been both more "orthodox" and more "catholic" than theirs—for I was *just* orthodox and *just* catholic, and neither Greek nor Roman!

In that discourse, I set forth a thesis that I wish we could keep on the table for discussion: *A united church will have an open pulpit, open communion, and open membership.* I claimed that any church that practices any of the "opens" should—to be consistent—practice all three, and we must practice all three to be truly catholic.

223

In Churches of Christ, we practice only open communion—which we should cease doing if we reject the other two. Nothing is a greater expression of fellowship than the Lord's supper!

I also told the seminarians that the only thing that should be required for unity and fellowship is faithfulness to Christ—or Christlikeness—and that this was the position taken by the founders of the Restoration Movement. We can and should frankly discuss our differences—such as baptism—*within* the fellowship, not as a condition *for* fellowship. It is the only unity possible—unity in diversity. The alternative is continued division, which is a horrid evil and a sin against God, as the Restoration pioneers put it.

The Presbyterians responded graciously, but they asked Larry and Chris if their church really believed what I had said. They appropriately answered, "Some of us do."

Chapter 18

When Brethren & Enemies Are The Same

When Carl Ketcherside was criticized by his fellow editors, such as being branded "Blind in one eye" by Reuel Lemmons in the *Firm Foundation,* he would sometimes joke about it. He pointed out that, while the Lord taught him to love his enemies as well as his brothers, that wasn't a problem in his case, for his brothers and enemies were the same!

I soon learned that if I had any "enemies," they were not on the university campus where I made my living as a professor, or in the city where I have lived for forty years. Rather they were in the church where I served as an editor and teacher—or so it seemed.

While I never really thought of them as "enemies," they did sometimes seem to behave as enemies might. To me, they were always my brothers and sisters in the Lord, and I've had no problem loving them—even when their behavior was questionable.

Often asked how I endured it all, my answer was that it was never much of a problem, perhaps because I understood the concerns of my critics. After all, I was once where they were. Too, I've always figured that if my lover's quarrel was well-intentioned, and if my critics did not respond in kind, that was their problem rather than mine.

In offering some of these stories, I not only let the reader in on some of the things that have happened, but I allow him or her to see what the quarrel was about and what the issues were. It was sometimes as pathetic as it was stormy, and as amusing as incredible.

———————

At one Christian Church where I was doing a seminar with Marshall Leggett, afterwards president of Milligan College, I was dealing with the nature of the church as understood by our pioneers. Noting that Thomas Campbell used "Church of Christ" or "Christian Church" in a universal sense, as being composed of all Christians everywhere, I expressed concern that we used the terms in a sectarian way. To make my point, I ventured that Billy Graham is a member of the Christian Church or Church of Christ the same as we are. I was told afterward—in no uncertain terms—that Billy Graham was a Baptist and *not* a member of the Christian Church!

I didn't help myself any when I explained that by Christian Church I meant the one body of Christ, referred to in Scripture, not to the "Christian Church" associated with the North American Christian Convention. One irate sister accused me of being "a wolf in sheep's clothing," which surprised me since I had been eminently biblical in my teaching on the nature of the church.

I was used to being called names in Churches of Christ, but this was a Christian Church. I was to learn that some in Christian Churches can be as sectarian as any of the rest of us, and sometimes just as unchristian.

———————

I also had a problem with fundamentalists in Christian Churches. In a lecture one summer at the Week of Ministry, conducted at Milligan College in Tennessee, I revealed that I didn't believe in biblical inerrancy. I pointed out that the Bible makes no such claim for itself. Some folks were unhappy with me. It didn't help when I noted that those who pursue truth have nothing to fear from modern biblical research and

226

that "textual criticism," as we now call it, was anticipated by our own pioneers.

Fundamentalists among us seem unaware that Alexander Campbell, who also didn't believe in the inerrancy of Scripture, was among the first modern translators to "mess with the Bible." To the dismay of his brethren, in his *Living Oracles*, a translation of the New Testament (1827), he deleted Acts 8:37—one of their favorite prooftexts. He left it out because it lacked sufficient support from ancient manuscripts. To him it was a matter of being honest with the Bible.

For the same reason, Campbell left out the doxology of the Lord's Prayer ("Thine is the kingdom, and the power, and the glory forever. Amen!") as the Catholics do. When Edgar Goodspeed, over a century later, was criticized for omitting the doxology in his modern version, he defended himself by noting that Alexander Campbell had done likewise back in 1827.

I likened the fundamentalist preoccupation with the verbal exactness of the Bible to an astronomer who is so concerned with the mechanics of his telescope that he misses out on what can be seen through it. After all, God saved us by giving us a Person, not a book. The book reveals the Person, and it is the Person that is the end, while the book is the means. The book might never have existed—the New Testament at least—if Christ had come again within the first century, but the Person was absolutely essential.

I'm not saying that fundamentalism was a big problem in my ministry. It was a problem only among ultra-conservatives in the Christian Churches, who made an effort to keep me off their programs. To them, I had other sins, such as associating with Disciples of Christ. But in general, the Christian Churches provided me with many open doors, and over the years I've made many enduring friendships.

Some early opposition took interesting turns. The Cahaba Valley Church of Christ in Birmingham scheduled me for a series, but the elders cancelled it when preachers in the area protested my coming. Choosing to be free and not dictated to by our clergy, the elders risked rescheduling me for a later date. Since my appearance was controversial, I decided to speak on less provocative subjects than those that were making me infamous.

While the elders agreed to this, some of the members protested, saying it didn't make sense for Leroy Garrett to come and talk about prayer. They wanted to know what the fuss was all about—why area preachers would make such a big deal about my coming. The elders relented. Once I presented my case on unity and fellowship, they understood why I was a lightning rod, whether they agreed with me or not. I thought that was an interesting turn of events. I was willing to come in a peaceful, pastoral role, but the church wanted to hear the call for repentance from a reformer—even if they had to take flak for it from other churches!

———

Unfortunately, things sometimes got mean and nasty. An African-American brother named Ivory James, Jr., a Churches of Christ minister in Palm Beach, Florida, was known to express views reflective of those of Ketcherside and Garrett and to reach out to believers in other churches. He was not only labeled a "liberal" by the powers-that-be in the black Churches of Christ, but was eventually brought to trial. The charges included inviting Baptists into his pulpit, believing there were Christians in other churches, and not making instrumental music a test of fellowship. Neither did he preach baptism the way they did—charge enough for a trial.

Since he was to be on trial with excommunication as a possible sentence, Ivory asked his prosecutors if he could have a defense attorney. When they assented, he said, "I choose Leroy Garrett as my advocate."

I flew to Miami where the trial was conducted in a Holiday Inn, with hundreds in attendance—all black. At first I was the only white person there, but on the second day of the trial the prosecution team imported Ira Rice, Jr. from California.

The "somewhats" of the black Churches of Christ who conducted the trial included Jack Evans, president of Southwestern Christian College, and such noted ministers as Roosevelt Wells, Eugene Lawton, Nokomis Yeldell, and James Maxwell. It had the makings for real drama.

If it was fire and brimstone they wanted, they didn't need Ira Rice. I never witnessed such vitriolic abuse heaped upon a brother in Christ as they imposed on poor Ivory. They called him everything except what he was—their own brother in the Lord. They used the Bible as a club, applying to him verses that condemned pagan idolatry—such as Revelation 18:4 ("Come out of her, my people, lest you share in her sins"). It was a case of twisting the Scriptures in order to browbeat one for whom Christ died, incredibly cruel and abusive.

In my defense of Ivory, I shamed them for the way they were treating their blood brother in Jesus, whose crime was not idolatry or thievery or womanizing or disloyalty to Christ. It was nothing more than disagreement over marginal issues and matters of opinion. I told them I was shocked that they—as preachers who ought to know better—would twist and warp the Bible in order to put down a brother.

I insisted, moreover, that Ivory's ministry was none of their business to start with, that theirs was a kangaroo court. If they had any charge against him, they were to take it to his church and his elders, for only they have the right to discipline him. His elders and his church, in fact, were present and stood by him.

Ivory told me after one presentation, "Leroy, as long

229

as they live, they'll never forget that speech." When I saw one of them seventeen years later at ACU, I don't think he had forgotten!

An interesting note about that debacle, one that would interest sociologists of religion, was that Ivory and I had occasion to recognize Martin Luther King, Jr. as a brother in the Lord "because he believed in Christ and was baptized just as we." Ivory's critics were outraged, insisting that King was "a Baptist and no Christian." They showed little appreciation for him, which I thought odd. There I was, a white man in a black world appreciating Martin Luther King, Jr. while black people repudiated him. It shows that sectarianism is thicker than race!

Well, Ivory and I lost our case in *that* court. That the prosecutors were also the jury left us little chance. In the end, we were excommunicated! It was the first time (and the only time) that any segment of the Churches of Christ had formally withdrawn fellowship from me. But the charge against me was never clear; I presume it was for defending Ivory.

I found some redemption in the verdict of the one-woman jury. Toward the end of the disgraceful episode, an aged, black lady, matronly and dignified, a take-charge kind of woman, stood and read the riot act to the kangaroo court: "I don't like this," she told them, measuring her words, "This is a mess! I don't like the way you're treating this brother." On and on she went. By the time she sat down, "the powers that be" of the African-American Churches of Christ knew who had been taken to the woodshed. And they said not a word in response to her charge. Verdict enough!

I left Miami with my usual optimism. There is justice in the world after all—even if I had been excommunicated!

In 1974, all editors among Churches of Christ were

invited to attend the International Evangelism and Bible Conference conducted by the White's Ferry Road Church of Christ in Monroe, Louisiana. This church has long conducted a School of Preaching, with some 100 students at that time, and World Radio—one of the more successful outreach ministries among us.

This meeting allowed us editors to get together and discuss our common problems and to say to each other whatever we pleased. That the School of Preaching students were with us made it all the more interesting.

I was impressed that some of the things *Firm Foundation* editor Reuel Lemmons said on that occasion were what Carl Ketcherside and I had been saying for many years: "I am concerned about all the sectarianism in the Churches of Christ," he lamented. "Disagreements are wholesome, while disfellowship is deplorable." And again, "Some people don't know the difference between disagreement and disfellowship."

Reuel—who had the aura of an editor-bishop—could get by with saying things that Carl and I were hammered for saying. That was great. We welcomed any help we could get.

There were fourteen of us editors there and it was a great experience, sharing with the students and the local church folk. But on the last day of the conference, some gremlins came out of the woodwork and almost spoiled the party. Since I was the only infamous editor present, some students who were curious about what I believed had invited me the night before to a gathering in one of their homes for friendly conversation. When some of the faculty heard about it and got upset, it was reminiscent of the Freed-Hardeman affair twenty years earlier—though I had no fear this time of going to jail. Remember, as Carl Ketcherside said, that could happen only at Freed-Hardeman!

A professor at the school, whose daughter was among the students eliciting my attention, deemed it appropriate to issue a warning from the pulpit. Calling

231

my name, he warned the students of my evil influence: "He is not a man of peace, and his fruits are not good," he told them, and so they should be on their guard.

Some of the students asked me if the professor's charges were true. I conceded they might be— depending on how one looks at it. To one who is protective of the *status quo* in Churches of Christ, I suppose I would not be seen as a man of peace. I reminded them that Reuel Lemmons had said some of the same things I was saying. Was he "a man of peace"? After all, when it's time for drastic change, we might have to be like our Lord, and bring not peace but a sword.

What made this altercation different was that I had my son Benjy with me on this trip, then fifteen years old. He had his temporary driver's license. With an adult at his side, he could drive. He drove our flashy Pontiac Firebird all the way from home to Monroe and back again. He loved it!

But he was confused about all the fuss about his dad. As he drove us home, I tried to explain it: "Sometimes you believe changes should be made," I said, "But when you try to make them, there are those who will oppose you by doing not-so-nice things. They are good people and mean well; but they feel threatened, so you have to be ready to take the abuse."

Then he said, Truman-like, "You mean that if you can't take the heat you'd better get out of the kitchen." And I said, "That's it. You've got it." Then he told me what he might not have otherwise related. Following my public repudiation, a student, learning that he was my son, said to him, "Your dad has been a great help to me, and others as well. I think he's doing a great service for the Church of Christ."

There is "the rest of the story" to this particular episode. Two decades later, I got a telephone call from that professor. He wanted to know if I remembered what happened in Monroe back in 1974. He wanted to apologize. He had been studying, had read more of my writings, and he had changed his mind. He was sorry that he had been rude. A gracious letter with more apologies followed this call. Moreover, he told me that the climate had entirely changed at White's Ferry Road. He supposed that by now all the staff at the School of Preaching would agree with me.

His call really impressed Ouida. "You mean after twenty years he called and apologized!" But I told her, and I wrote the professor, that this was *his* victory, not mine. When people can admit being wrong and do what they can to correct it, *they* are the winner. He wins freedom, and what a victory that is!

During his last years, Carl Ketcherside and I would share our experiences with those who called or wrote to apologize for the way they had treated us. While we saw this as a sign of progress, Carl would always say, "It is their victory."

But it was sometimes amusing, for while apologizing to us they would complain about those who were now treating them the way they once treated us! Carl and I noticed through the years that our harshest critics were usually those who never seriously considered what we were saying. When they gave us an honest take, they would sometimes have a change of heart.

———————————

Often it seemed that there was no honest take of my position. This included some people in my own hometown, where the attitude toward me has sometimes been fierce. One would think it unlikely that in any church one Christian might say to another, "You are going to hell." But that happened to me at one of the Annual Denton Lectures, conducted each fall at the Pearl Street Church of Christ.

The judging brother, a preacher, was a stranger to me. Once he had announced my eternal destiny, I asked if he wanted to tell me why he made such a severe

233

judgment. I was a false teacher, he charged, but it wasn't clear to me why he thought that—unless it was that I accepted as Christians those that he did not. That would even include some in other Churches of Christ whom he did not fellowship.

Through the years, these lectures had created a straw man out of "Ketcherside-Garrett" —usually in terms of our "unity-in-diversity" heresy, referred to in chapter 13. Now and again, when in the audience, I received public censure from some lecturer. I was branded as a false teacher, or as a liberal, or a divider of churches—or all of the above. I was sometimes responsible for others being so labeled. On one occasion, Royce Money, president of ACU, was castigated because Leroy Garrett had commended something he had written!

These are not evil men. They are gospel preachers "defending the truth," as they see it. Perhaps they feel threatened, but unnecessarily so, as I view it.

Ouida would scold me when I would attend these Lectures each fall: "Why do you go there and suffer abuse?" she would ask with good reason. I would tell her that they too are my sisters and brothers. I love them also, and I must show the same acceptance towards those to my right as I do towards those to my left. It always turned out that I would meet a few daring souls who were not only courteous, but also were willing to read what I was writing.

These public censures sometimes took on an incredible dimension. These same brethren in 1976 conducted what they called "The Debate of the Century" between Anthony Flew, a British atheist, and Thomas Warren, Churches of Christ minister and professor. They paid Flew's expenses—flying him from England—to make the debate possible. People came from across the country, especially preachers. It gave me opportunity to visit with old friends—James D. Bales of Harding College being one of them. As the big debate took place in the evenings, the brethren met during the

234

days to preach to each other.

At one of these sessions I attended, Andrew Connally, whom I knew when we were young, was the speaker. He departed from his prepared speech to attack Leroy Garrett. Besides branding me with the usual epithets, he accused me of only recently dividing the Welch Street Church of Christ in Denton, referring to a split that produced a new congregation.

Afterwards, I privately explained to Andrew that he had his facts wrong: in fact, I had urged the Welch Street brethren *not* to leave their congregation and start a new one. I had urged them to stay and, in a spirit of love, try to work out their problems. Moreover, I told him there were former elders of said church nearby who would confirm the facts as I had related them—but I would leave it to his good judgment as to whether he should correct what he had said publicly.

At this Andrew showed amazing creativity: "Well, if I was wrong about that point, there are so many other things that you're guilty of that what I said still stands!"

———————————

It got sort of pathetic and a bit amusing when some local brethren included Ouida in their opposition to me. In 1990, Ouida and I placed membership with the Singing Oaks Church of Christ in Denton after being members for fifteen years of a "progressive" congregation in town that had disbanded. I met with the Singing Oaks elders in advance, assuring them that we would not place membership if they thought I would be a problem to them. Having been berated themselves in other onsets by the same people, they encouraged us to cast our lot with them.

When the elders of the Pearl Street Church of Christ, the congregation that conducts the Annual Denton Lectures, saw Ouida and me listed as new members in the Singing Oaks bulletin, they had this reaction: "In the April 5 Singing Oaks Bulletin (from Singing Oaks

235

Church of Christ, Denton) it is announced that Leroy and Ouida Garrett placed membership. That they were thus readily accepted is sadly [sic] but further confirmation of the degree to which the Singing Oaks congregation have [sic] set their course away from the Truth."

I had fun with Ouida over that one, assuring her that she had now arrived in the pantheon of renowned heretics—publicly branded as such! For a church to receive Ouida into its membership was evidence that it had turned away from the truth!

This notion of one church criticizing another church for receiving certain ones into its membership led me, in my writings, to pose a question: *Does a congregation have the scriptural right to choose its members?* May it accept only whites or only the affluent or only those who pass a doctrinal litmus test? I can see that a church may refuse membership to one who has been disciplined by another congregation, but must it not otherwise have to accept any faithful Christian who applies? I suggested a proposition for discussion, after the order of the Jesuits: *A member is free to choose a congregation, but a congregation is not free to choose its members.*

An editor's task, as I have perceived it, is to open up new avenues of thought, plow new ground, challenge sacred cows, and suggest different ways of looking at things. I've never supposed I had to be absolutely right before placing an idea on the table for discussion. I believe if an idea is reasonable and relevant—what William James called "a live option" —it deserves a hearing.

An instance of my role was in a 1985 *Restoration Review* editorial in which I raised the question, *Is the Virgin Birth Part of the Gospel?* It was one more way to elicit discussion on the nature of the gospel—a live issue at that time since our opponents insisted that everything

236

in the New Testament is the gospel.

I made it clear at the outset that I believed in the virgin birth because of the testimony of Scripture, particularly Dr. Luke's account, who may have interviewed Mary. But I ventured that it isn't part of the gospel. Mark introduced his testimony as "the gospel of Jesus Christ the Son of God," but he makes no reference to the virgin birth. John emphasizes the supernatural character of Christ, but included nothing about the virgin birth. Even though Paul referred to Jesus' birth, such as "born of woman" (Galatians 4:4), he never even alludes to a virgin birth in any of his writings. All through Acts, the gospel is proclaimed but the virgin birth is never mentioned. Apparently it was not part of the apostolic proclamation.

I noted that Mark and Paul either didn't know of the virgin birth or didn't consider it relevant to what they had to say. But they *did* repeatedly set forth the gospel. I allowed that there must have been many early Christians who lived and died having never heard of the virgin birth. But they certainly heard and obeyed the gospel. I explained that, while the doctrine of the virgin birth is biblical, it isn't part of the gospel. Not everything in the New Testament is the gospel!

I suppose it was too much to expect that thesis to get a fair hearing. If my critics were to admit that anything at all in the New Testament is not the gospel, they might have to surrender their position that one's view on instrumental music is a test of his fidelity to the gospel. Or congregational cooperation. Or Sunday schools. Or the millennial question. Or the issue of marriage and divorce. Our failure to understand the nature of the gospel has been our undoing.

To Mike Willis, editor of *Guardian of Truth*, my article was one more indication that "Leroy Garrett, editor of *Restoration Review*, continues to move more and more toward modernism." He titled his remarks about what I had to say as "Belief in Virgin Birth Not

237

Necessary." As for my question as to whether the virgin birth is part of the gospel, he said, "Yes, it is recorded in Matthew 1:18-25 and Luke 1-2." Moreover, he told his readers, "Such a man is a dangerous false teacher who undermines confidence in the revealed word of God."

About this time, I happened to be with the renowned Dale Moody, longtime professor at Southern Baptist Theological Seminary in Louisville, at a conference in Conway, Arkansas. Known for his conservative scholarship, I tried my question out on him: "Is the virgin birth part of the gospel?" I asked him, realizing he was void of anything "liberal." At first taken aback, as if he had not been asked that before, he proceeded to affirm his belief in the virgin birth. Then I said, "I understand that it is biblical, but is it part of the gospel?" He paused for a moment and then said, "No. It is not part of the gospel."

Both Alexander Campbell and C. H. Dodd, noted British scholar, would agree with Moody. Each of them, a century apart, composed a definitive list of what precisely made up the gospel, based on the proclamation of the gospel in Acts. Their lists—centered in the death, burial, and resurrection of Jesus Christ—were virtually identical. Neither included the virgin birth. And yet both, like Moody and me, believed in the virgin birth.

If one wonders why some leaders among us become anxious over a different drumbeat, it may be that Mike Willis himself answered that question nearly twenty years after the above incident took place. In a 2001 editorial in *Truth Magazine,* he reviewed the struggles the "non-institutional" Churches of Christ, the group with which he is identified, have had with the "grace-unity movement" led by Carl Ketcherside and Leroy Garrett.

Tracing developments from the 1960s and 1970s to the present, Mike estimates that "Approximately 100 younger preachers from non-institutional churches were influenced in the direction of the grace-unity

238

With Carl Ketcherside, Maple St. Church of Christ, Hartford, Illinois, 1987, two years before his death.

Movement."

One hundred preachers lost to the Ketcherside-Garrett unity movement! Willis didn't add that they were usually among the better educated and most promising.

This surprising admission may explain why party leaders sometimes respond abusively when absolutist claims are questioned and numbers decimated. Abuse is often resorted to when the party's very existence is threatened. It was why the chief priests resolved to do away with Jesus and why the pope excommunicated Luther.

In his review of his own party, Mike Willis does more than recount the Ketcherside-Garrett struggle of years past. He identifies more recent departures from the party line, such as the "liberal teaching on marriage and divorce." These accounts led many of them to brand even Homer Hailey, one of their most exemplary leaders, as a false teacher. Moreover, there are "liberal"

239

views taught at Florida College, the school long identified with this group, in reference to "the big bang theory" and the creation story in Genesis. Some professors are allowing that the six days of creation couldn't be literal 24-hour periods.

Mike sees all this as consequences of the unity-in-diversity movement. He warned his people that if this doctrine, which he also describes as "agreeing to disagree," is allowed to open the door to one issue, there is no end to the false doctrines that will creep in. The door that might be opened to new ideas must be kept shut and guarded by the party faithful. Differences are not allowed in areas identified as "matters of faith," which are always the issues—however marginal—that identify the particular party. The Mormons have theirs, the Baptists have theirs, and groups and sub-groups within Churches of Christ have theirs.

Mike Willis has rather ably described the fallacy of modern Protestantism and denominationalism. Since "agree to disagree" or "unity-in-diversity" is not allowed on "the issues" mandated by each party, a proliferation of sects is the only possible result. That is why there are several brands of Mormons, scores of different kinds of Baptists, upwards of twenty different Presbyterian churches, and on and on it goes.

———————————————

Some count as many as twenty-six different kinds of Churches of Christ. It goes on seemingly endlessly—dividing and sub-dividing. It cannot be otherwise, considering the demand for doctrinal conformity. "Faithful" has come to mean, not devotion to Jesus Christ, but loyalty to "the issues" as defined by the party.

This is why the Stone-Campbell Movement emerged on the American frontier—to correct this devastating fallacy. The genius of the Movement was to show that we can differ and still be united. "In essentials, unity" meant to them that we unite upon the core gospel. "In opinions, liberty" meant that we allow for differences or "agree to disagree" on non-essentials—theological opinions, theories, methods.

Yes, of course, this means there will be errors to be tolerated, which is always the case when people are free to think and interpret the Bible for themselves. We are all in error about some things—except those among us who are perfect in understanding! If the church has to be error-free to be united, then unity will never be and cannot be attained. We can no more see everything alike than we can look alike. It's not a question as to *whether* there will be error, but *what kind* of error.

Alexander Campbell was careful to distinguish between errors of the heart and errors of the mind. When there are errors of the heart, such as a factious spirit or sinful pride, fellowship may be impossible. But errors of the mind or understanding, which we all have, are embraced in the biblical mandate to "Receive one another even as Christ has received you" (Romans 15:7). None of us was free of error when Christ received him or her.

The dream our pioneers had for the unity of the church at large I have had for my own Churches of Christ. If I have persuaded some that they do not have to believe the sectarian bill of goods that has been imposed upon them, and that they can enjoy fellowship with other Christians without sacrificing any truth they hold, then it will have been a quarrel—a lover's quarrel—worth waging.

Chapter 19
The Sunset Years

Driving a school bus was such an adventure for me that it's a story that can hardly be left out. I chose to do this in order to regain my Texas teacher pension status. On retiring from full-time teaching, I withdrew the funds to invest in a business venture. To return the money and qualify for retirement benefits, it was necessary to do two more years of full-time service. Several years of part-time teaching at Richland College didn't count as full-time service, but bus driving did, even if it required only a few hours a day.

Once certified as a driver, I was hired by our own Denton Independent School District, which takes its transportation obligations quite seriously. I had taught a special course in philosophy at Denton High School for six years while a professor at Texas Woman's University, and was not an unknown commodity. But I still had to demonstrate to them that a bus load of children would be safe with me as their driver. It was 1980, and I was almost 62—a little old for a school bus driver.

I keenly felt the responsibility, especially in inclement weather. But over a two-year period, I transported hundreds of kids for thousands of miles without incident or accident—and that includes no discipline problems, the usual headache for drivers. I scored well with the kids, who would board the bus chanting, "Leroy is our hero!" They thought it cool that they had a Ph.D. for a bus driver!

One of my favorite students was Mark McCallon, son of a good friend of mine, Earl McCallon, a professor at the University of North Texas. Mark, then in middle school, grew up to be a librarian at Abilene Christian University. He tells the story around campus of having me for his school bus driver—and how, on one occasion I was talking to him about philosophy, and he was so interested that he missed his stop. In due time, I performed the marriage ceremony for him and his lovely Beverly. Mark has the rare distinction of being married by his school bus driver!

School bus driving turned out to be the most profitable job I ever had. For nineteen years now, I have drawn teacher retirement that I wouldn't have had otherwise, and which Ouida will continue to receive if widowed. And there is health insurance coverage for both of us, including prescription drugs. A few years after driving the bus, I went to a world-renowned hospital in Houston for radical prostate surgery. The bill was $25,000, virtually all of it paid by Medicare and my teacher retirement insurance. Only recently Ouida commented, after going through some expensive tests, "It is just as well that you drove that school bus!"

While I was driving the school bus, Harvard asked me to represent the university at the inauguration of the new president of the University of North Texas, Dr. Frank E. Vandiver, on November 13, 1980, an academic courtesy among universities. I drove the bus as usual that morning. In order to arrive at the event on time, the dispatcher allowed me to take the bus to the University rather than return it to the barn. Amidst all the congestion, I parked it on the campus green and hurried to the affair with my academic robe flowing in the breeze.

At all such events, the one from the oldest university leads the academic parade. Since Harvard dates back to 1636, that meant that I was first in line. (I once had to yield to someone from a Scottish university that was founded in the 15th century!) There I was first in line, putting on my academic regalia, preparing to lead the notables from Yale, Princeton, Stanford, Texas, Rice, and on and on.

It is understandable if the dignified professors considered it odd for a schoolbus driver to be leading their academic procession. And not only that but one who had the audacity to park his bus out on the campus lawn! I knew, of course, that one may park a school bus anywhere and get away with it. They are sacrosanct!

Years later Harvard asked that I personally deliver a certificate of congratulations—elegantly embossed—to another new University of North Texas president. That time it was without my schoolbus!

———————

One of my good friends, Gene Wilborn, a Denton businessman and a Christian brother, delights in telling my schoolbus stories, which admittedly are a bit unusual. In mentioning Gene, I have another story to tell. For some time during the middle 1990s (I was an old man by then), Gene and I did Meals-on-Wheels together. We delivered hot meals in Styrofoam containers to the dozen or so homes on our route, mostly to African-American families. I was impressed with the high quality of the meals, which were prepared in a hospital kitchen.

Most were shut-ins; some were disabled and bedfast. Gene drove, and I delivered. I came to know some of our folks quite well, occasionally sharing their problems and dreams. Some were able to meet me at the door, but others asked me to come inside, occasionally all the way to the kitchen table. One bedfast lady had me go to her kitchen, fetch silverware, unwrap the meal, and serve her in bed! It was a joyous ministry that went well with preaching and teaching. A preacher or teacher would do well to be able to tell an occasional Meals-On-Wheels story.

Gene and I shared a lot of quality time, and we had lunch together on those days. A treasured memory! My only complaint was with those who seemed to take advantage of the program. I recall saying to Gene after delivering two meals to an affluent, able-bodied couple (that I would see out shopping!), younger and more robust than myself, "They ought to bring meals to me!"

I would occasionally help with other routes, including white families. I may have created a problem at one home—the couple receiving the meals were members of the Church of Christ in town that had publicly labeled me as a heretic. While we always got along handsomely, I wondered what the "powers-that-be" at their church might say. It was a problem not unlike those addressed in the Jewish Mishnah, where the Pharisees determined how far one might go before breaking the law, such as "One may spit on the Sabbath day so long as it is not on a porous surface, thus causing nature to work." I could hear the church authorities say, "You may receive a meal from a heretic so long as you do not speak to him." Fortunately, the couple didn't see it that way.

Ouida and I decided in 1990 that we would cease publishing *Restoration Review* after two more years. We advised readers to renew "for the duration," with the last issue coming in December 1992—the subscription price declining with each passing issue. As the time drew near to close, the requests that we continue were so persuasive that we decided that we would keep in touch for a while longer by way of a newsletter. Everyone on our mailing list would receive it free of charge. We had funds left over from *Restoration Review*, so we would send out the newsletter as long as the money lasted. New names would be added upon request—all gratis.

In March 1993, we sent out our first issue of the newsletter with the title of *LAST TIME AROUND— An occasional newsletter from Leroy and Ouida Garrett*, to over 2,000 homes. The lead article was "Transformed Or Conformed?" which concluded with "Transformation means freedom; conformity means bondage. Isn't it good news that we have a choice?" By the time we had issued fifteen newsletters, longtime reader Kathy Wyler, then of Kerrville, Texas, persuaded us to change the name. She didn't like the implication of *LAST TIME AROUND.* She suggested *ONCE MORE WITH LOVE,* with which we agreed. Since February 1996, we have sent out forty-two newsletters with that title, making fifty-seven in all, and counting.

By the end of 2002, I had been an editor—if the newsletter counts—within the Stone-Campbell tradition for fifty years, which sets a record. Alexander Campbell went for forty-three years and David Lipscomb for forty-seven. But I never had the aura of an "editor-bishop" that they had, nor, of course, the talent. However, I have had the satisfaction of putting ideas on the table for discussion and calling for meaningful change. I have even called for repentance, and like Campbell and Lipscomb, I have had a lover's quarrel with my own church.

Leonard Allen, in graciously dedicating his book, *Things Unseen,* to me, succinctly described my half-century as an editor among Churches of Christ: "To Leroy Garrett, prophet and priest, in season and (mostly) out." Roger Ledlow, of Tallahassee, put it another way in a recent e-mail: "Have enjoyed your voice crying in the Church of Christ wilderness for many years." But Cecil Hook may have best pinpointed one thing I have sought to do all these years. In *Our Heritage of Unity and Fellowship,* which is a selection of essays by Carl Ketcherside and me that he edited, he said of me: "He disturbs our superficialities." Cecil could have added that Socrates got himself killed doing that!

Even though my out-of-season, disturbing voice may have gone largely unappreciated in the early decades, in my extended sunset years there seems to have been a remarkable transformation, especially evident in the increasing number of congregations that have felt free to

247

invite me to take part in their programs. These are mostly churches that would be considered more traditional than progressive, to whom I would have been off-limits not that long ago.

Looking back on only the past decade—the years most reflective of the change—I spoke at these churches during that period, 1992-2002. This list includes assignments only with Churches of Christ.

Alabama:
Landmark Church of Christ, Montgomery

Arkansas:
Calico Rock Church of Christ, Calico Rock

California:
Northside Church of Christ, Santa Ana

Indiana:
Eastside Church of Christ, Terre Haute
North Central Church of Christ, Indianapolis
Speedway Church of Christ, Indianapolis

Delaware:
Cedars Church of Christ, Wilmington

Kentucky:
Pennyrile Church of Christ, Madisonville
Portland Avenue Church of Christ, Louisville
Southeast Church of Christ, Louisville
Westport Road Church of Christ, Louisville

Louisiana:
Airline Drive Church of Christ, Bossier City
Amite Church of Christ, Amite
Causeway Blvd. Church of Christ, Mandeville

Maine:
Greater Portland Church of Christ, Portland

Massachusetts:
Brookline Church of Christ, Brookline

Michigan:
Troy Church of Christ, Troy

Missouri:
Lafayette Church of Christ, Ballwin

New Jersey:
Liberty Street Church of Christ, Trenton

Oklahoma:
Dayspring Church of Christ, Durant
Eastview Church of Christ, Miami
Memorial Drive Church of Christ, Tulsa
Thackerville Church of Christ, Thackerville

Oregon:
Westside Church of Christ, Beaverton

Texas:
Allen Church of Christ, Allen
Argyle Church of Christ, Argyle
Aubry Church of Christ, Aubry
Buckingham Road Church of Christ, Garland
Burbank Gardens Church of Christ, Grand Prairie
Central Arlington Church of Christ, Arlington
Downtown Church of Christ, El Paso
East First Street Church of Christ, Dumas
Garden Ridge Church of Christ, Lewisville
Golf Road Church of Christ, Midland
Park Hill Church of Christ, Fort Worth
Pecan Grove Church of Christ, Greenville
Pitman Creek Church of Christ, Plano

249

A gracious welcome back, Liberty Street Church of Christ, Trenton, New Jersey (near Princeton), 1998.

Plymouth Park Church of Christ, Irving
Pond Springs Church of Christ, Austin
Quaker Avenue Church of Christ, Lubbock
Round Rock Church of Christ, Round Rock
Singing Oaks Church of Christ, Denton
Town West Church of Christ, Taylor
Vandelia Church of Christ, Lubbock
West Amarillo Church of Christ, Amarillo
Westworth Church of Christ, Fort Worth
Woodland West Church of Christ, Arlington

Tennessee:
Forest Home Church of Christ, Franklin
Forest Mill Church of Christ, Manchester
Woodmont Hills Church of Christ, Nashville

In some of these congregations, my transformation was from heretic to hero. I have been introduced with "He was saying these things forty years ago, but we didn't listen; but now we are listening. Or, as David Edwin Harrell, Jr. put it in his *The Churches of Christ of the 20th Century* (2000), in reference to Carl Ketcherside and me, we were "prophets before our time." Harrell noted that, while we were "lonely liberals" in the 1960s, by the 1990s our views were widely accepted by Churches of Christ. Allen Dennis has pointed out that I am one of the few reformers who has lived to see some fruit for his labors.

Publications are also reflective of the change. All along I occasionally had essays in Disciples and Christian Church publications, but it wasn't until the 1990s that I was published in *Wineskins*—which may now be the leading journal among Churches of Christ—and *Leaven*, published by Pepperdine University. I served as a senior consultant and wrote several articles—including a major essay on Alexander Campbell—for the *Encyclopedia of the Stone-Campbell Movement,* an impressive joint effort of all three churches. Equally significant, many writers in various journals today are saying what it was "out of season" for me to say a generation ago.

The change is also evident in our colleges. I've referred to the unlikely circumstances of being honored by Pepperdine and Abilene Christian. Equally satisfying to me is the interest taken by students. Robert Griffin (Christian Churches) is presently doing a master's thesis at Harding Graduate School of Religion on "Leroy Garrett: Advocate of Christian Unity," which will be an analysis of my interpretation of the Stone-Campbell plea. A similar thesis was done by William Lee Wilbanks (Churches of Christ) as early as 1966, which included both Carl Ketcherside and me.

Wilbanks concluded that, in reference to unity and fellowship, our views were more liberal than those of Stone and Campbell. His study may have been too early for an in-depth analysis. I am persuaded he would have reached a different conclusion if he had done his work twenty years later. If anything, I believe Stone and Campbell were more liberal than Carl and I, particularly Stone.

There is an interesting story coming out of

Oklahoma Christian University. When Heather Duncan—an enterprising senior at that university—heard her history professor refer to me as one within Churches of Christ with a different view of things, she persuaded him to allow her to do her term paper on me. When Heather and her mother came to Denton to interview me for her research paper, the professor had them do a video of the interview as part of the university's "Living History" depository. I subsequently gave a lecture at Oklahoma Christian on Restoration history for their Christian Scholars Conference (2002).

I also did a "Living History" interview for Dr. Douglas Foster for the Restoration archives at Abilene Christian in 1993. Both Heather and Doug asked the kind of questions that will help future generations of our people in Churches of Christ to understand better the transition we are now going through. I envy those future researchers. How exciting it would have been in my own research to have a video of Raccoon John Smith talking about his adventures or Daniel Sommer reviewing his stormy life!

I am especially pleased to have played a part in putting together the Stone-Campbell Dialogue—which may prove to be the most promising development of this generation for all of our people in the Movement. John Mills, a leading minister among Christian Churches, and Robert K. Welsh, president of the Council on Christian Unity of the Disciples of Christ, agreed that there should be unity talks within the Stone-Campbell tradition. They asked me to form a representative group from Churches of Christ. It was decided that the Dialogue would begin with three persons from each wing of the Movement.

I consulted with Don Browning of the Farmers Branch Church of Christ in Dallas, who is not only wise but also well-informed about our people. We decided to ask Mike Armour of the Skillman Avenue Church of Christ in Dallas, who has had extensive experience in reaching across lines, and Douglas Foster of Abilene Christian, who has both heart and mind for such things, to stand in for Churches of Christ. They would choose the third person. They asked Phillip Morrison, then managing editor of *Wineskins* in Nashville, to join them.

The Stone-Campbell Dialogue—the name finally adopted—is especially significant because it was initiated by leading Disciples of Christ, who at last decided that unity efforts should "move in both directions," as they put it. They should not only seek unity with those outside Stone-Campbell but also with those inside. This is different thinking for the Disciples. Their committee, besides Welsh, was Richard L. Hamm, general minister and president of the Disciples, and Peter Morgan, president of the Disciples of Christ Historical Society.

The committee from Christian Churches, besides Mills, included Henry Webb, historian and retired professor of Milligan College, and James B. North, vice president and professor of church history at Cincinnati Bible College and Seminary.

Knowing all nine of the Dialogue members, I was excited from the outset about its potential for healing wounds. The nine men resolved that they should start by confessing to each other the sin of division, and the way we have misrepresented each other. They—we— would first get acquainted and learn to pray together as brethren too long divided.

Since its first meeting in 1999, there have been increased numbers from the branches for each successive meeting and has had an agenda that places no limitation on what can be discussed. I see it as the most important development in our history since the formation of the Commission on Re-study of the Disciples of Christ in 1934—which was an effort to restore peace to our fragmented Movement after two recent tragic divisions.

My "sunset years" are the best years of my life. My eighties are proving to be better than my seventies, just as my seventies were better than my sixties. Those in their sixties will tell you that they are better than the fifties. One's perspective is honed by the years, and one's appreciation for what really matters is enhanced. I rise around six, do floor exercises, and get in some reading, including the *New Jerusalem Bible* with its abundant footnotes by Roman Catholic scholars. Then I go for a brisk two-mile walk before joining Ouida for breakfast.

Ouida and I read to each other as part of our devotionals at breakfast (and dinner too). We are presently re-reading C. S. Lewis' *Mere Christianity*. I spend much of the day in my study and the computer room. I work the mail, answering letters and e-mails, write articles, and visit on the phone. We visit nursing homes together, keep house together, and put out our newsletter together. We are often with our daughter Phoebe and her husband Ernest Trammell, who also live in Denton. Our grandson Ashley Yeck and his wife Amy, and our only great grandchild Tyler, live in the county. Our son David (Benjy) and his wife Vickie visit from Missouri each summer. And we are blessed by numerous brothers and sisters in the Lord who come to see us from around the world.

I still visit somewhat among the churches, both far and near, frequently meeting congregations new to us. Ouida is often with me. We are also busy at our home congregation, the Singing Oaks Church of Christ in Denton. At this writing, I am doing a seven-part series to joint adult Sunday classes on Restoration history, and an extended series on the Holy Spirit at our Bible study group that meets in homes. We have cultivated strong ties of friendship and fellowship with many in our congregation. We love and are loved. They realize that I have been a controversial figure among Churches of Christ all these years—even in our own hometown—but they love me just the same.

254

The sunset years are the best of all.

I write these last paragraphs of my life story on our 58th wedding anniversary. I gave Ouida a potted plant and took her to one of our favorite restaurants. We reminisced and thanked God, not only for all the years together, but that we have had interesting things to do. And we have had dear friends with whom to do them.

I reminded Ouida of an essay I once wrote about Oliver Wendell Holmes, son of the poet of the same name and a Supreme Court justice. Near the close of his life, he referred to the cases he had tried—a thousand in all—noting that most of them were trivial and transitory.

Then the jurist said, "We cannot live our dreams. We are lucky enough if we can give a sample of our best, and if in our hearts we can feel that it has been nobly done." That well describes my own life. I have hardly realized my dreams—except in part—but it was nonetheless important to dream. Perhaps I have given a sample of my best, and I am pleased that in my heart I can feel that it was nobly done or at least nobly tried. It may be that

255

much of my life, like Holmes' life, has been trivial, but there have been many moments along the way that really mattered. Now and again I have been able to reach for the stars.

And my quarrel with my own church—sisters and brothers that I could never forsake—has not been in vain. That it was indeed a *lover's* quarrel has made the difference.

I do not ask that in the end our dear Lord will say, "Well done, good and faithful servant." If He but says, "Well tried, Leroy, well tried," that will be my glory!

When I visited the grave of dear old friend Perry Gresham in "God's Acre" at Bethany in 2000, I noticed that Elinor Lennen's poem was engraved thereon. It was a poem Perry often quoted as reflective of his own view of the meaning of life. Since I have bequeathed my body to science and will have no tomb on which to express such sentiments, I should like to engrave that same poem on my life's story, an expression of the direction I have sought for my own life.

> *Give me wide walls to build my house of life!*
> *The north shall be of love against the winds of fate,*
> *The south of tolerance that I may outreach hate.*
> *The east of faith, that rises bright and clear each day,*
> *The west of hope, that even dies a glorious way.*
> *The floor beneath my feet shall be humility,*
> *The roof, the sky itself, infinity.*
> *Give me wide walls to build my house of life!*

At home at 1300 Woodlake Drive, Denton, Texas, 76210. Come see us! Write! Soldier on!

My Testament Of Faith

I was impressed that when William Barclay, one of my favorite writers as well as one of my favorite people, did his *A Spiritual Autobiography* (1975), he included a "Testament of Faith." That statement about what he believed about various subjects was an informative supplement to his life story. It encouraged me to do something similar that might help my readers to understand better where I am coming from in my life story. These are hardly more than vignettes on subjects that could run volumes, but sometimes—as Shakespeare reminds us— "brevity is the soul of wit."

God

I often told my students how impressed I was by the teleological argument—the argument from design—for the existence of God. How can there be design without a Designer, a watch without a Watchmaker? How can there be intelligence without a higher Intelligence? It is so convincing to me that I marvel how anyone can reject it. And yet I do not try to *prove* the existence of God. The affirmation that God exists is an axiom that one accepts or rejects. It can be neither proved nor disproved. If it could be proved, it would be a matter of science rather than religion. We believe, based upon what we see as persuasive evidence, what we cannot scientifically prove. Jesus himself is our trusted witness. He never tried to prove the existence of God. He accepted it as a given, as an axiom. Jesus not only believed in God, but referred to him as "Abba, Father" —in the dearest of terms. Even though he is Creator and Ruler of the universe, He is our dear heavenly Father, who is abundant in mercy and eager to forgive.

Christ

I am awed that while we cannot see God we see in Jesus Christ the "express image of his person" and "the image of the invisible God." He is the interpreter (exegete) of God (John 1:18), and when we see him we see what God is like (John 14:9). The humanity of Jesus is as relevant as his divinity. He was "manifest in the flesh," becoming a human being like us—with all the weaknesses of humanity, except for sin itself. He was tempted in all points as ourselves. He feels our pain as well as our joy. He is our friend and companion as well as our Lord and Savior. God is in Him, reconciling the world to himself (2 Corinthians 5:19). I join Paul in exulting: "Thanks be to God for his unspeakable gift" (2 Corinthians 9:15).

Holy Spirit

While I do not use such language as "the trinity" or "triune God" – which are not biblical terms—I have no problem accepting whatever the Scriptures say about God, Christ, and the Holy Spirit. The Spirit is the helper or comforter that God gave to take Jesus' place when he left earth for heaven: a missionary to the church (John 14:6). He dwells within us, bearing witness with our spirit that we are God's children, and the Spirit helps us in our weaknesses, even making intercession for us (Romans 8:9,16,26). He thus helps us to worship God and Christ. The Spirit is given as a "guarantee" that our earthly bodies will one day take on heavenly glory (2 Corinthians 5:5). While some hymns would have us do so, I do not praise the Spirit or pray to the Spirit. I worship only God and Christ *through* the Spirit, which is what I understand the Scriptures to teach.

Church

I believe in the church as family, community, and congregation. It is the community of faith both in heaven and on earth. The church is a social entity, a body, and we are "members one of another." I disagree with those who go it alone and are a "church" unto themselves. We are to be in fellowship with "the whole family in heaven and on earth" (Ephesians 3:15). With Thomas Campbell, I believe the church is essentially, intentionally, and constitutionally one—a unity that is real even if not always realized. It is holy, apostolic, and catholic, as the ancients confessed. I accept all who are "in Christ" as making up the church—not because of, but in spite of, sectarian or denominational affiliation.

Bible

I view the Bible as Holy Scripture, the term Jesus used, rather than as the word of God, for only our Lord is ultimately "the Word of God" (Revelation 19:13). God speaks through Scripture, though some Scripture is not his word. But where God does speak through Scripture, it can be called the *written* word of God. Sometimes, as in most of the Psalms and much of Job, it is man's word: man speaking to God—not God speaking to man. But it is still Scripture, and it informs us. The Bible is a record of God's disclosure of himself through mighty deeds toward the redemption of humankind—what he says and does (facts). The Bible is also a record of the human response to that revelation. While I believe in the reliability and integrity of Scripture—and in its inspiration—in that it adequately conveys what God intends, I do not believe in its inerrancy, a claim that it does not make for itself. I also

261

believe that modern biblical research is useful—if not necessary—to understanding the nature of Scripture. I am not, therefore, a fundamentalist.

Faith

One of the great contributions of our Restoration pioneers was the proposition that faith is personal rather than doctrinal, centered in the Person of Christ. "Faithfulness" is not to be measured by loyalty to creeds and dogmas, however important these may be, but by fidelity to Jesus as Lord. One might be sincerely mistaken in doctrine, but right in his relationship to Christ. In a universal sense, faith is having a heart for God, and the Bible teaches that such faith reaches beyond biblical revelation, as is evident in such "believers" as Abram, Rahab, the Ethiopian nobleman, and Cornelius. It is this "spirit of faith" that justifies. While it is true that faith is based on testimony, as our pioneers insisted, we are to realize, as they did, that God speaks to us through three books, not just one. He reveals himself through the book of nature and the book of human nature, as well as through the book of Holy Scripture.

Baptism

It is tragic—and inexcusable—that in the history of the church baptism has become the water that divides. Baptism may well be the most beautiful and meaningful of all God's ordinances in that it is a reenactment of the gospel itself: death, burial, and resurrection. It is a beatific metaphor in that in it the believer is buried with Christ in the likeness of his death and raised in the likeness of his resurrection. It is God's work of grace in that it is something God does to us rather than something we do ourselves—the circumcision of Christ (Colossians 2:11-12). To me, the design of baptism appears in Scripture to be clearly connected to salvation (Mark 16:16), forgiveness of sins (Acts 2:38), putting on Christ (Galatians 3:27), and the answer of a good conscience (1 Peter 3:21). However, I must—due to the long history of confusion on the subject—be tolerant of divergent views. I agree with Alexander Campbell that we cannot make our position of baptism a test of fellowship.

Unity

The oneness of the church has long been my passion, and I have grown in my understanding of it. The principle that most impresses me is that unity is not ours to create, whether in unity meetings or ecumenical research, but it is God's to give. It is a gift to be received, not a work to be accomplished. We are to "preserve the unity of the Spirit in the bond of peace" (Ephesians 4:3), not to create it. Love and forbearance are the means of receiving the gift. We unite upon the center who is Christ, allowing for differences on marginal issues. The old slogan, handed down from the Protestant Reformation, and adopted by our own Movement, says it well: "In essentials, unity; in opinions, liberty; in all things, love."

Human nature

I agree with Reinhold Niebuhr that the human being is "a strange mixture of good and evil," and that the direction one's life takes toward good or evil depends on the circumstance of birth and opportunity, especially education. We are fallen beings with a propensity towards evil, but there is also something of God in us all. We are not wholly corrupt. We have capacity for philanthropy and decency. Even when Jesus spoke of us as "you being evil," he at the same time recognized that we "give good gifts" (Luke 11:13). He also spoke of the

263

"honest and good heart" and he saw noble impulses in the prodigal son in the pig pen. But that we are sinners in need of redemption is apparent enough. I suspect it is true that we sin because we are sinners, and not sinners because we sin.

World

We are in the world but not of it. We are here to bless the world by being the light of the world and the salt of the earth. In the sense that our mission is its redemption, we are to love the world, like God does. The world is interesting and challenging—calling us to greatness in service—but we are never to forget that we are pilgrims passing through. We look for that city whose builder and maker is God. When we leave planet earth we do not leave home, we go home.

Hermeneutics

In our passion for "a new hermeneutic," we may make it harder than it is, and yet I realize that biblical interpretation is not all that easy. But surely Paul (as in Ephesians 3:4) and John (as in John 20:31) wrote so as to be understood. There is virtue in Alexander Campbell's "common sense" method: "When I at last took the naked text and read it with common sense, the Bible became a new book to me." I like his rule, "We must come within understanding distance" —which is to say that heart as well as head should be involved in making sense of the Bible. One of my rules is that all Scripture must be interpreted in reference to the spirit of Christ. To put it another way, our Lord is himself the interpreter of Scripture.

Human Suffering

There appears to be no satisfactory answer to "How could a loving and powerful God have been at

Auschwitz without preventing Auschwitz?" Just as God is incomprehensible, so is meaningless suffering—particularly the suffering of the innocent. We can only endure it with trust and courage. If there is an answer, it is that Friday (suffering) is followed by Sunday (victory). In the end God wins—and he will be there for us, just as he is now with us in our suffering. The question should not be *"Why do we suffer?"* but rather *"How are we to respond to suffering?"*

Ethics

I believe in the ethics of virtue—the classical virtues (courage, generosity, honesty, loyalty) and especially the Christian virtues (love, mercy, forgiveness, self-denial). It means to take seriously the dignity of all persons—irrespective of color, race, or station in life. But not taking oneself too seriously! A sense of humor is also a virtue. The essence of "doing right" is embodied in the Golden Rule, which is found in one way or another in all the great religions—a starting point for world peace and unity.

Money

I have sought to follow these "down home" rules—live simply, live within one's means, be frugal, stay out of debt, give money away. I am convinced that the money one gives away is the money best spent. Money and things are not to possess us; we are to possess them. What wealth we have is from God; as *stewards* (a great word!), we are to use what is God's to alleviate human suffering. I like the idea of Christians dying broke.

Work

I see work as basic to life; it gives meaning to life. That is why when I can no longer be busy at something constructive, I want to be taken. Since work is inherent to life, I believe it is eternal. He who sits upon the throne has promised he will make all things new. This surely includes work—new *heavenly* work, perhaps on distant planets. This is why retirement can be a change of pace, but not a cessation of meaningful employment. I have been especially blessed in that for much of my life I've been paid for what I would have done without pay.

The Living of These Days

Alexander Campbell got it right: "We live not for time but for eternity," except that I would put it: "We live in time in view of eternity." Our time on planet earth is only part of God's plan for us. We are being made ready for the main event—or as one poet put it, life in this world is "a vale of soul-making." That is why we must live precipitously. For the sake of truth and justice, we must be willing to get our nose bloodied.

God's Tomorrow

I believe in a tomorrow—God's tomorrow. There will be a "new earth" – which may well be heaven's capital (Revelation 21:1-3), as well as "new heavens," the rest of heaven. We will have new names, new bodies, like unto Christ's body, new tenantries, new employment. Like angels, we will move about the heavenly universe, in service to God, instantaneously. We now see as through a glass darkly, but then face to face. "O the depths of the riches, both of the wisdom and knowledge of God! How unsearchable are his judgments and his ways past finding out!" (Romans 11:33)

Addendum 2
What I Want
For Churches of Christ

A listing of some of my major concerns for Churches of Christ may help the reader to understand where I am coming from better. Now that we have begun to look at ourselves more objectively as a church—even more critically—I hope these proposals might find a place on the table for discussion. While some of these items apply uniquely to Churches of Christ, most of them are more or less applicable to churches in general. If we in Churches of Christ are presently in "an identity crisis," as some of our leaders put it, it is no less the case with many denominations. Hopefully, these "musts" will be helpful in the identification process.

1. Let us recover our heritage as a unity people.

If Churches of Christ need to redefine themselves, as some of our leaders suggest, this is the place to start. The Restoration Movement was "born of a passion for unity, and unity has been its consuming theme," as Robert Richardson puts it, and its mission was "to unite the Christians in all the sects."

Alexander Campbell referred to unity as his "darling theme," and Barton Stone's motto was "Let Christian unity be our polar star." The principles they forged on a rugged frontier were unity principles; their founding documents were unity documents; their slogans were unity slogans. And they themselves, at first two separate movements, became one unity movement as early as 1832.

One would incorrectly suppose that we in Churches of Christ, with all our divisions, have a heritage of factionalism. Somewhere along the line, we got off track. We must repudiate our divisive ways, and re-connect to our true heritage. Once we see ourselves as the unity people we are supposed to be, we will position ourselves to be a blessing not only to ourselves but to the larger church as well. This is our message to divided Christendom: "In essentials, unity; in opinions (and methods), liberty; in all things, love."

There are many encouraging signs that we have begun to make this mid-course correction. A recent instance of this is a statement made by Max Lucado in an interview in the *Christian Chronicle* (July, 2002). In response to a question as to what Churches of Christ might do, Max referred to our heritage in Stone-Campbell as "the days when we did it best." Referring to how Stone and Campbell were "passionate in love" and "tolerant in controversy," he went on to say, "They accepted all who accepted Christ and disagreed agreeably."

2. Let us resolutely and absolutely renounce our more recent sectarian heritage.

Once, when I had set forth in some detail our unity heritage in Stone-Campbell, a disturbed brother said, "But that is not my heritage in Churches of Christ." He was, of course, right. Since our separation from the Disciples of Christ, which was solidified by the time of the census in 1906, we have divided or sub-divided again and again. It's not unusual for us to have four or five different kinds of Churches of Christ in the same community, none of which have any fellowship with the others. We often "solve" problems by dividing. We have divided over both opinions and methods, which is contrary to the principles that gave us birth as a people. This is what we must summarily repudiate as sinful, disgraceful, and scandalous. We must renounce our sectarian ways and reclaim our true heritage. We must proclaim with moral clarity, "We have been wrong!" — in our journals, in our schools, and in our pulpits. We must do what Roman Catholics did in 1965 at Vatican II. They repudiated their long-standing practice of rejecting other Christians as "erring schismatics" and acknowledged them as true sisters and brothers in Christ. They looked at their own history with a critical eye, decided they had been wrong, and then confessed it. We need to have our own Vatican II.

3. Let us, in particular, repudiate our historic position of making instrumental music a test of fellowship and a cause of division.

We have not been wrong in singing a cappella. All churches sometimes sing a cappella. We have been wrong in making it a test of fellowship and in allowing it to become a cause for division. We have rejected others as equals in Christ because of their use of instruments in worship. It should embarrass us that it has become a means of identifying who we are—the church that doesn't use instruments of music! Our sin has been to treat a matter of opinion (or method) as if it were an essential. We have made it part of the core gospel, when it is but a marginal issue.

Our position must now be that, while for conscience's sake we will remain non-instrumental, we will no longer make it a test of fellowship. We must now realize that instrumental music is an issue upon which Christians can differ and still be one in Christ. We can have "instrumental" churches and "non-instrumental" churches and still accept each other as equals. It is a matter of congregational preference. Some of us in Churches of Christ can even believe that for us to sing with instruments would be a sin without insisting that it is a sin for others. We can even believe that we are closer

269

to the spirit of the New Testament when we sing a cappella, as I believe, without rejecting those who differ from us.

The good news is that instrumental music is increasingly becoming a non-issue among us. But we must do more by being proactive in denouncing this sectarian dogma that has done so much harm for so long.

4. While we are to continue to be Churches of Christ, let us become what Churches of Christ truly ought to be—in the light of Scripture and our own true heritage.

I disagree with those progressive, avant garde Churches of Christ who seek to escape legalism and sectarianism by leaving their heritage and becoming some other kind of church. They change their name to something other than "Church of Christ." They risk throwing out the baby with the bath. Rather than to renounce their heritage, let them resolve to be what they believe a true "Church of Christ" should be. If one's mission is to help renew and reform the church, it is a mistake to leave. Changes are best effected from within. Just as a leopard cannot change its spots, we cannot change who we are. We are not Lutherans or Presbyterians or Baptists or Methodists. We are who we are: Churches of Christ with our own distinct history and heritage.

We are to grow and bear fruit where we have been planted. If we need to make changes—and we do—then let the work begin from within in a loving and forbearing way. We do not help our people by leaving. Those we can help the most are our own people. We are to stay put and work for renewal where we are: a solution I would advise for every concerned believer, regardless of denomination. We are adrift when we become a "cut flower" people, separated from our roots.

This appeal conforms to Scripture. Most all the

churches in the New Testament had something wrong with them. The "faithful" among them were never told to leave and start a "loyal" church. The church at Sardis was "dead," but there were a "few" who "walked with Christ" (Revelation 3:4). They didn't walk out—but did their walking where they were, in that church!

5. *Let us become part of the body of Christ at large, cooperating with other Christians in the work of redeeming the world.*

We can do this without surrendering any truth we hold, and without approving of any error on the part of others. We can work with other believers, not because we agree on every doctrinal issue, but because of our common devotion to Jesus Christ. There is truth in the adage, "Service unites; dogma divides." Those who build a "Habitat" house together or join hands to help in some natural disaster learn that doctrinal differences become marginal, while their mutual love for Christ moves to the center. As our communities become more pluralistic, with Buddhists and Muslims as our neighbors, we Christians are coming to see that we have far more in common than not.

As we experience unity in mutual service with other Christians, we may all come to see the inappropriateness of our sects and denominations. Like Barton W. Stone, we may eventually be willing to say of our own Churches of Christ, "Let this body die, be dissolved, and sink into union with the body of Christ at large." When that day comes—no more denominations, just the body of Christ—we will have realized the dream of our pioneers. That is who we are—or who we are supposed to be!

6. Let us reject our radical congregationalism and become more responsibly organized for the tasks before us.

We have yet to learn what Alexander Campbell taught over a century ago—that the church is more than the sum total of its congregations. No local church, nor group of area churches, can do what the church as a whole can do. We have paid a heavy price for what we call "congregational autonomy," given all our duplicate programs, ineffectiveness, and work left undone. Considering the restrictions we have imposed on ourselves, based on the myth that it is biblical, it is amazing that we do as well as we do.

If we were properly organized for missionary and benevolent work—with centralized ministries responsible to the congregations—the results would be remarkable! We organize for maximum results in all other areas of life—businesses, schools, government, social agencies. Only our churches are required to limp along with an incompetent polity.

7. Let us become more responsibly biblical.

This must start by correcting some fallacies that have been our undoing, beginning with the "restorationist" mentality or the patternistic method of interpretation. The myth that there is in the New Testament a golden age of pristine purity of the church that we are to "restore" in our day has had deadly consequences. Our leaders have seen that "pure church" or "the pattern" in different ways, and, by assuming that it can be only one way, they have produced faction upon faction, each claiming to be the true church built "according to the pattern."

The basic fallacy has been to make the New Testament into something that it is not. We have supposed that the New Testament produced the church, when in fact it was the church that produced the New Testament. The earliest churches could not have been built "according to the pattern" (the New Testament), for they existed for generations before there was the New Testament! Those churches were the result of the *kerugma* (the thing preached) or the apostolic proclamation of the gospel. They were guided by the *didache* or the teaching of the apostles, which included the teachings of Christ that they passed along. As time passed, those churches had problems and needed further instruction, so the apostles and evangelists wrote letters to address those problems. After a generation or so, the "gospels" were written, preserving stories about the teachings of Jesus. When these were all canonized several generations later, it came to be called the New Testament.

We can say, then, that out of the experiences of the first-century community of faith—the apostolic congregations—came the New Testament. That makes it a vital witness to what the church is to be (or not to be) and therein is revealed the word of God, but this does not make it a detailed pattern for all aspects of church life for all ages to come. The New Testament is more *descriptive* of what the church should be (or not be), than *prescriptive*, as if a code of law. This is why unity is in diversity rather than in conformity. This is why the demand for conformity—interpreting the pattern *my* way—produces factions.

If Alexander Campbell had his way, one would approach the Bible with a common sense method. That meant to Campbell that the Bible should be read as one would read any other literature, by the rules of common sense. He proposed one rule that is particularly informing—*we must come within understanding distance.* He meant that we are to read with the heart as well as the head. It was the rule our Lord gave in John 7:17: "If anyone wants to do his will, he shall know concerning the doctrine." Understanding begins with

273

the heart's desire.

As for a practical hermeneutics, one could hardly do better than Campbell's approach to the Bible: "Experience has taught me that to get a victory over the world, over the love of fame, and to hold in perfect contempt human honor, adulation, and popularity, will do more to make the New Testament intelligible, than all the commentators that ever wrote" (*Mill. Harb*, 1830, p. 138).

I suggest one basic rule of interpretation, a negative one, that I call "the spirit of Christ rule." I think it will prove to be liberating, especially for us in Churches of Christ: *No interpretation is to be accepted that runs counter to the spirit of Christ.* That means that if Jesus would not believe it or accept it, we should not. We are to interpret the Bible in reference to Christ, not the other way around. The Scriptures are subject to Christ, not Christ to the Scriptures. We are not to mutilate the Lord, cutting Him down to our size, so as to make him fit our view of Scripture.

If one interprets certain Scriptures to support slavery, racism, or segregation, then we must reject the interpretation, however logical it may appear—for it runs counter to the spirit of Christ. Likewise, when the Bible is used to justify division among Christians, to impose a gender test in the life of the church, or to treat divorced people as less than equal, we are to resist. We have preachers who can quote verses endlessly to prove that "We are right and all others are wrong," but is the conclusion consistent with the spirit of Christ?

8. *Let us realize who the enemy is.*

We have fought among ourselves long enough, dividing into warring factions. We have too long declared war on "the sects" or "the denominations." The enemy is not that other Church of Christ across town with which we have no fellowship. Nor is the

274

enemy the Baptists, Methodists, or Presbyterians—not even the Catholics!

If this was the mentality of Churches of Christ in our earlier history, don't suppose that we have it completely behind us. We are still reluctant to have anything to do with other churches. And those we still call "denominational preachers" are seldom, if ever, guests in our pulpits. We treat other churches and other Christians as if they were the enemy.

Since we as Christians are at war, it is vital to know who the enemy is. The New Testament describes our enemy as "the rulers of the darkness of this age" and as "the spiritual hosts of wickedness in the heavenly places" (Ephesians 6:12). He or it is further described as "arguments and every high thing that exalts itself against the knowledge of God" (2 Corinthians 10:5). In 1 Peter 5:8, "the devil" is named as our adversary, and he is likened to a roaring lion on the prowl seeking whom he may devour.

If we take our warfare too lightly, it may be because we don't realize the deadly power of the enemy. The modern church might be likened to the society lady at a garden party who was told there was a lion loose in the neighborhood: "Really?" she said, as she took another bite of her cucumber salad. Once we take measure of our enemy in all his horrid reality, we will be more likely to circle the wagons with all other believers, including those we once supposed to be our adversaries, and fight the good fight together.

9. Let us cease shooting our own wounded.

We sometimes reject our sisters and brothers in Christ when they need us most. It may be when they are going through a divorce, or when once divorced, they plan to remarry. Some have made a big issue out of "divorce and remarriage," treating it as an unpardonable sin. They would even break up homes, causing even

275

deeper wounds, on the pretext that the couple is "living in adultery"—even when they now have a second family and have their lives back on track!

When Homer Hailey, one of my professors at ACC in the 1940s, sought to correct such pharisaical brutality in a liberating book on the subject, our people shot *him*, branding him as a "false teacher." They didn't hesitate to consign him in his old age to a life of rejection, even after seventy years of faithful service. As incredible as it may seem, it was seriously debated in some journals whether Homer Hailey could be "fellowshipped" – because he at last, in his old age, revealed that he held a different view on divorce and remarriage!

We've been known to shoot our missionaries in the field if they become "liberal" or depart from the party line through exposure to the larger Christian world, leaving them to get home the best they can. And many a preacher has been fired the same afternoon of the Sunday he gave that "moving" sermon!

We haven't been pastoral to our troubled people. A preacher with gnawing doubts has to keep them to himself. A teacher hesitates to say anything "different" in his or her class, however liberating the idea might be (as do those in the class). A sister who delights in her exciting experiences at Bible Study Fellowship is reluctant to reveal what she's been up to. And if one is troubled about his or her sexuality—whether he or she might be gay or lesbian—it is just as well to deal with the problem alone. Like many other churches, we shoot our rejects. We have had a bad habit of neglecting the heart.

Our Lord sought to redeem the wounded rather than to condemn them. He was compassionate and merciful towards the ostracized of society. He even died for them. We must learn to be like him.

10. Let us bring women into the church as equals; let us cease being male-dominated.

It must impress visitors to our assemblies as odd that our services are exclusively led by men. Women do not even have such servant roles as making announcements or serving at the Lord's table. Little boys may pass out attendance cards, but not little girls. Teenage boys may read Scripture and lead prayer, but not teenage girls or adult women. Among churches generally, we are virtually alone in our model of being all-male. We are open to the charge of being "a chauvanistic church." Do we really believe that this is biblical?

If we claim that Scripture mandates such a stance, we have some explaining to do, for the Bible has it both ways when it comes to the woman's role in the assembly. If one passage requires her to be silent (1 Corinthians 14:34), another says she may speak—even preach or prophesy—if she has her head covered (1 Corinthians 11:5). If one verse says she is not to teach but be in subjection to man (1 Timothy 2:12), another tells of an evangelist who had four daughters who were preachers (Acts 21:8)! Moreover, an inspired apostle insisted that ,just as there is to be no racial test in the church, there is to be no gender test—for we are all equal in Christ (Galatians 3:28).

This problem is not beyond solution when we recognize that, while most apostolic teaching is permanent and always applicable, some is temporary and applicable only to a given situation. It is evident that some commands or examples were temporary in nature: communal living in Acts 4:32; kosher food in Acts 15:29; the holy kiss in 2 Corinthians 13:12; long hair for women in 1 Corinthians 11:15; and washing feet in John 13:14. While any of these might still be practiced by the church—as some sects do—the church has generally seen them as culturally determined.

Why then can't this be the case with the passages

277

that subjugate the woman? Were they too not dictated by cultural conditions? In first-century Corinth, it is understandable that Paul would say "It is a shame for a woman to speak in the assembly" (1 Corinthians 14:35). Since it was seen as inappropriate for a woman to speak in *any* assembly in that culture, he enjoined against it in the church. But would Paul say the same things today in a culture where women address, with complete acceptance, every conceivable kind of assembly in the world?

Paul's language in Gal. 3:28 is of a different nature. He lays down an eternal principle—in the church there is to be no distinction made in reference to race, sex, or social standing. Never! The apostle wrote that in a world where upward of half the world's population was in slavery, women were marginalized, and there was a social caste system. The church was caught up in all that; the apostle presented an ideal that was beyond where the church was at the time.

Is not the church today to reflect the ideal—no racism, no class distinctions, no gender tests? None! This is a double imperative for Churches of Christ. If we don't become more Christian in our treatment of women, we will come up short of being part of the "one, holy, catholic, and apostolic church." We will, moreover, compromise our witness to a culture that is increasingly giving women their proper place.

11. Let there be renewal in our assemblies.

We must find ways to make our assemblies more exciting and fulfilling. I've long been persuaded that many of our people attend out of duty more than out of joy. They often leave dissatisfied, if not discouraged. We are losing a lot of people to the newer churches—a problem for all mainline denominations. In this postmodern era, denominational loyalty has less appeal and there is a lot of "church shopping" going on. The growing churches today are not enlisting people from the world as much as from other churches. Whether we like it or not, churches are in competition with each other.

Our preaching often lacks passion and a sense of urgency, and even when it is soundly biblical, it may be neither relevant nor interesting. Preachers who are good storytellers and apt illustrators seem to be the most effective. It may be true that preachers are not to be entertainers, but there is nothing wrong with being interesting! I've been impressed with two essential rules for the preacher: he must be sincere and he must be enthusiastic. Two other rules can always be added: he must have something to say and know how to say it. If the one in the pulpit lacks any of these, his hearers are deprived.

We don't take the public reading of Scripture seriously enough, and we don't do it well enough. We seem to think that anyone can read the Bible before a congregation, including novices. It should be taken as seriously and given the same careful preparation as preaching or teaching. After all, God is speaking to the church through the reading of Scripture. When a congregation *stands* in reverence before and open Bible and hears God's word read well, it can be the most uplifting part of the service. Recently, I heard a woman reading Scripture over the radio. I was so impressed that I called Ouida to listen. I said to her, "If we could only have reading like that in our assemblies!" But that gifted woman wouldn't even be allowed to read in our churches! Perhaps that is why we don't read well. We have less than half the congregation from which to select the readers—and it is probable that our most gifted readers are among those against whom we discriminate!

It is not all that different with our public prayers. It's not just any one who can take a congregation before God's throne in prayer. Prayer can be and should be edifying, and sometimes even awing. If there are but few

279

who have the gift of public prayer, then only those few should be called on—until others cultivate the gift. The one thing the apostles asked Jesus to teach them was to pray. Yes, one can be taught to pray. Only those who are "taught" in public prayer should be used. And those who have learned to lead public prayer know better than to impose long, tedious, repetitious, boring prayers upon a helpless congregation.

It is in music that Churches of Christ have historically excelled—and with grace. All these years, we have sung heartily and we have sung well, generally speaking, and always a cappella. The irony is that it is our music that is the most troubling issue these days. Lynn Anderson has told us for years that "Music is the coin of the realm" and that if we do not get with it in our singing we will be left behind. This might call for special music, which challenges one more of our sacred cows. It certainly calls for spiritually-exciting, well-prepared "making melody in the heart."

The churches that have heeded Lynn's warning and are making music the coin of the realm are growing, and they are miles ahead of the other churches. One big change is the use of praise teams, which are not unlike cheerleaders at a basketball game. They rev it up, which is not exactly like us! And those who do it best have a good mix of both new songs and the great hymns of the church, which has been a point of contention. Even in renewal—especially in renewal—there should be, and must be, balance.

There must also be reformation at the Lord's table. Let us begin by being more biblical in that we use "the words of institution" like Jesus did, which we usually neglect to do. It warms our hearts to hear our Lord say, "This is my body, which is broken for you" and "This is my blood of the new covenant, which is shed for many for the remission of sins." We should hear these words each time we commune together, and we do not have to editorialize with such language as "This *represents* his body." Allow the mystery to remain in what Jesus actually said, "This is my body ... This is my blood." In some churches, the participants say these words to each other as they serve one another.

And let us do away with the Matzo crackers and quit serving crumbs. The Greek word usually rendered *bread* actually means *loaf.* Let's place a loaf of bread on the table—such as a large French loaf, which would beautifully symbolize our unity—and break the loaf together. It is another of our myths that it must be unleavened bread. Jesus simply "took bread (the loaf)." In the Orient, I have "broken rice" with believers, the only bread they had. If Jesus took unleavened bread, he didn't *choose* it. Since it was Passover, unleavened bread would have been the only bread in the house, but still a loaf or loaves.

Cracker crumbs violate the symbolism of the apostle's language, "We, being many, are one loaf, and one body, for we all partake of that one loaf" (1 Corinthians 10:17). And it is a *table* we gather around, not an altar. It is not a call for repentance and forgiveness, but of fellowship and celebration. It would be exciting if "around the table" we shared with each other what Jesus means to us, or use it as an opportunity to share our love for each other.

You may have noticed that I have not referred to these things as *worship.* I am not calling for renewal of our "worship services," but renewal of our assembly. To recognize this difference is itself part of the renewal I seek. The New Testament makes no reference to a "worship service," and the things we call worship— preaching, singing, reading, Lord's supper—are never called that in Scripture. Worship, which means to bow down to God, is the whole of the believer's life. Taking a child to the park is as much worship as singing; going to work is worship as much as prayer. Believers are already worshippers when they assemble at 9:45 A.M. on Sunday to "begin worship."

Such notions as "the call to worship" or "the five acts of worship" – and that worship begins and ends at set times—have led us to strange and irrational conclusions. We can sing with an instrument at home but not at church because "it is not part of the worship"! A visiting college choir may not perform "during worship," so we dismiss the service—worship ends—and then the choir may sing, which is not worship! Such dogma cons us into believing that we worship God only at church, and only at a certain hour.

It all reflects a gross misconception of the nature of the assembly, which is not "to worship God" – we're already worshipping him! – but to edify and encourage one another, and to remember our Lord around his table. It is an assembly of the saints, not a "worship service."

It is refreshing to attend the Garden Ridge Church of Christ in Lewisville, Texas where this is understood. There are no "Hours of Worship" but "Time of Assembly," and no "Order of Worship" but "Assembly Schedule." There are no invitations to "worship with us" but to "assemble with us." The members probably realize that if they sing hymns on a piano at home it is as much "worship" as if done in the assembly of the saints!

Finally, the assembly must somehow be rescued from the predominance of the professional minister—assuming that we are for the time being stuck with "the minister system." God has called every Christian to be a minister, and we must find ways for this to be realized in our assemblies. We might start with a different view of the assembly. If it is like a theater, then the people are not to be the audience (which is the way it is now) but the performers. God, the angels, and all of heaven are the audience. The minister or leader is the prompter, not the entertainer or the performer.

An example of this might be the story Steve Eckstein told me about what he did some years ago at his

282

assembly in Portalis, New Mexico. Rather than his usual sermon on this particular Lord's day, he told the congregation, "We're going to talk about what Jesus means to us." The microphone was passed to those in the pews. Several gave moving testimonies, men and women alike. Steve said an aged sister, longtime member of the congregation, spoke in the assembly for the first time ever. Her account of how the Lord had been both Friend and Savior during a very difficult life touched the hearts of all those present. The saints went on to embrace each other as sisters and brothers. They sang and prayed together, and broke bread together. Steve said it was his most memorable assembly.

On that particular Lord's day, Steve Eckstein, the minister, was not the entertainer or the performer, but the prompter. The people were the performers. God was the audience, and we can believe that he was well pleased.

12. Let us be a colony of heaven—Cross-shaped, grace-oriented, Spirit-filled.

My favorite image of the church is that of "We are a colony of heaven," as one modern version renders Philippians 3:20. Other versions read, "Our citizenship is in heaven." The apostle Paul may have been drawing an analogy between the city of Philippi, which, as a Roman colony, was to reflect the glory of Rome, its capital, and the community of believers as an outpost of heaven. As Philippi was a colony of Rome, the church was to be a colony of heaven, reflecting its goodness and beauty.

That sums up what I see as the ongoing reformation of the church. We are always in the crucible of becoming more like Christ. The ultimate destiny of the church is Christlikeness, both in this world and the next. As a colony of heaven we await our Lord's coming, who at that time will transform our bodies into the body of his

283

glory. We, therefore, will eventually be like him in body as well as in spirit.

That makes us Cross-shaped, a people crucified *with* Christ and crucified *to* the world. It means we are grace-minded and grace-oriented, a people who are what we are—a redeemed community—only by the grace of God. As a Spirit-filled people we bear the fruit of Christlikeness—his love, longsuffering, forgiveness.

This is what I want for my people in Churches of Christ: to be a people who bear witness to the Cross by being themselves a cruciform church; to be a people saved and sustained by God's grace; and to be a people not drunk on the wine of self-importance, but filled with the Holy Spirit.

Index

A

Abilene Christian College (University), 19, 20, 35-39, 49, 51, 65, 77, 183, 184, 218, 220, 230, 244, 251
ACU Press, xiv, 221
Allen, F. G., 27
Allen, Leonard, 247
American Association of University Professors, 97, 103
"An Address to the Churches of Christ," 194
Anderson, Lynn, 280
Andrews, Donald H., 112
Aristotle, 100, 107
Armour, Mike, 252
Armstrong, Jim, 152, 153
Arndt, William F., 53
Annual Denton Lectures, 125, 233-234
Annual Unity Forum, 90, 133, 134, 137
Atchley, Rick, ix
Arthur, William, 150
Atlanta Christian College, 133
Auer, J. A. C., 60-61

B

Bacon, Francis, 30, 98
Bacon, Margaret Hope, 58
Baird, James, 20, 30, 47
Bakewell, Selina (Campbell), 118
Bales, James D., 74, 116-117, 234
Banta, Doyle, 71

Barclay, Julian, 91-92
Barclay, William, 146, 161, 259
B. D. Phillips Lecture, 216
Bell, Buddy, 123
Baylor University, 222
Beck, Mack and Shirley, 176
Belcher, Gilmer, 36, 41
Berrier, Mark, 108
Bethany College, 82, 86, 88-91, 133, 211, 216-217
Bevis, Jim, 195
Bible Talk, 67-70, 76, 79, 80, 104, 111, 185
Bilak, Epi Stephan, 181
Bishop College, 102-106, 109
Blackwood, Andrew W., 48
Blakemore, W. B., 147, 149
Blampeid, Ray and Marge, 173
Bland, Billy, 187
Blowers, Paul, 211
Boles, H. Leo, 21
Boll, R. H., 21
Boone, Archie and Margaret, 121
Boone, Pat and Shirley, 121
Boston University, 61
Brannum, C. W., 71
Brewer, G. C., 69
Brigance, L. L., 20, 29
British Millennial Harbinger, 199
Brown, Margaret, 89
Browning, Don, 252
Brooker, David and Heather, 169
Brooker, Ron and Dot, 171-172
Brush Run Church, 89, 190-191
Bryant, "Bear," 7
Buttrick, George, 90

C

Cadbury, Henry J., 57-60, 62, 84

Campbell, Alexander, xii, 42, 53, 61, 67, 69, 83, 84, 87-89, 90, 92, 93, 112, 113, 117-118, 120, 129, 135, 149-151, 154, 170, 172, 173, 183-191, 197-200, 208, 210, 212-214, 222, 227, 238, 241, 247, 251, 262-263, 265, 267, 272-273

Campbell, Joan, 177

Campbell, Margaret (Brown), 89, 118

Campbell, Selina (Bakewell), 118

Campbell, Thomas, 90, 130, 148, 149, 150, 154, 187, 192, 212, 226, 261

Campbell, Wycliffe, 92

Cannon, Bob, 121

Carlingford Theological College (Australia), 172

Carrilet, George, 180

Cawyer, W. F., 134

Chafer, Lewis, 45, 47

Chapman, Graeme and Eileen, 172

Chiang Kai-Shek, 143-145, 168

Chiangmai Bible Institute, 156

Chick-A-Go-Go, 109-110

Christian Baptist, 203, 210, 219

Christian, C. W., 222

Christian Chronicle, 268

Christian Standard, 108, 213, 215

Churches of Christ
  Airline (Bossier City, LA), 248
  Allen (TX), 249
  Amite (LA), 248
  Amy (Cooper, TX), 25
  Argyle (TX), 249
  Aubry (TX), 249
  Bering Drive (Houston, TX), 221
  Blaney Avenue (Cupertino, CA), 133
  Broadway (Lubbock, TX), 137
  Brookline (MA), 249
  Blytheville (AR), 30
  Brookvalley (Atlanta, GA), 221
  Buckingham Road (Garland, TX), 249

Burbank Gardens (Grand Prairie, TX), 249
Burke Road (Pasadena, TX), 221
Cahaba Valley (Birmingham, AL), 228
Calico Rock (AR), 248
Castlemilk (Scotland), 150
Causeway (Mandeville, LA), 248
Cedars (Wilmington, DE), 248
Central Arlington (Arlington, TX), 249
Central/Plymouth Park (Irving, TX), 221
Chisholm (AL), 52
"Commonly Called Glasites or Sandemanians"
    (Scotland), 151
Coplaw (Scotland), 150
Dawson (Australia), 169
Dayspring (Durant, OK), 249
Downtown (El Paso, TX), 249
East First Street (Dumas, TX), 249
Eastside (Terre Haute, IN), 248
Eastview (Miami, OK), 249
Eatontown (NJ), 51
Farmers Branch (TX), 221
Forest Home (Franklin, TN), 250
Forest Mill (Manchester, TN), 250
Garden Ridge (Lewisville, TX), 249, 282
Golf Road (Midland, TX), 249
Greater Portland (ME), 52, 249
Grote Street (Australia), 170
Hampton Place (Dallas, TX), 44, 130
Henderson (TN), 28
Highland (Abilene, TX), 36
Hobart City (Australia), 173
Horsham (Australia), 169
Howrah (Australia), 172
International (Boston), 172
Lafayette (Ballwin, MO), 249
Lake Highlands (Dallas, TX), 221
Landmark (Montgomery, AL), viii, ix, 248
Laurel (DE), 52

Liberty Street (Trenton, NJ), 46, 51, 221, 249
Memorial Drive (Tulsa, OK), 249
Murry River (Canada), 176
North Park (Abilene, TX), 36, 39
North Central (Indianapolis, IN), 248
Northside (Santa Ana, CA), 248
Oak Cliff (Dallas, TX), 15, 19
Oak Hills (San Antonio, TX), ix
Old Park (Ukraine), 181
Ochanomizu (Tokyo, Japan), 155
Park Hill (Ft. Worth, TX), 249
Pearl Street (Denton, TX), 233, 235
Pecan Grove (Greenville, TX), 249
Pennyrile (Madisonville, KY), 244
Pitman Creek (Plano, TX), 249
Point Sturt (Australia), 170
Pond Springs (Austin, TX), 250
Portland Avenue (Louisville, KY), 248
Quaker Avenue (Lubbock, TX), 137, 221, 250
Round Rock (TX), 250
Singing Oaks (Denton, TX), xiv, 235, 250, 254
Southeast (Louisville, KY), 248
Speedway (Indianapolis, IN), 248
St. Andrews (New Zealand), 174
Sunset (Dallas, TX), 19, 23
Tabernacle (NJ), 52
Thackerville (OK), 249
Tom's River (NJ), 51
Town West (Taylor, TX), 250
Troy (MI), 249
University (Conway, AR), 221
Vandelia (Lubbock, TX), 250
Welch Street (Denton, TX), 235
Westworth (Ft. Worth, TX), 250
West Amarillo (Amarillo, TX), 250
Westchester (Los Angeles, CA), 221
West Islip (NY), 133
Westside (Beaverton, OR), 249

Westport Road (Louisville, KY), 248
White's Ferry Road (Monroe, LA), 231, 233
Wollongong (Australia), 172
Woodland West (Arlington, TX), 250
Woodmont Hills (Nashville, TN), ix, 250

Churches of Christ of the 20th Century, The, 250
Churches of Christ Theological College (Australia), 172
Clark, Harvey, 169
Clevenger, Eugene, 20
Cochran, Louis and Bess, 186
Colley, Flavil, 131
Compton, Ron, 134
Conant, James Bryant, 5, 56, 62-63
Concordia Seminary, 53-54
Connolly, Andrew, 235
Coulter, David and Ann, 174
Crimean Christian College, 180
Crow, Paul, 147
Curry, Melvin, 102
Cutts, Jack; Ross; Walter; Ernest, 52

D

Dallas Christian College, 106-108, 214
Dallas Times Herald, 45
Dallas Theological Seminary, 45, 47
Dampier, Joe, 214
Daniel Baker College, 18, 32
Darnell, David R., 116
(David) Lipscomb University, 117, 211
Davies, Eliza, 170-171
Davis, Chris, 223-224
Davis, John, 42
Davis, Phil, 206-207
Davis, M. M., 183
Davis, W. O., 30
Dawson, Ken and Erma, 169

Dean E. Walker Memorial Lecture, 213-214
Declaration and Address, The, 192-193
DeGroot, A. T., 134, 217
DeHoff, George, 70
Dennis, Allen, ix, 123, 251
Denton High School, 82, 100-101, 243
Descartes, Rene, 98
DeWelt, Don, 138, 139, 203, 204
Dillenberger, John, 63
Disciples of Christ Historical Society, 207, 209-211,
    216
Dixon, H. A., 71-72, 75
Dodd, C. H., 128, 129, 238
Dobson, Ken, 158
Duncan, Heather, 251-252
Dunn, G. A., Sr., 19, 21, 45, 71

E

Eckstein, Steve, 282-283
Eddy, Sherwood, 85
Educational Philosophy of Alexander Campbell, The, 43
Ellis, Carroll, 134
Emerson, Ralph Waldo, 56
Emmanuel School of Religion, 214, 216
Encyclopedia of the Stone-Campbell Movement, 207,
    251
Endsley, E. R., 20, 29
Erasmus, Desiderius, 71
Etter, Carl L., 117
Eubanks, Allen and Joan, 157
European Evangelistic Society, 213
Evans, Jack, 229

F

Fanning, Tolbert, 69
Farmer, Keith and Margaret, 172

Faulkner University, 52
Ferguson, Everett, 136
Fiers, A. Dale, 133
Fife, Robert O., 136, 147
Filbeck, David and Delores, 157
Firm Foundation, 225
Flew, Anthony, 234
Ford, Arthur, 85-87
Ford, Henry, 208
Foster, Douglas A., 138, 211, 219, 220, 252, 253
Fox, Logan J., 117
Fudge, Edward, 134
Franklin, Benjamin, 69
Franklin, Cecil, 117
Freed-Hardeman College/University, 19-22, 27-33,
    35, 36, 52, 56, 71, 73-77, 108, 183, 231
Frost, Robert, xi
Folsom, James "Big Jim," 53
Fritsch, Charles T., 48
Fuller, Andrew and Kathy, 159

G

Gardiner, Andrew, 150
Garrett, Annie Olive (Heath), 2, 11-13, 24
Garrett, Beeler, 5, 9
Garrett, Benjamin Joseph, 1, 24
Garrett, Clyde, 4, 5
Garrett, David Benjamin "Benjy" and Vickie, 88, 93,
    110, 161-162, 232, 254
Garrett, James Leo, 222
Garrett, Joann "Toer," 6, 12
Garrett, Olin, 3, 13
Garrett, Ouida (Pitts), xiv, 13, 25, 43-44, 47-48, 52-
    53, 62, 73-74, 77, 91, 93-94, 105, 109-110, 142,
    150, 158, 161, 163-165, 170-171, 173-177, 215,
    233-236, 244, 246, 254, 279
Garrett, Philip Herbert, 93-94, 110

Garrett, Ray, 4, 6
Garrett, William J. "Bill," 6-7, 12
Garrett, Zinn, 5, 9, 17
Garrison, W. E., 197
Garst, Charles E., 155
Gehman, Henry S., 50-51
Gingrich, G. W., 53
Glasgow University, 149
Goble, Elmer, 38
Goff, Clyde, 134
Goodpasture, B. C., 21, 70
Goodspeed, Edgar, 227
Gospel Advocate, 69, 70, 75, 111
Gospel Guardian, 76
Graham, Billy, 131, 226
Graham, Ralph, 36, 37, 46, 47, 49, 51, 117
Gregory, Mike, 101
Gresham, Charles, 136, 138
Gresham, Perry and Aleese, 88, 89, 90, 92, 133-138,
    217, 256
Griffin, Barry, 170
Griffin, Robert, 251

H

Hailey, Homer, 21, 33, 36, 42, 183, 239, 275-276
Haldane, James and Robert, 151
Hall, W. Claude, 20, 21, 29, 31
Hamm, Richard L., 253
Hancock, Ralph, 109
Hardeman, Dorsey, 21
Hardeman, N. B., 19-24, 28, 29, 31-33, 35, 36, 43,
    56, 183
Hardeman, Mrs. N. B. ("Miss Jo"), 21, 22
Hardeman, Pat, 117, 133
Hardin, Arnold, 133, 134
Harding Graduate School of Religion, 251
Harding, James A., 69

293

Harding College/University, 20, 74
Harrell, David Edwin Jr., 250-251
Hartford Forum, 136
Harvard University, 54, 55-65, 75, 80, 244
Hawkins, Jack, 38
Headen, Jerry and Pam, 157
Heeter, Gabriel, 8
Herring, Cliff and Norma, 176
Herring, Jane, 177
Highers, Alan, 125
Hines, J. L., 19, 23
Holmes, Oliver Wendell, 255
Holt, Charles, 71, 134
Holt, Jack, 76
Hook, Cecil, 247
Hope, Norman V., 48
Hopkins, A. C., 135
Houtz, Laverne, 134
Howe, John, 147
Hromadka, Joseph A., 48
Hudson, Charles, 52
Hughes, Richard, 218, 219
Hull, William, 71

I

Ibaraki Christian College, 155

J

Jackson, D. N., 38
Jacobs, Lyndsay and Lorraine, 213
James A. Garfield Award, 215
James F. Cox Speech Contest, 36
James, Ivory, 228-230
Jefferson, Thomas, xii-xiv
Johnson Bible College, 76, 216
Johnson, Ed, 109

Johnson, John T., 200
Johnson, Leonard, 52
Jones, Joseph, 180
Jurji, Edward J., 48

K

Karekin I (Catholicos of Armenian Church), 179
Ketcherside, Carl, v, ix, 67, 76, 78, 84, 112, 125-126, 128-139, 218, 222, 225, 228, 231, 233, 238, 239, 247, 251
Key, Roy, 117
King, David, 199
King, Martin Luther, Jr., 105, 230
Kirkpatrick, Lawrence V., 134
Knox, John, 151
Knowles, Victor, 138
Koone, Dorothy, xiv
Kurfees, M. C., 135
Kyker, Rex, 36

L

Lambert, O. C., 38
Langford, Thomas, 133, 134, 138
Lard, Moses E., 69
Last Time Around/Once More With Love, 246-247
Last Will and Testament of the Springfield Presbytery, The, 208
Lawton, Eugene, 229
Leaven, 251
Lee, Allan, 147, 212-213
Ledlow, Roger, 247
Leggett, Marshall, 226
Lemmons, Reuel, 225, 231, 232
Lennen, Elinor, 256
Lewis, C. S., 254
Lewis, Jack, 146

Lewis, LeMoine, 64-65
Lilly Endowment, 81, 82, 99-100
Lincoln Christian College, 216
Lipscomb, David, 69, 111, 211, 247
Loetscher, Lefferts A., 48
Lovel, Jimmy, 76
Lowell, James Russell, 103
Lown, W. F., 134
Lubbock Christian College/University, 133
Lucado, Max, ix, 268
Luther, Martin, xii, 53, 71, 181, 184, 188-189, 208, 239
Lynn, Mac, 222

M

Mackay, John A., 48
Mackey, Jack and Joan, 176
MacMurray College, 80, 81-83, 85, 88
Mahoning Baptist Association, 190
Maritime Christian Fellowship, 176
Maritime Christian College, 177
Massey, George, 94
Masterton, Ken, 169, 172
Maxwell, James, 229
McAllister, Lester, 210
McCallon, Earl, 243
McCallon, Mark and Beverly, 243-244
McCullough, Victor, 177
McGarvey, J. W., 27, 29
McLean, Archibald, 89
McLean Institute, 158
Memoirs of Alexander Campbell, The, 198
Metzger, Bruce M., 48-49
Meyers, Robert, 116
Miller, Perry, 61
Milligan College, 133, 216, 226
Millennial Harbinger, The, 42, 184, 198, 203

Mills, John, 252
Mission Messenger, v-vi
Mitchell, Dan, 150
Money, Royce, 137, 234
Montgomery Bible College, 52, 80
Moody, Dale, 238
Moore, George Foote, 61
Moore, W. T., 67
Morfew, Ray and Gwen, 173
Morgan, Peter, 211, 253
Morris, Don H., 32, 37
Morrison, Philip, 253
Mossman, Charles, 36
Mother Teresa, xii
Moyer, Lloyd, 134
Murch, James DeForest, 134
Music, Goebel, 187

N

Nakarai, Toyozo, 214
Neal, Denton, 71
New Jerusalem Bible, 254
Newland, Wayne and Alice, xiv, 52
Newton, John, 188
Nichols, Gus, 21, 33
Niebuhr, Reinhold, 263
Nock, A. D., 60
Nomura, Moto and Yorika, 155
Norris, Louis W., 81
North American Christian Convention, 226
North, James B., 253

O

Oklahoma Christian College (University), 20, 251-252
Olbricht, Tom, 134, 219
Oliphant, W. L., 15, 19

Oliver, A. C. and Ruth, 176
Oneil, Rhoda, 177
Osborn, Ronald, 193, 208
"Our Heritage At Its Best," 213
Overstreet, Harry and Bonaro, 112
Owen, Robert, 189
Ozark Christian College, 137

P Q

Paton, Jack, 150
Paul Quinn College, 102
Peck, M. Scott, 189
Pendleton, William. 89
Pennybacker, Albert, 177
Pepperdine University, 117, 216, 218, 220, 221, 251
Pfeiffer, Robert H., 61
Phillips, B. D., 216-217
Phillips, J. D., 132, 151
Phillips, Richard, 134
Phillips, Thomas W., 216
Phillips University, 217
Philosophy In High School, 82
Pike, James, 87
Piper, Otto A., 48
Pitts, D.B.; Mr. and Mrs. (Mother Pitts), 43, 46, 163
Plato, 100, 107
Powers, Mary Nell, 20
Princess Diana, 175-176
Princeton Theological Seminary, 36, 45, 46-54, 62, 223
Pusey, Nathan, 62

R

Redstone Baptist Association, 190
Reid, Thomas, 150
Restoration Forum, 92, 137, 207

Restoration Quarterly, 83
Restoration Review, vi, viii, 88, 104, 111-112, 115-118, 163, 192, 218, 236, 246
Reviving the Ancient Faith: A History of Churches of Christ, 219-220
Rice, Ira Jr., 229
Richardson High School, 41, 184
Richardson, Robert, 89, 198-199, 267
Richland College, 106, 243
Rigdon, Bruce, 178
Roberson, Charles H., 36, 49
Roberts, J. W., 36, 37, 83
Rogers, Samuel, 195
Roland, C. P., 20, 72, 74
Roosevelt, Franklin D., 28, 39
Rushford, Jerry, 218

S

Sanders, J. P., 117
Sanders, Rex, 109
Sanderson, L. O., 21
Scarritt College, 133
Shakespeare, William, 259
Schlesinger, Arthur Jr., 61, 112
Scott, Alfred R., 153-154
Scott, Walter, 67, 114-115, 197-198, 210, 212
Seenlee, Ahtapa, 156-157
Shaw, Knowles, 156
Shelburne, Gene, 134
Shelly, Rubel, 187
Short, Howard, 136, 210
Sims, Harold, 155
Smith, Huston, 90
Smith, Raccoon John, xii, 195-197, 201, 252
Smith, Richard E., 64, 93
Smith, W. R., 36
Socrates, 98, 100, 107, 247

Sommer, Daniel, 21, 252
Southeastern Christian College, 133
Southern Christian University, 52
Southern Methodist University, 42, 183
Spain, Carl, 42
Spencer, Claude E., 209
Sperry, Willard, 65
Spinoza, Baruch, 98
Spiritual Sword, The, 125
Stallings, Gene, 7
Stendahl, Krister, 63-65
Stewart, David, 134
Stewart, R. W., 20
Stone, Barton W., 67, 88, 108, 113, 129, 172, 185,
    194-195, 197, 208, 212, 251, 267, 271
Stone-Campbell Dialogue, 207, 252-253
Stone-Campbell Journal, 207
*Stone-Campbell Movement: An Anecdotal History of
    Three Churches, The*, 203-209
Sturt, Charles, 170
Sweet, W. W., 192

T

Tant, J. D., 22, 128
"Ten Years of High School Philosophy," 83
Texas Christian University, 217
Texas Woman's University, 43, 82, 93, 97-99, 101,
    108, 145, 243
Theology Today, 223
Thomas, Harold, 221
Thurston, Danny, 164
Toney, Larry, 223, 224
Trammell, Phoebe Anna (Garrett), 62, 85, 93, 110,
    158-159, 254
Truth Magazine, 238
Turner, Rex A., 52, 70
Twain, Mark, 141

U

Union Seminary (Richmond), 223
University of Dallas, 106, 108
University of North Texas, 102
University of Tulsa, 133

V

Vandiver, Frank, 244
Van Tuyl, Warren and Norma, 51
Vatican II, 269
Vaughn, Norman, 23
Vinson, Bryan, 133
Voices of Concern: Studies in Church of Christism, v,116
Voltaire, 101

W

Walker, Dean E., 136, 213, 214
Walker, Richard, 36
Walker, Townsend, 36
Wallace, G. K., 21, 33, 67, 128
Wallace, Foy E., 21
Walling, Jeff, ix
Walters, Farrell, 133
Wardell, Clinton, 173
Warren, Charles E., 117
Warren, Thomas, 234
Waters, Ervin, 132, 136
Watson, Max, 64
Webb, Henry, 134, 253
Wells, Roosevelt, 229
Welsh, Robert K., 252
Wen, Jordan, 144
Wesley, John, 208
West, Earl, 20
Westwood Christian Foundation, 218
Wetzel, Robert, 137, 215

Wharton, W. L., 18
Wheeler, Donald, 49
White, Edward, 20
Wilbanks, William Lee, 251
Wilborn, Gene, 245-246
Wilder, Amos, 63
Wilkerson, C. L., 21, 31
Willis, Mike, 237-240
Wineskins, 251, 253
Wilson, Seth, 134, 138, 139
Witt, Robert L., 72, 74
Wolfson, Harry A., 61
Woods, Guy N., 38, 69, 70, 73
World Convention of Churches of Christ, 147, 164, 169, 173-174, 207, 209, 212-213
Wrather, Eva Jean, 209-210
Wright, Conrad, 63
Wyler, Kathy, 247
Wynnewood Chapel, 6, 131-133, 137, 217

X Y Z

Yale University, 54
Yan, Allen, 166-167
Yeck, Ashley and Amy, 254
Yeck, Christi, 158-162
Yeck, Tyler, 254
Yelland, Graham and Edna, 170
Yeldell, Nokomis, 229
Young, Norvel and Helen, 219

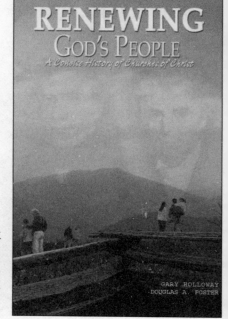